W9-CLE-625

GLOUCESTER COUNTY COLLEGE LIBRARY
PR4681 .K6
Knoepflmacher, U. C.
George Eliot's early novels;the limits o

3 2927 00005 7329

PR
4681   71-00512
K6

DATE DUE

GLOUCESTER COUNTY COLLEGE
WITHDRAWN FROM
SEWELL, NEW JERSEY 08080
RCSJ LIBRARY

 George Eliot's Early Novels

George Eliot's Early Novels

THE LIMITS OF REALISM

U. C. KNOEPFLMACHER

UNIVERSITY OF CALIFORNIA PRESS

BERKELEY AND LOS ANGELES, 1968

University of California Press
Berkeley and Los Angeles, California

Cambridge University Press
London, England

Copyright © 1968 by
The Regents of the University of California

Library of Congress Catalog Card Number: 68–23005
Printed in the United States of America

In Memory of
GEORGE A. KNOEPFLMACHER, RUTH MARTIN,
and RICHARD P. BLACKMUR
—*three irreplaceable teachers.*

Acknowledgments

The circumstances of this book's composition were greatly eased by two generous grants: one from the American Council of Learned Societies and the other a Humanities Research professorship awarded by the Chancellor of the University of California at Berkeley. I want to acknowledge the help of many colleagues: Thomas Flanagan, John H. Raleigh, and Ernest Tuveson kindly read the manuscript at different stages of its growth; Paul Alkon, Stephen Booth, John S. Coolidge, Stanley Eugene Fish, John E. Jordan, Joseph Kramer, Morton Paley, and Wayne Shumaker resolved some of my queries; my good friend Masao Miyoshi lived up to my expectations as a thoughtful reader, exacting censor, and most persistent gadfly. To my students in English 151 in general, and to Myra Goldberg Riddell and Lee Sterrenburg in particular, I express my indebtedness—they stimulated much that I have to say here; to Miss Elizabeth Walser, my unabated admiration—she made this manuscript far more intelligible than it would have been without her labors. I also thank the Yale University Library and the J. Pierpont Morgan Library for allowing me to quote from manuscripts in their possession, and the editors of *Victorian Newsletter* and *ELH: A Journal of English Literary History* for allowing me to reprint, in somewhat altered form, those portions of chapters three, four, and six which previously appeared in their journals.

U. C. K.

Contents

Abbreviations

Citations in this book
refer to the Cabinet Edition (Edinburgh, n. d.)
of George Eliot's novels.

 George Eliot's Early Novels

Introduction

George Eliot's novels are dominated by two conflicting impulses. She wanted to unfold before her readers the temporal actuality she believed in; yet she also wanted to assure them—and herself —that man's inescapable subjection to the flux of time did not invalidate a trust in justice, perfectibility, and order. This double allegiance drew her, over almost twenty years, to seek fictional modes that could accommodate both the actual and the ideal laws she wanted to portray. Instead of faithfully copying the circumstances of external life, George Eliot arranged reality to make it substantiate her moral values. In giving form to her ideas, she always proceeded, as Henry James shrewdly recognized, "from the abstract to the concrete."[1] Fully aware of the exploratory nature of her art, George Eliot herself spoke of her novels as being the outgrowth of "successive mental phases."[2]

The novelist wanted her contemporaries to be fully aware of the manifold interconnections between her mental phases. When John Blackwood barely hinted that she consider delaying the publication of *Silas Marner*, she stressed most emphatically that her writings ought "to appear in the order in which they are written" (GEL, III, 382–383). Earlier, after the success of *Adam Bede*, she had asked that her three *Scenes of Clerical Life* be republished in order to reach a wider audience: "first, because I think it of importance to the estimate of me as a writer that 'Adam Bede' should not be counted as my only book; and secondly, because there are ideas presented in these stories about which I care a good deal, and am not sure that I can ever embody again"

[1] "George Eliot's Life," *Atlantic Monthly*, LV (May 1885), 673.
[2] *The George Eliot Letters*, ed. Gordon S. Haight (New Haven, 1954– 1955), III, 383. Hereafter this edition is referred to as GEL.

(GEL, III, 240). In fact, as I hope to show, her movement from the pastoral *Scenes* to the rural epic of *Adam Bede* to the tragedy of *The Mill* was quite as deliberate and programmatic as the classical Virgilian movement from pastoral beginnings through georgics and on to the epic.[3]

The changes experienced by George Eliot's generation were especially disheartening because of their abruptness. The mid-Victorians suddenly had to shift from tradition—a mode of life based on the repetition of sameness—to the insecurity of an existence in which men could neither hark back to time-honored norms nor confidently predict the outcome of the innovations around them. George Eliot's "mental phases" strikingly illustrate the extent to which she, like Matthew Arnold, was caught between two eras, the one dying and the other as yet unborn. In her own efforts to find meaning in this world of flux, the novelist returned at regular intervals to the 1830's, that era of reform and agitation, which she regarded, after the manner of other Victorian prophets, as marking the beginning of England's entrance into a modern age of doubt and instability. "Amos Barton," "Janet's Repentance," and *The Mill on the Floss*, like *Felix Holt* and *Middlemarch* later on, are set in that period; the abrupt historical changes which act as a background in each of these works have a direct bearing on the future, which is the author's present. Alternating with these novels, however, are the works belonging to a second series in which the action is removed into a more remote and usually more quiescent past. Hence it is that "Amos Barton"—a tale which opens with an emblem of change (the altered appearance of Shepperton Church)—should be followed by "Mr. Gilfil's Love-Story," a novella which gradually winds back into a more placid eighteenth-century past; that "Janet's Repentance," again set in a near-present of conflict and commotion, should be succeeded by *Adam Bede*, located in the

[3] See pp. 163–164, below.

tranquil, mythical world of Hayslope; that *The Mill*, where industrial St. Ogg's displaces the agrarian existence at Dorlcote Mill, should lead the novelist back to the pastoral world of *Silas Marner* and further back to Florentine history in *Romola*. Similarly, *Felix Holt, The Radical* is followed by the epic of *The Spanish Gypsy*, set in fifteenth-century Spain; *Middlemarch*, by *Daniel Deronda*, a novel which, though set in the author's present, reaches back into history to find a religious fountainhead for her own irreligious age.

George Eliot's hope that her readers might appreciate the sequential relations among her novels has unfortunately gone unheeded by her critics. We possess a number of outstanding essays on some of her individual works. But the path which led the novelist from the simple "Amos Barton" in 1857 to so ambitious a construct as *Daniel Deronda* in 1876 has never been carefully retraced. I first conceived of this study as a direct offshoot of my *Religious Humanism and the Victorian Novel* (1965), in which I examined the divergent roads taken by three novelists who wanted to impose meaning on the evolutionary order with which they suddenly had been confronted. Although I was able to treat the whole development of both Pater and Butler, the very bulk of George Eliot's fiction forced me to restrict myself to her last two novels. By stressing the considerable differences between the modes of *Middlemarch* and *Daniel Deronda*, I hinted at some of the artistic difficulties their author had met in expressing her values. Yet I felt that a more thorough and comprehensive study of her earlier fiction was definitely called for. As I began to reread the novels and look again at the extant book-length studies of George Eliot, my aims became more ambitious, for not a single study had treated *all* her novels in the order of their composition. Those critical works which were chronologically arranged invariably omitted some of her less successful or less well-known fiction; and those studies that did not approach her novels in the order of their composition were not meant to be all-inclusive. A recent book on the novelist's apprenticeship, *George Eliot's Scenes of Clerical Life*, called attention to a work commonly slighted by previous critics. But its author, Thomas A. Noble, failed to grasp the significance of the differences among these three experimental novellas and thus disregarded their implications for George Eliot's artistic growth.

Since the appearance of Dr. Leavis' influential articles on George Eliot more than two decades ago, nine critical books have been devoted to her fiction. Her reputation once again approaches that which she held in her own times. Yet it is regrettable that those most interested in establishing her eminence as a major English novelist should so consistently have shied away from her artistic failures. To dismiss George Eliot's lesser works altogether is as shortsighted as to overpraise them. For only by examining all of her experimentations can we fully assess her achievements. The failure of *Romola* or *The Spanish Gypsy* is as incontestable as the success of *Middlemarch*, but it is seldom recognized that this success stems largely from those very failures. The lack of control which mars the conclusion of *The Mill* led the novelist to the mastery of form and meaning in *Silas Marner*. Nor is a story like "The Lifted Veil" to be regarded as a curious anomaly, somehow unbecoming to a "realist" who had in her essays once attacked "the remote, the vague, and the unknown" as unfit subjects for art.[4] To the contrary, this horror tale (and *Daniel Deronda*, with its similar temporal distortions) must be interpreted as an expression of the selfsame search which connects all of George Eliot's fiction.

George Eliot's development as a novelist can be divided into two distinct stages. The first of these is the subject of this book. From 1857 to 1861, the novelist was engaged in a period of intense productivity, eagerly testing out her double aims through a variety of forms of ever-increasing sophistication. In those five

[4] "Worldliness and Other-Worldliness: The Poet Young," *Westminster Review*, LXVII (January 1857), 42.

years, she wrote the three novellas which make up *Scenes of Clerical Life* (1857–1858), *Adam Bede* (1859), "The Lifted Veil" (1859), *The Mill on the Floss* (1860), "Brother Jacob" (written in 1860, but not published until 1864), and *Silas Marner* (1861). In the second stage, from 1862 to 1876, she moved away from the pastoral novel she had perfected in *Silas Marner* and sought to stimulate sympathy for "the historical life of man" on that wider plane she had first tried out in *The Mill* (GEL, IV, 97). *Romola* (1863), *Felix Holt* (1866), *The Spanish Gypsy* (set aside in 1865, rewritten in 1867, and published in 1868), *Middlemarch* (1871–1872), and *Daniel Deronda* (1876) are the five major works of her later phase.

Even though the novelist's ethical concepts remained constant throughout her career, her continued experimentation with form suggests the difficulties she encountered in delineating those beliefs.[5] Despite their common pastoralism, her first three novellas differ markedly. In "The Sad Fortunes of the Reverend Amos Barton," a story set in the "electric" 1830's, George Eliot set out to shatter a complacent and commonplace clergyman's indifference to the sufferings of his fellow mortals. The plot is mechanical and sentimental: the unexpected death of Barton's "sweet" wife Milly impresses on him the precariousness of earthly life and forces him into an awareness of George Eliot's own temporal "religion of humanity." Incongruously welding satire and idealization, "Amos Barton" hovers uneasily between the grotesque and the sublime. The story revealed to its author that the dual aims inherent in her brand of "realism" could not be carried out through a domestic tale or "slice of life." She was

---

[5] "George Eliot's Quest for Values," the subtitle of Bernard J. Paris' recent study, *Experiments in Life*, strikes me as inappropriate. George Eliot's quest as a novelist was not for values, but rather for the forms with which to express those values. Mr. Paris' inattention to the novelist's mode of persuasion, to the shape and texture of her variegated experiments in life, seriously mars an otherwise valuable book.

led to consider a new mode of presentation that might allow her to dignify the ordinary aspects of life with greater integrity and forcefulness.

Her next novella, "Mr. Gilfil's Love-Story," ingeniously exploits the gap left by "Amos Barton." Departing from the near-contemporary and domestic reality she had portrayed, George Eliot turned to an extraordinary setting. Teasing her readers into believing that the story of Tina Sarti, an exotic Italian orphan living in an English Gothic manor, would contain an unusual romance, she cleverly exploited these false expectations and tried to demonstrate instead that a different kind of romance could lurk beneath the commonplace, everyday realities of life, represented in this tale by the gnarled, gin-drinking Mr. Gilfil, a figure as wizened as Wordsworth's Michael or the old Leech-Gatherer. Still, her final description of the aged Mr. Gilfil betrayed her dissatisfaction with his lot; like some of her later figures, this clergyman was primarily an innocent victim of capricious reversals. Thus, in her third and longest novella, "Janet's Repentance," George Eliot tried to counter the negative conclusion of her previous tale. Moving to the 1830's again, she depicted a clash very much like those in *The Mill on the Floss*, *Felix Holt*, and *Middlemarch*. Through the invention of Milby, a provincial town similar to St. Ogg's, Treby, or Middlemarch, she tried to portray the predicament of a creature such as Maggie, Esther, and Dorothea were to become. Like those later figures, Janet Dempster despairs over "the dreary persistence of measurable reality" (SCL, II, chap. 14, p. 211). But the intervention of an extraordinary outsider with a romantic past of guilt and expiation rescues the heroine from the town's negativism. Like Romola or Esther or Dorothea, the matured Janet learns to face the future with far greater confidence than Mr. Gilfil had.

George Eliot was ready for the larger canvas of *Adam Bede*. Again, as in "Mr. Gilfil's Love-Story," she returned to an agrarian past. By proclaiming that even this sheltered Arcadia was not immune to the harsh natural laws that governed her own present, she could fulfill her double objectives. On the one hand, she could point to the irrevocability of the laws of change; yet on the other, with her firm grasp of Warwickshire life, she could detach from an earlier rural world those ethical principles that were solid enough to withstand the test of change. What is more, the novelist turned away from the naturalism inherent in her previous three *Scenes*. Recognizing the need for a medium which would heighten the import of her ethical beliefs, she converted her novel into a modern retelling of the Christian myth of the Fortunate Fall. Like his prototype in *Paradise Lost*, her Adam must accept his banishment into the temporal world; yet, unlike his predecessor, he cannot predicate his acceptance on the Son's promise that he and his descendants shall someday be delivered from Time. Instead, Adam the carpenter's son must be his own savior; his redemption is to come through his fellow men. Amply compensated by the fecundity of Loamshire, a terrestrial Eden, he and Dinah are reconciled to their lot in the present without the prophetic look into the future granted to Milton's Adam.

The dire consequences of escaping the bounds of time are taken up, however, in "The Lifted Veil," the supernatural tale which George Eliot published anonymously between *Adam Bede* and *The Mill on the Floss*. The Gothic horrors visited on a man capable of foreseeing his future would hardly seem to be the proper domain for the "realist" who had chastened Amos Barton and Adam Bede. Yet the story of Latimer, the disappointed visionary, indicates the extent to which George Eliot needed to purge her own misgivings about the natural forces that operated in *Adam Bede*. In that novel, Hetty Sorrel's destruction of her own child had come to represent for the author the cruelty of a natural world impassive to universal suffering; rather uneasily, she had replaced Hetty with *Adam Bede*'s Dinah Morris, the believer in the emanations of universal Love. In "The Lifted Veil," Hetty's place is taken by the vampire-like Bertha; Dinah's, by the idealistic Latimer. The former emphasis is reversed. Surrounded by Adam Bede's "solid world," the visionary Dinah could front the limitations of a life without foresight; sundered from his fellow men by his gifts of insight and foresight, Latimer the Seer succumbs to Bertha's evil. On lifting the veil which protects the illusions of ordinary mortals, he sees the horror recognized also by Melville's Captain Ahab and by Conrad's Kurtz. He dies, destroyed by his vision of nothingness.

In *The Mill on the Floss*, the most ambitious of the experimental novels of her first phase, George Eliot tried to explore the tragic implications of her deterministic philosophy of time. Like "Amos Barton" or "Janet's Repentance," *The Mill* depicts a collision between opposites. But tradition and innovation, illusion and actuality, in this case prove to be irreconcilable. Maggie the dreamer and Tom the pragmatist are destroyed by the waters of the Floss. Although their union in death at least allows the author to elegize the childhood Eden they have lost, their fate is almost as capricious as Latimer's. Maggie wants, but cannot receive, "some explanation of this hard, real life" (MF, IV, chap. 3, p. 28). Caught between past and present, she can find no outlet for her aspirations. The rural world that had supported Adam Bede has crumbled away. Janet Dempster was saved from the puerility of Milby by the example of the Reverend Edward Tryan; but Dr. Kenn, the clergyman who briefly shelters Maggie in St. Ogg's, is an impotent bystander who, for all his sympathy and understanding, cannot save "the strugglers tossed by the waves" (MF, VI, chap. 9, p. 264). Perhaps unexcelled in its early portions, *The Mill on the Floss* is also important as a preparation for *Middlemarch*. Nonetheless, the unquestionable failure of the novel's resolution illustrates George Eliot's persistent difficulties in reconciling the discrepant realities of the actual and the ideal. Like Matthew Arnold, whose classical tragedy *Merope* had appeared two years earlier, George Eliot found that she could not displace her inner doubts and reservations by resorting to the exaltation of a tragic heroine.

This frustration led the novelist to search for a less "somber" and less expansive form. After the relief provided by "Brother Jacob," a comic short story, she found her first perfect means of balance in the "legendary tale" of *Silas Marner*. In the more stylized world of the fable, she could at last create a reality true to her dual aims. Resorting to the double plot she would thereafter use in all her later novels, she depicted simultaneously Silas' regeneration and Godfrey's punishment, without having to provide the logical "explanations" she had sought in *Adam Bede* or *The Mill*. Silas the doubter is miraculously rescued from the despair to which Latimer and Maggie succumbed; Godfrey, on the other hand, is punished by the same relentless forces which had turned on Hetty Sorrel, that other repudiator of a child. Through their interaction, George Eliot could convincingly portray the "remedial influence of pure natural human relations" (GEL, III, 383). In remote Raveloe, a mythical world not unlike that of Shakespeare's romances, the laws which clashed in the earlier novels coalesce and coincide: "realism" blends with the coincidences of the fairy tale.

But George Eliot still chafed at the limitations on which this achievement was based. The story of Silas had merely "thrust itself" between *The Mill on the Floss* and *Romola*, where she once again turned to an epic stage for her concern with universals. Yet her literal attempt to exercise the role of novelist-historian was a failure. She could extricate Romola from the historical actuality of Florence (a city which in her treatment resembled Milby or St. Ogg's) only by taking her heroine to an extraneous atmosphere such as the rural setting which had sustained Adam Bede or Silas Marner. *Romola* convinced the novelist of the impossibility of welding history with the fabrications of romance. Increasingly aware of these new difficulties in blending the actual and the ideal, she began to separate the two by oscillating between prose fiction and poetry. *Felix Holt, The Radical* is predominantly ironic: by showing the insufficiency of all purely political attempts to improve man's moral life, George Eliot implicitly advanced her own ethic. *The Spanish Gypsy*, the long narrative poem in blank verse which she rewrote after a visit to Spain, is predominantly heroic: by explicitly personifying the aspirations of an entire people, she tried to give grandeur to the same moral choices made by the historically insignificant characters of her previous fiction.

It was the framework of *Middlemarch* that finally allowed the novelist to regain the balance she had struck on a modest scale in her first stage in *Silas Marner*. She once again devised a form that was intended to fuse romance and history, the heroic and the prosaic. In *Romola*, the two had remained apart: the fairy-tale atmosphere of the novel's conclusion had sharply clashed with the treatment of actual Florentine politics. In *Middlemarch*, however, George Eliot managed to combine the epic strain of *The Spanish Gypsy* with the political ironies of *Felix Holt*. Relying on paradox, she constructed an epic which questioned the possibility of an epic life in a world of motion and change. The ideal and the actual could now be held in perfect equipoise. She could create still another Madonna, as ardent and noble as Romola had been, and yet at the same time portray the natural laws which prevented such a creature from attaining a heroic stature. She could give full play to the teachings of history; but, whereas in *Romola* the figures of Savonarola and Machiavelli had belonged to an order of reality different from that of her fictional characters, history here became but a frame of reference, a mere analogue to the "unhistoric acts" examined in the foreground. She could still portray the remedial influences of human relations which she had dramatized since "Amos Barton," but the wishfulness inherent in the fable of Fred Vincy's regeneration by

Mary Garth could be played down and subordinated to the more somber fates of Lydgate and Dorothea.

In *Middlemarch* George Eliot thus balanced and reapportioned all the elements which had warred in most of her previous fiction. Fully profiting from each of her earlier successes and failures, she devised a form which drew on all the modes she had previously used: the domestic tale, fable, romance, epic, tragedy, and satire. Artistically, *Middlemarch* was the culmination of her second period, just as *Silas Marner* had been the culmination of her first. Nevertheless, she could not yet bring herself to accept the mandates of that "hard unaccommodating Actual" to which Dorothea must submit. In *Daniel Deronda* she tried to transcend that "Actual" by splitting it into an ordinary world of causality and an extraordinary realm of coincidence and romance. In the earlier novels, figures like Adam Bede, Godfrey Cass, or Gwendolen Harleth's closest prototype, Esther Lyon, had elevated their "animal life into religion" within the sphere of a common, everyday experience (DD, chap. 42, p. 385). Now, however, such fulfillment became limited to the exclusive sphere of Deronda. Whereas the values adopted by the earlier characters had been applicable to the tangible, time-bound world of ordinary life, in *Daniel Deronda* they are encased in the transcending visions of Mordecai the Prophet, a figure whose unusual ability to foresee the future is not treated with the horror visited on the narrator of "The Lifted Veil."

The primary purpose of this book is to discover a rationale for George Eliot's growth as a philosophical novelist. In it I propose to examine those seven "mental phases" which make up the first stage of her development.[6] In discussing those seven works, I shall link them to each other and to the fiction of the novelist's second stage, which I expect to re-examine more fully in a later

[6] An eighth work, "Brother Jacob," is only discussed in passing in Chapter Seven.

volume. Throughout, I hope to demonstrate how her gradual mastery of new fictional forms and techniques allowed her to combine, as Wordsworth had done in his poetry, the ordinary and temporal existence she accepted with the extraordinary and ideal realm she yearned for.

But even if my main purpose is to dwell on the meaningful connections between the novelist's works, there are also further aims. George Eliot's and George Henry Lewes' dicta on "realism" have, I think, been adopted too unquestionably as a glossary for her own practices as an artist. Although her novels try to meet the standards of empirical veracity that she had upheld in her essays and reviews, her fiction gradually reacted on her theory and led her away from the naturalistic presentation of "Amos Barton." In my *Religious Humanism*, I dwelt on the relation between George Eliot's humanist ideals and the Christianity she rejected; in this study, I relate her art to that of her Romantic predecessors. Just as her "religion of humanity" represented an attempt to counter, as well as to conserve, the elements of Christian belief, so does her fiction involve both a reversal and a continuation of the modes and attitudes of the English Romantics. My first chapter opens with Wordsworth's and Coleridge's disputation over "reality" in art; this dispute acts as a backdrop for much of what I say about George Eliot's craft. If Victorian poetry reverberates with echoes from Milton, Wordsworth, Goethe, and Keats, George Eliot's fiction likewise profits from the efforts of those among her forerunners who had grappled with the problems of belief and knowledge in the mutable world. Her imaginative appropriation of the works of the Romantic poets and novelists, her successful adaption in *Adam Bede* of Milton's epic theme, her reliance on Shakespeare's tragedies and romances, although unnoted by previous critics of her novels, are areas essential to a full appreciation of her philosophic art.

Lastly, frequent connections have been made to the works of other Victorians, to novelists like Dickens and Thackeray, to poets like Arnold and Tennyson, to critics like Carlyle and Pater. George Eliot's preoccupation with time and reality resulted from her desire to reconcile the empirical laws of nineteenth-century science with the teleology of her lost belief. Her purpose was shared by all those who hoped to steer their iron age toward a better future. If, in our own times, the golden era they yearned for has hardly materialized, we can at any rate participate in their imaginative refashioning of the past. As George Eliot understood so well, each age, though irrevocably separated from that preceding it, must nonetheless reinterpret the past it has lost in order to arrange its own disordered present.

It was her refusal to accept some of the logical implications of her own outlook which led this highly logical woman to seek new theoretic forms which would accommodate reason and faith, the promptings of the head and heart. Her philosophical system was destined to remain inconsistent, as likely to be superseded as our own feebler efforts to account for the dualistic nature of life. Yet the very inconsistencies of her creed permitted her to create at least two acknowledged masterpieces whose artistic reality exceeded by far that of her underlying ideas. The Milton of *Paradise Lost* resorted to a mythical Ptolemaic universe as a means of justifying existence in the world of Kepler and Galileo; the George Eliot who sought to order the world of Darwin and Huxley was driven to invent in *Middlemarch* a power not unlike the Deity she had dismissed as myth. Paradoxically enough, the very imperfections of her philosophy led to the perfection of her art.

1. From Philosophy to Fiction

Poetry, therefore, is a more philosophical and a higher thing than history: for poetry tends to express the universal, history the particular.

—ARISTOTLE, *Poetics* IX. 3

What a mind was Aristotle's . . . ! But he confounded science with philosophy, which is an error. Philosophy is the middle state between science, or knowledge, and sophia, or wisdom.

—COLERIDGE, *Table-Talk*

GEORGE ELIOT AS A PHILOSOPHICAL NOVELIST

George Eliot's desire to find a form which would allow her to steer her characters from temporal anarchy to a higher order of experience, was not unlike that of Henry Fielding, a full century before her time. Somewhat anticipating Coleridge's conflict with Wordsworth, Fielding had reacted against the simulated "reality" of Richardson's fiction by conferring on his own novels the ideal dignity of classical form. Through the deliberate artifice of his plots and the calculated effect of his digressions, Fielding could imply the existence of a reasonable order, even though this order was only dimly perceived by the characters peopling his teeming "histories." The apparent amorality of ordinary life thus merely masked the workings of a providential disposition as capable of rewarding benevolence as of punishing the unjust.

George Eliot also sought a form that would validate the mandates of some higher ethical order; despite her affiliation with Continental thought, she, too, was deeply rooted in the English moralistic tradition. But the novelist whose *Middlemarch* had been accused by Henry James of being "too often an echo of Messrs. Darwin and Huxley,"[1] could no longer avail herself of Fielding's Christian, atemporal frame of reference. To James, "Fielding was didactic—the author of *Middlemarch* is really philosophic."[2] In that novel, the closest in mode to Fielding's "epic comedies in prose," George Eliot made sure to dissociate herself from his example. Though a "great historian" and colossus, Fielding lived in a simpler age, unburdened by the preoccupations inherent in her own time-bound philosophy: "But Fielding lived when the days were longer (for time, like money, is measured by our needs), when summer afternoons were spacious and the clock ticked in the winter evenings."[3] As a "belated historian" who tells the story of a late-born Theresa, the narrator of *Middlemarch* protests that his task is more limited. He must content himself with examining the texture of life on this earth and not disperse his light over "that tempting range of relevancies called the universe."

This protestation is telling. For far from belittling her own role as a novelist, the narrator's faint irony calls attention to George Eliot's own very definite preoccupations with the universe. For it is the altered nature of that universe which is the true object of her comparison. Fielding, confident of a divinely ordered world, can well afford to spend his days on earth by chatting slowly in all "the lusty ease of his fine English." But time is far more precious to the belated historian. As a moralist and lawgiver, George Eliot cannot "linger" after Fielding's example. Her predecessor, she claims, has had the happiness to have lived over a hundred and twenty years ago, in a secure and static eighteenth century. The narrator of *Middlemarch*, how-

---

[1] Henry James, "George Eliot's 'Middlemarch,'" reprinted in *NCF*, VIII (December 1953), 170.

[2] *Ibid.*, p. 169.

[3] References in this and the following paragraph are from *Middlemarch*, Bk. II, chap. 15, pp. 213–214.

ever, lives in an era in doubt of its future. Unlike Fielding, this narrator must become a genuine historian. A scientist, who "cares much to know the history of man, and how the mysterious mixture behaves under the varying experiments of Time," he must, on his own, find those laws which previous novelists could take for granted. And, what is more, this narrator-historian must extricate those laws from the casual web of actuality: "I at least have so much to do in unravelling certain human lots, and seeing how they were woven and interwoven. . . ." George Eliot's distinction is clear. Despite her affinity to Fielding, despite her affection for the didactic lectures so resonantly delivered from his armchair, she cannot mount the same "proscenium." The traditional forms of the novel can no longer satisfy the needs of a philosophical writer steeped in the evolutionary lore of the mid-nineteenth century.[4]

As a lifelong admirer of Wordsworth and Scott, George Eliot regarded herself as a continuator of those English Romantics, who at the beginning of the nineteenth century had claimed to be philosophers whose visionary intuition could apprehend in the factual, particular world of experience the "indwelling law, which is the true being of things."[5] Wordsworth, much to Coleridge's chagrin, had not only extended the status of philosopher to children, madmen, and rustics, but also regarded their language as "a more permanent, and a *far more philosophical* language, than that which is frequently substituted for it by Poets."[6] In the *Biographia Literaria*, Coleridge took issue with

---

[4] See George Henry Lewes' extremely unfair attack on Fielding in "A Word About Tom Jones," *Blackwood's Edinburgh Magazine*, LXXXVII (March 1860), 331–341.

[5] *Biographia Literaria*, ed. George Watson (New York, 1956), chap. 15, p. 179.

[6] "Observations Prefixed to *Lyrical Ballads*," in *Criticism: The Foundations of Modern Literary Judgment*, ed. Schorer, Miles, McKenzie (New York, 1958), p. 31; italics added.

such statements. Fearful of any imitation of the accidental circumstances of "low and rustic life," he adduced "the principle of Aristotle, that poetry as poetry is essentially *ideal*."[7] According to Coleridge, it was Wordsworth's own unusual "philosophic pathos," rather than any emulation of the ordinary and commonplace, which ranked him with England's two poet-philosophers, Shakespeare and Milton.[8] For himself, Coleridge reserved the role of philosophical critic and legislator. When, in 1817, he exhorted Wordsworth and those young Wordsworthians of "strong sensibility and meditative minds" to follow the principles necessary for the production of a "Genuine Philosophic Poem," he was attempting nothing less than to chart the future course of literary creation in nineteenth-century England.[9]

Near the end of the century, almost seventy years after Coleridge's exhortation, a group of meditative minds took a retrospective look at the work of the most Wordsworthian of English novelists, George Eliot. She had died in 1880, and by then the attitude towards philosophical art had perceptibly changed. Though Frederic Harrison still hailed her as the "most philosophic artist, or the most artistic philosopher in recent literature," W. H. Mallock guardedly described her fiction as but a "gradual setting forth of a philosophy and religion of life, illustrated by a continuous succession of diagrams."[10] Henry James remonstrated again: "The philosophic door is always open, on her stage, and we are aware that the somewhat cooling draught of ethical purpose draws across it." Almost reluctantly, he conceded that the novelist's constant reference to ideas had allowed her to shape a reality beyond that of the ordinary novel: "Her preoccupation

[7] *Biographia*, chap. 17, p. 192; italics added.

[8] *Ibid.*, chap. 22, p. 270.

[9] *Ibid.*, chap. 14, p. 170; chap. 22, p. 275.

[10] "The Life of George Eliot," *Fortnightly Review*, XLIII [O.S.] (March 1885), 315; "George Eliot on the Human Character," in *Atheism and the Value of Life* (London, 1884), p. 165.

with the universe helped to make her characters strike you as also belonging to it; it raised the roof, widened the area, of her aesthetic structure."[11]

Coleridge would have agreed that George Eliot's art, like that of the Romantics, was "philosophic" in its intentions. In two or three paragraphs of closely reasoned prose, the sage of Highgate might well have protested that his beloved Fielding had mediated, as much as George Eliot had, between "science, or knowledge, and sophia, or wisdom." Although he might also have belittled the too scientific foundations of George Eliot's beliefs and argued that her realistic mode merely compounded the same difficulties he had already spotted in Wordsworth's own efforts to portray "*real* life," the author of "The Ancient Mariner" would definitely have lauded the creator of *Silas Marner* and *Middlemarch* for her "preoccupation with the universe." Like James, who regarded *Silas* as her most perfect fiction, he would have singled out that work as his favorite and chided her for assuming that only Wordsworth, among her predecessors, could have appreciated its design.[12] For Coleridge would have regarded it and her other novels as expressions of that "indwelling law" which he, like George Eliot, believed it was the philosophical artist's task to discover and to interpret.

For George Eliot the search after such universal laws was fraught with considerable difficulty. In 1819, the year in which she was born, Shelley could still invoke the West Wind, identify himself with its fierce "spirit," and ask it to scatter his words among mankind: "Be through my lips to unawakened earth / The trumpet of a prophecy." To the Victorian prophets, however, the earth had come to seem for more imperturbable. The world of fact no longer yielded the conceptions of the Great and

[11] "George Eliot's Life," *Atlantic Monthly*, LV (May 1885), 673.

[12] George Eliot wrote to John Blackwood about *Silas Marner*: "I should not have believed that any one would have been interested in it but myself (since William Wordsworth is dead)" (GEL, III, 382).

Whole on which the Romantics had been able to predicate a poetic faith:

> Hither and thither spins
> The wind-borne, mirroring soul
> A thousand glimpses wins
> And never sees a whole:
> Looks once, and drives elsewhere, and leaves its last employ.[13]

Thus it was Thomas Carlyle, not Coleridge, who pointed out the new direction: "Sentimentalist and Utilitarian, Skeptic and Theologian, with one voice advise us: 'Examine History, for it is "Philosophy Teaching by Experience." ' "[14]

George Eliot heeded this advice. Like Carlyle, Mill, Arnold, and Newman, she sought to detach from man's evolution in time the semblance of an indwelling law. But as a skeptic who, like Matthew Arnold, had come to regard the Scriptures as but a "series of historical documents,"[15] she extended her skepticism to history itself. Just as Arnold's Empedocles and Tennyson's Lucretius find that their atomistic philosophies strip life of all direction and meaning, so does George Eliot's fiction illustrate her latent distrust of the same temporal order to which she had given her assent. In her anonymously published short story, "The Lifted Veil," the Shelley-like protagonist despairs of the flux which kills all ideals; in *The Mill on the Floss*, Tom and Maggie Tulliver cannot find that "cheerful faith" which another brother and sister had found by the banks of "this fair river" Wye. Instead, they become the passive victims of the ever-flowing Floss.

Despite Carlyle's advice, then, George Eliot could hardly extract from history the philosophic sanctions available to both sen-

---

[13] "Empedocles on Etna," II. 82–86.

[14] "On History," *Critical and Miscellaneous Essays*, II, *The Complete Works of Thomas Carlyle* (New York, 1901), p. 61.

[15] "Evangelical Teaching: Dr. Cumming," *Westminster Review*, LXIV (October 1855), 446.

timentalist and theologian. Far from yielding Carlyle's subjective belief in the operations of a mystical *Geist* or Newman's faith in the revealed doctrines of the apostolic church, history remained for her a force firmly grounded by that progression of unheroic events which she called "worldliness." Nor could she ever fully share the historical optimism of the utilitarian. J. S. Mill's unswerving confidence in man's reason and perfectibility enabled him to prescribe the dialectical rules for an orderly advance from past error to future truth. Though hopeful of a similar end, George Eliot, the former Calvinist, found little comfort from the somber picture of a human animal whose irrationality and imperfection permeated all of the capricious movements of past and present. Rather than justifying a belief in progress, the new "development hypothesis" only seemed to her to accentuate the invariability of human blindness, error, and suffering.[16]

And yet, despite her deep distrust of a temporal order which seemed erratic and amoral, George Eliot insisted in her early essays that only by understanding its laws could men derive the principles needed for their perfection. The natural world was no longer, as it had still been for the Romantics, a mere veil hiding a higher reality. It had become that reality itself. The distinctions once drawn between reason and understanding, revelation and science, mystery and fact, no longer held their former meanings. Coleridge—and, in their own way, Victorians like Carlyle and Newman—upheld the superiority of the philosophical knowledge gained by faith or intuition to the scientific knowledge obtained by natural philosophy. But for George Eliot, as

---

[16] For further information on George Eliot's religion of humanity, see my *Religious Humanism and the Victorian Novel* (Princeton, 1965), pp. 24–71. The reader unacquainted with qualities of her unbelief should also consult Gordon S. Haight, GEL, I, xliii–xlv; Bernard J. Paris, *Experiments in Life: George Eliot's Quest For Values* (Detroit, 1965), pp. 1–148; Basil Willey, *Nineteenth Century Studies: Coleridge to Matthew Arnold* (London, 1960), pp. 204–236.

for Matthew Arnold, the distinction itself seemed to have lost its validity. The material and the moral worlds had almost become identical. In her early essays, Marian Evans urged what she later would try to accomplish with ever-increasing zeal in her novels: she asked that the same undeviating laws already acknowledged as "the basis of our physical science" be likewise applied to "our social organization, our ethics, and our religion."[17] The former opposition between faith and science no longer existed. For religion had been reduced to ethics, while philosophy had come to mean natural philosophy only: "In this view, religion and philosophy are not merely conciliated, they are identical; or rather, religion is the crown and consummation of philosophy."[18]

But if ethics and science had become identical, George Eliot soon found that their laws were hardly interchangeable. She gradually realized that a strictly scientific study of "the inexorable law of consequences," which ruled in the material world, could not by itself direct men toward that stability and perfection which had been the goal of both orthodox and Romantic faiths. George Eliot shared the "religious fervor" which Coleridge had spotted in Wordsworth's poetry; even as an agnostic, she found inspiration in the works of John Milton. The residue of her Puritan idealism prompted her to infuse historical actuality with a teleology of epic proportions. Yet, by squarely rejecting all appeals to any order beyond the empirical phenomena surrounding human experience, she could no longer hold up a Faerie-land or Miltonic Heaven as guides for earthly conduct. Years before the composition of "Amos Barton," her first work of fiction, she had already expressed her need to idealize existence in the finite world. With premature confidence, she asserted that a "nobler presentation of humanity has yet to be given in resignation to in-

[17] Review of Robert William Mackay's *The Progress of the Intellect, as Exemplified in the Religious Development of the Greeks and Hebrews* in *Westminster Review*, LIV (January 1851), 355.

[18] *Ibid.*, p. 356.

dividual nothingness than could ever be shewn of a being who believes in the phantasmagoria of hope unsustained by reason" (GEL, II, 49).

The fierce reason with which she disparaged such false hopes in her essays on the evangelical theologian Dr. Cumming and on the poet Young might well have gone into a projected philosophical treatise on *The Idea of a Future Life.* To the theologian, the historical flux to which all life was subject would end in the eternity of a resurrection in Christ; earthly salvation was predicated on a belief in immortality, a future existence outside of time. George Eliot's materialist standards roundly denied this eschatology. Man was mortal; the brevity of his existence only underscored his vulnerability to the onslaught of time. Yet she was not to become an iconoclast. In her fiction, she chose the harder task of ennobling her enforced resignation to "individual nothingness." Unlike the twentieth-century existentialist, willing to create meaning in spite of nothingness, she could not quite bring herself to confront a world devoid of some "indwelling law." Thus she was led to demand a "sort of transhumanation" similar to that made possible by a Christian belief in the hereafter or by the Romantic faith in the power of the imagination (GEL, I, 280).

In the figurative mode of her novels, George Eliot thus tried to recreate what had formerly been promised by religion only— the annulment of time. Through the promise of a divine redemption, Christian poets like Milton had justified death, suffering, and evil in the mutable world; through the power of their imaginations, the Romantic poet-philosophers had likewise hoped to transcend the bonds of time: for Keats, "axioms in philosophy are not axioms until they are proven by our own pulses."[19] George Eliot hoped to effect a similar "transhumanation" through the medium of her own philosophical art. This transcendence, like that inherent in Romantic poetry, was to be achieved through the con-

[19] Letter to Reynolds, *Letters of John Keats: 1814–1821*, ed. Hyder Edward Rollins (Cambridge, 1958), I, 279.

junction of feeling and thought; like Wordsworth, George Eliot hoped to rely on the power of "memory" in her attempts to reach out to a larger life. But the Romantics had glimpsed infinity through their inward reliance on the imagination: Shelley escaped the "heavy weight of hours" by his imaginative identification with the West Wind. The time-burdened and time-conscious observer whose persona George Eliot was to develop in her novels, addresses his creed not only to the rare individual endowed with an aesthetic faculty like Coleridge's "secondary imagination," but to all men capable of feeling: "Through my union and fellowship with men I *have* seen, I feel a like, though a fainter sympathy with those I have *not* seen; and I am able to live in imagination with the generations to come, that their good is not alien to me, and is a stimulus to me to labor for ends which will not benefit myself, but will benefit them."[20]

Through the power of the historical imagination, by exercising sympathy for fellow creatures imprisoned by time and space, man can alleviate the burden of his own mortality: his self-annulment can lead to salvation. Both Christianity and Romanticism placed this redemption in a numinous realm outside the veil of ordinary life. Following the lead of post-Hegelians like Feuerbach, George Eliot places it within the temporal world. In her ethical system, man can still defeat time, but only by acknowledging its hold over all his endeavors. Just as in Thomas Carlyle's more metaphysical scheme there is Time the Destroyer, Chronos, and an Eternity-in-Time, so in her fiction, two different orders, both rooted in the temporal, usually coexist. Yet while the one proves to be illusory and transitory—a phenomenal world of appearances—the other reaches out beyond the momentary data of the senses to an awareness of a larger and more permanent rhythm. The characters unable or unwilling to recognize the mandates of this higher order are invariably punished by the

[20] "Worldliness and Other-Worldliness: The Poet Young," *Westminster Review*, LXVII (January 1857), 33.

deterministic sequences they engender: Amos Barton, Lawyer Dempster, Hetty Sorrel, Godfrey Cass, Tito Melema, Mrs. Transome, Nicholas Bulstrode, Tertius Lydgate, and Gwendolen Harleth must pay for disregarding both the guidelines of the past and the impending consequences of the future. Though suffering from the same lack of foresight, George Eliot's protagonists, Adam Bede, Janet Dempster, Silas Marner, Romola, Esther Lyon, Fedalma, Dorothea Brooke, and Daniel Deronda are eventually brought to understand their relation to broader social and historical forces.

Their understanding marks a triumph over their temporal selves. For their expanded sympathies create a "transhumanation" which connects their present to a meaningful past and links their actions to a future which they are partially allowed to shape. The reader, who participates vicariously in the widened awareness of these characters, thus senses the same "laws" which they come to perceive. The characters conquer the isolation enforced upon them by time. The reader, similarly oppressed by change and transition—by that modern age in which, according to Arnold, "we hear already the doubts, we witness the discouragement, of Hamlet and of Faust"—can likewise regain his confidence, emerge fortified, and face a dim and hidden future. Just as Milton's Christian reader is conducted toward an acceptance of his fallen nature by a vatic poet who can justify the ways of God to man, so is the reader of *Middlemarch* manipulated by an omniscient historian-philosopher "teaching by Experience."

The Divided Aesthetic of "Realism"

George Eliot's concern with time thus acts as a convenient key both to her thought and to her craft, to her monist view of existence and to her increasingly skillful presentation of this existence as a framework for her moral ideals. This presentation, however, is hardly uniform. For the confidence which the novelist wanted to instill in her readers is often marred by her own doubts and inner revulsion over the temporal Nature whose ways she wanted to justify. In chapter five of "The Sad Fortunes of the Reverend Amos Barton," her first published story, the narrator challenges those who would have him portray actions which have no counterpart in the actual world. Addressing a hypothetical lady reader, he mocks the expectations of a reading public that prefers "the ideal in fiction," to whom tragedy means ermine tippets, and comedy, the adventures of some unusually droll personage. Amos Barton, the narrator protests, is by no means either an 'ideal or exceptional character"; quite to the contrary, he is 'palpably and unmistakably commonplace." Yet it is out of the "homely details" of such ordinary lives that poetry and pathos, tragedy and comedy must be drawn: "Nay, is there not a pathos in their very insignificance—in our comparison of their dim and narrow existence with the glorious possibilities of that human nature which they share?" (FAB, I, chap. 5, p. 67). George Eliot's first story, printed in the January and February 1857 issues of *Blackwood's Edinburgh Magazine*, is replete with similar statements. The narrator professes himself unable to "invent thrilling incidents"; he suggests, after the manner of Wordsworth, that his main accomplishment "must lie in the *truth* with which I represent to you the humble experience of ordinary fellow-mortals. I wish to stir your sympathy with commonplace troubles—to win your tears for *real* sorrow: sorrow such as may live next door to you...." (chap. 7, p. 94; italics added.)

The frequency of such utterances, as well as George Eliot's private statements to her publisher John Blackwood, reveal the new novelist's eagerness to justify the nature of her art. The taste for domestic fiction had become well established in the late fifties; writers like Trollope and Mrs. Oliphant (who had serialized her novels in previous numbers of *Blackwood's*) were themselves writing successfully about men of an "insignificant stamp." The attacks, in "Amos Barton" and in George Eliot's 1856 essay on "Silly Novels by Lady Novelists," against the "many remarkable novels, full of striking situations, thrilling incidents, and eloquent writing," had long been anticipated by Thackeray's parodies of genteel fiction. But George Eliot was, of course, concerned with more than defending a literary vogue. Her early pronouncements (which anticipate the aesthetic creed more fully expounded in *Adam Bede*) stem directly from her philosophic outlook. She wanted, as a practicing novelist, to remain as faithful as possible to the empirical veracity she had already upheld in her essays and reviews. And yet, her early pronouncements contain inferences which have not seen sufficiently questioned;[21] her first three novellas possess serious discrepancies which have never been explored. For, far from displaying the perfect assurance of a novelist whose theory fully corresponds to her practice,[22] the George Eliot of *Scenes of Clerical Life* exhibits pronounced contradictions—contradictions which, with characteristic integrity, she strove to resolve in her art.

In a letter to John Blackwood, who had been troubled by the increasingly somber character of her three sketches of clerical life, the novelist began to re-examine her intentions: "Art must be either real or concrete, or ideal and eclectic. Both are good and true in their way, but my stories are of the former kind. I undertake to exhibit nothing as it should be; I only try to exhibit some things as they have been or are, seen through the medium as my own nature gives me." Although in these lines George Eliot comes close to pretending that she is nothing more than a chron-

---

[21] See, however, Richard Stang, "Realism with a Difference: George Eliot, Meredith, Lewes," in *The Theory of the Novel in England, 1850–1870* (New York, 1959), pp. 159–166. See also William J. Hyde, "George Eliot and the Climate of Realism," *PMLA*, LXXII (March 1957), 147–164; Thomas A. Noble, "Theory and Practice," *George Eliot's Scenes of Clerical Life* (New Haven, 1965), pp. 27–54; and Bernard J. Paris, *Experiments in Life*, pp. 242–250.

[22] Noble, "Theory and Practice," p. 49.

icler or historian, her last clause qualifies the preceding assertion.
For the medium of her own nature compels her, after all, to
rearrange things as they have been or are in order to suggest how
they ought to be. Her next sentence tries to define this medium:
"The moral effect of the stories of course depends on my power
of seeing truly and feeling justly; and as I am not conscious of
looking at things through the medium of cynicism, or irreverence, I can't help hoping that there is no tendency in what I write
to produce those miserable mental states." (GEL, II, 362.)
There is a curious ambivalence about this aesthetic. Like John
Ruskin, whose realism she had praised in one of her reviews, the
writer wants to be faithful to the details of actuality, and yet at
the same time be allowed to moralize or interpret these same details. Ruskin had demanded an almost photographic accuracy in
the observation of natural phenomena; George Eliot insists that
she is merely a natural historian exhibiting "things as they have
been." But whereas Ruskin freely allegorized the didactic prop-
erties of clouds and grass without the slightest self-consciousness,
George Eliot is irritated to find that she must now insist that her
"medium" is, after all, highly moralistic.

In her essays and in her early fiction, George Eliot tried to
lead her readers toward the acceptance of a reality which was
finite and unheroic. Yet the exact nature of this reality became
more problematic when transmuted by her art. Was the "real"
merely the observable, phenomenal world of experience? George
Eliot rebelled against such an assumption. She could not place
her faith in the fortuitous evolutionary world she regarded as
real. The very opening paragraph of "Amos Barton" evokes a
world dominated by the relentless flux of time. The Shepperton
Church which once housed Amos and his clerical precursors is
irrevocably altered: "that dear, old, brown, crumbling, picturesque inefficiency is everywhere giving place to spick-and-span
new-painted, new-varnished efficiency" (chap. 1, p. 4). Only the
"substantial stone tower" and its prominent village clock have re-

mained the same. Gradually, by recalling the structure's past shape, the narrator-historian also reconstructs the shape of his childhood past. In the fashion of Proust, her later admirer, the novelist combines irony with a genuine elegiac sadness in sorting out the worn layers of time. In a passage which, significantly enough, she omitted from the published version of the story, the narrator recalls his early illusions. Like those held by the small Maggie in *The Mill*, his beliefs have been shattered by his later experiences, by the "reason" of adult knowledge: "Oh that happy time of childish veneration! It is the fashion to regret the days of easy merriment, but we forget the early bliss of easy reverence, when the world seemed to us peopled with the great and wise."

In "Amos Barton" and its sequel, "Mr. Gilfil's Love-Story," George Eliot's presentation of a "dim and narrow existence" seriously clashed with her unsatisfied yearning for the "glorious possibilities" which that existence seems to deny. She therefore tried to impose "poetry and pathos" on the mundane and un-heroic, to discover significance in insignificance, to detect—as Wordsworth had done—the extraordinary in the ordinary. In her first two stories, such efforts are largely unsuccessful. The idealization of Milly Barton—the first in George Eliot's gallery of matronly Madonnas—jars with, rather than elevates, the satirical treatment of her hopelessly uninspiring husband; the con-version of Caterina Sarti—the prototype for Maggie Tulliver, Esther Lyon, and Gwendolen Harleth—is robbed of its full im-pact by a change in emphasis: Caterina's unexpected death brings back the focus on her husband's enforced resignation. Only in the third of her *Scenes of Clerical Life*, "Janet's Repentance," was George Eliot able to give more weight to the "glorious possibil-ities" of human nature without compromising her negative pic-ture of man's limitations. Through Janet's redemption at the hands of the Reverend Mr. Tryan she was able to provide the balance between the actual and the ideal that was lacking in her former tales. Her first attempts to work out her ideas in fictional form thus created difficulties she had not foreseen. Philosophically, these difficulties had been anticipated by Hegel's distinction between "reality" and "existence"; artistically, by Coleridge's astute remarks about the "realistic" aims of Wordsworth's poetry.

Hegel, in the spirit of German idealism, could readily distinguish between the two axioms, "Whatever is *real* is reasonable" and "Whatever *exists* is reasonable," by elevating "reality" above existence and identifying it with the infinite spiritual quality of "reason." For George Eliot, rooted in the monism of Comte, Spencer, and Feuerbach, such metaphysical subtleties were impossible. She too, sought a higher order in which "Right" and "Reason" could once again be synonymous.[23] But what she called reality was perilously close to the very actuality she wanted to improve. By rejecting "otherworldly" standards such as Hegel's, she was burdened with the task of justifying man to man. Her own personal experience of social injury and alienation made this task all the more difficult.[24] Out of the imperfect and egoistic human being she portrayed so convincingly, she had to carve a man-god capable of validating her precept that the "fundamental faith for man" was nothing but a "faith in the result of a brave, honest, and steady use of all his faculties."[25] Out of the petty society which defamed Edward Tryan, Maggie Tulliver, and Will

[23] "Evangelical Teaching," p. 462. The Beinecke Library at Yale University possesses a manuscript (possibly in George Eliot's hand) giving a detailed criticism of Lewes' treatment of Hegel in *Biographical History of Philosophy* (1845–1857). The author of the manuscript complains: "Being and Existence are here treated as identical terms—And we here want to be told what Hegel means by Being, which I have not seen quite satisfactorily explained anywhere in the chapter."

[24] See, for instance, her friend Barbara Bodichon's reaction on first hearing that this social outcast had captured the Victorian reading public with *Adam Bede*: "That YOU *that you* they spit at should do it!" (GEL, III, 56.)

[25] "Evangelical Teaching," p. 462.

Ladislaw, she had to create an agency whose mandates, though severe and painful, were also irrevocable and just. Out of history itself, the summation of actions riddled by error, she was forced to create in her later novels a power corresponding to the exacting Miltonic God which she had rejected.

The inconsistencies of such a creed were not unlike those inherent in the materialist philosophy of a very different school. In his *Conditions of the Working Class in England* (1845), Friedrich Engels, another disciple of Hegel and Feuerbach, idealized the "comfortable and peaceful existence" of England's rural past in order to counter its grim industrial present.[26] His picture of a "righteous, God-fearing, and honest" peasantry almost evokes the idyllic pastoral existence led by the Poysers or the Winthrops in George Eliot's pastoral novels. Yet the historicism of Engels and Marx, with its belief in inevitable progress, clashed with this idealized reality. In the Communist Manifesto, written three years later, the past is no longer upheld, but merely seen as an inferior historical stage for the complexity of the present. In a shift of emphasis not at all unlike that which accompanies George Eliot's own shift from the Poysers to "these emmet-like Dodsons and Tullivers," Marx and Engels now denounced the dulled *"Idiotismus"* (stupefaction) of the English peasant.

George Eliot's own ironic detachment from the "rustic stupidity furnished by the farm-laborers" (FAB, chap. 2, p. 33) allows her to exploit the simplicities of an irretrievable past for the enlightenment of her own present. By exercising the role of an ironic novelist-historian, she manages to avoid some of the artistic flaws which Coleridge had detected in Wordsworth's realism. Wordsworth, his friend insisted, should not have adopted the point of view and language of his rustic puppets, but should have gone beyond the "insulated facts" of their experience to discover

[26] *The Condition of the Working Class in England*, ed. W. O. Henderson and W. H. Chaloner (London, 1956), pp. 10–11.

those connections or bearings from fact to fact "from which some more or less general law is deducible."[27] To do otherwise, he emphasized, was to "take away the liberty of a poet, and fetter his feet in the shackles of an historian," that is, to represent reality "in the manner of De Foe's [novels], that were meant to pass for histories, not in the manner of Fielding's"[28] According to Coleridge, a great philosophic poet should consequently adopt a "contemplative position," to remain, like Milton, *"Spectator ab extra."*[29] He should distinguish himself by his own prospectiveness of mind, "that *surview*, which enables a man to foresee the whole of what he is to convey."[30] The latter phrase aptly describes that "steadiness and clarity of ironic contemplation,"[31] which George Eliot was to perfect in both *Silas Marner* and *Middlemarch*.

Nonetheless, Coleridge's quarrel with Wordsworth's "equivocation in the use of the word 'real' "[32] is definitely applicable also to the writer who had started out in her career by pretending, as Wordsworth had, to be nothing but an uncultivated observer of ordinary life. George Eliot's letter to Blackwood suggests that she was highly irritated to discover that her moralism had either gone entirely unperceived or even been mistaken for "cynicism" and "irreverence." Her choice of words is significant. For she

[27] *Biographia*, chap. 17, p. 197. In her essay on "The Natural History of German Life," *Westminster Review*, LXVI (July 1856), 51–79, George Eliot echoes Coleridge when she argues that English and German novelists are mistakenly transferring their own exalted thoughts and feelings to ploughmen and woodcutters who are devoid of such higher emotions.

[28] *Ibid.*, chap. 22, pp. 251, 256.

[29] *Specimens of the Table-Talk of Samuel Taylor Coleridge* (Edinburgh, 1905), p. 186.

[30] *Biographia*, chap. 18, p. 201; Coleridge's italics.

[31] W. J. Harvey, *The Art of George Eliot* (London, 1961), p. 88.

[32] *Biographia*, chap. 17, p. 198.

may well have wanted to dissociate herself from the example of Thackeray, who had been accused of producing those very same "miserable mental states." Blackwood had already commented on the "harsher Thackerayan view of human nature" which he claimed to have detected in the first installment of "Janet's Repentance"; he had applauded one of the story's scenes as being "something" in the style of the master who, as he jokingly suggested, might well be disposed to claim the new author as his latest disciple (GEL, II, 344–345). George Eliot was not amused. Although she had shown an acute interest in Thackeray's reaction to her first two stories, she now veered in the opposite direction. Icily, she informed her correspondent: "I am not conscious of being in any way a disciple of his, unless it constitute discipleship to think him, as I suppose the majority of people with any intellect do, on the whole the most powerful of living novelists" (GEL, II, 349).

It is significant that, immediately upon the publication of *Scenes of Clerical Life* in book form, it should have been Dickens and not Thackeray who detected the "womanly touches in those moving fictions." In a highly effusive letter addressed to the still unknown "George Eliot Esquire," Thackeray's rival unreservedly praised "the man or woman who has written so charmingly." The very novelist who had once claimed that *Vanity Fair* had produced in him those same unbearable mental states she spoke of in her letter to Blackwood, now vowed that he would "yield" himself to all future utterances from this new competitor "with a perfect confidence in their making me wiser and better" (GEL, II, 424).

Dickens' tribute is important. It attests to his recognition of the intensely idealistic character of the stories which John Blackwood, misled by George Eliot's emphasis, had mistakenly felt to be anti-idealistic. Gradually, the novelist began to amplify her previous definitions. Her "realism," she now recognized, merely demanded a close faithfulness to probability, not a rejection of the "ideal or eclectic." Indeed, George Eliot's art became more and more eclectic. After the composition of "Amos Barton," she began to experiment with the correlatives of romance and the epic, while at the same time maintaining that real life was primarily unromantic and unheroic. When one of her readers claimed that the figure of the Reverend Edward Tryan in "Janet's Repentance" was a true copy of his long-deceased brother, she retorted that Mr. Tryan was "not a portrait of any clergyman, living or dead. He is an *ideal* character, but I hope *probable* enough to resemble more than one evangelical clergyman of his day" (GEL, II, 375; italics added). When, after the publication of *Adam Bede*, it was held that the novel depicted incidents actually experienced by its author, she was forced to insist that her story was imaginary: "The details which I knew as facts and have made use of for my picture were gathered from such imperfect allusion and narrative as I heard from my father, in his occasional talk about old times" (GEL, III, 176). She rejected the contention that Dinah Morris' preaching was the result of her having "seen journals and notes of sermons" kept by her Methodist aunt:

Now this supposition is simply a proof of the low conceptions of art that are prevalent, and the narrow, ignorant views of religious history and religious life. *Truth* in art is so startling, that no one can believe in its art; and the specific forms of religious life which have made some of the grandest elements in human history are looked down upon as if they were not within the artist's sympathy and veneration and intensely dramatic reproduction. (GEL, III, 185; her italics.)

Yet the confusion between "truth in art" and historical truth had not been totally the fault of her readers. She had herself encouraged it by resorting to the fiction of an untutored provincial observer who had personally known Amos Barton, Mr. Tryan, Dinah Morris, and Adam Bede. Only after her public began to attribute her works to the impostor Joseph Liggins,[33] did George Eliot devise a new narrative persona in the shape of an erudite and sympathetic historian. What is more, the split between artistic and historical truth would still remain. It is most apparent perhaps in what could easily have become her masterpiece, *The Mill on the Floss*. In the "Life on the Floss," her faithfulness to the empirical standards she had adopted clashes with her idealistic purpose. She warns the reader that Maggie's destiny is to be shaped by heredity and environment: "irreversible laws within and without her" will bring about the girl's doom. But Maggie's tragic fate, so meticulously prepared for, becomes, when it does manifest itself, arbitrary and capricious. The fortuitous circumstances which cause Maggie's death suggest that, far from being irreversible, her accidental drowning acts as a convenient escape from an unbearable reality. For George Eliot invokes the waters of the Floss only after the girl has returned to St. Ogg's and fully expiated her fault. Victimized first by the slanders of her society and then by the churning waters of the river, the rounded and consistent character we have grown to understand and like suddenly turns into a flat and passive exemplum in a homily on the need for sympathy in an imperfect world. While Mr. Tulliver dies by blindly defying a changing world whose reality he cannot fathom, Maggie's and Tom's execution by an emblematic agent of that world remains arbitrarily superimposed by an author unable to dispel her vision of "individual nothingness" through an insistence on the redemptive qualities of Love.

Throughout her career, George Eliot's desire to be faithful

---

[33] Liggins, a resident of Nuneaton in Warwickshire, encouraged rumors that he was the author of *Scenes of Clerical Life* and *Adam Bede*. George Eliot was much annoyed to have her work attributed to this "base worldling." She asked Blackwood to write a letter of denial to the *Times*, wrote several letters herself under her pseudonym, and was finally forced to reveal her authorship to quell the persistent rumors (see GEL, II, 337, 366; III, 21, 44, 46–47, 49, *et passim*).

to the conditions of actual existence clashed with her efforts to transcend or dignify the meanness of those conditions. While the Hardy of *Tess of the D'Urbervilles* gloomily recreates the laws of an evolutionary universe in order to lament the capriciousness of the cosmos, the George Eliot of *The Mill on the Floss*, though every bit as gloomy, tries to enlist these laws to validate her belief in "Right" and "Reason." While the Thackeray of *Vanity Fair* is content to reproduce a corrupt, secular society for whose imperfections he can provide few alternatives, the George Eliot of *Middlemarch* tries to infuse this same social organism with the principles necessary for its perfection and growth. Therefore, while Thackeray and Hardy can paradoxically pretend that the invented world of their novels corresponds to nothing more than the world of fact, George Eliot's similar claim is far more sophistical. Although the fabricated "reality" of her stories is held out as an equivalent to that of the external world, it also acts as a corrective, containing within it the very ideals which that world would seem to deny. In this sense, her aims are far closer to Dickens' than to those of Thackeray. Like her two great predecessors, George Eliot is obsessed by the obstacles in the path of man's aspirations towards goodness and perfection. But, unlike Thackeray and very much like Dickens, she wants to rescue her characters from their bondage to time, to carry her pilgrims beyond the temporal anarchy of Vanity Fair and the City of Destruction into a higher, more universal plane. Dickens achieves this aim, not through philosophic art, but through the startling use of fairy tale, symbol, and myth. His peculiar genius allows him to make the actual seem unreal and the unreal seem distinctly possible: in a novel like *Our Mutual Friend*, the oppressive reality of the world-as-it-is can gradually be laughed away as it becomes displaced by an incredible society of "mutual friends," an incorporeal world-as-it-might-be, to which, despite its utter unreality, we must and do extend our belief.

For George Eliot such a practice is suspect. Notwithstanding her later friendship with Dickens, it is clear from her and Lewes' dicta on the novel, that she would have regarded such an enforced suspension of disbelief as being almost tantamount to artistic irresponsibility.[34] Through the irrational persuasiveness of his art, Dickens has succeeded in annulling the reality of the time-bound world. But, George Eliot would protest, he has done so subjectively by imposing his own idiosyncrasies on that world and has failed those readers who are bound by its inescapable logic. In her own novels she would try to adhere to the logic of the real world and yet attempt to guide her readers towards an apprehension of the ideal: "Falsehood is so easy, truth so difficult" (AB, chap. 17, pp. 267–268). Even in those works where her "truth in art" was to be impeccable, she would also strictly observe the truth of real life.

Unwilling to give up the conflicting standards which first manifested themselves in "Amos Barton," George Eliot the novelist thus embarked on the career that was to end almost twenty years later with the publication of *Daniel Deronda*. The norms that she had set for herself in "Amos Barton" were ultimately repudiated when she aggrandized Deronda into an "ideal or exceptional character" of Carlylean proportions. Still, her journey was hardly circular. In its course, she would produce *Silas Marner* and *Middlemarch* and master the truth that was so difficult. In her greatest novel she adopted that "prospectiveness of mind" which Coleridge had in 1817 declared to be essential to the genius of a great philosophic poet. Almost a hundred years later, Henry James re-examined George Eliot's work for the last time in his life. Though more lavish in his praise, the American novelist still

---

[34] For the best exposition of George Eliot's and Lewes' views, see Stang, "Realism with a Difference." Both she and Lewes felt that Dickens' idealizing disposition had led him to create stereotypes. In "The Natural History of German Life," she holds that only Dickens' disregard for psychological accuracy prevented his books from becoming "the greatest contribution Art has ever made to the awakening of social sympathies" (p. 55).

refused to speculate on the place which "the author of Middle-march and Silas Marner may be conceived to have in the pride of our literature."[35] Fifty years later, her place seems far more secure. For the "beauty and humanity, of applied and achieved art," which even James professed to find in her fiction, ranks George Eliot among those few English writers who dared to explore the "middle state" between knowledge and wisdom which is the exclusive domain of philosophic art.

[35] *The Middle Years* (London, 1917), p. 60.

2. Sentimentalism and Death: "Amos Barton"

These Faytours little regarden their charge
While they, letting their sheepe runne at large,
Passen their time, that should be sparsely spent,
In lustihede and wanton meriment.
  —*The Shepherdes Calendar*

Altogether, as matters stood in Shepperton, the parishioners were
more likely to have a strong sense that the clergyman needed their
material aid, than that they needed his spiritual aid—not the best
state of things in this age and country, where faith in men solely
on the ground of their spiritual gifts has considerably diminished,
and especially unfavorable to the influence of the Rev. Amos, whose
spiritual gifts would not have had a very commanding power even
in an age of faith.

  —"AMOS BARTON"

In December of 1857, Marian Evans, already at work on *Adam Bede*, looked back at the beginning of a "new era" in her life: the year which was coming to a close had been marked by the serial publication of her three "Scenes from Clerical Life."[1] The onetime editor of the *Westminster Review* had been encouraged by George Henry Lewes to find a new outlet for her intellectual powers: "his prevalent impression was that though I could hardly

[1] "How I Came To Write Fiction," GEL, II, 406ff. The three novellas were printed in eleven consecutive numbers of *Blackwood's Edinburgh Magazine*: "Amos Barton" appeared in the January and February issues; "Mr. Gilfil's Love-Story" was published in four parts from March to June; "Janet's Repentance," in five parts from July to November.

38

write a *poor* novel, my effort would want the highest quality of fiction—dramatic presentation. He used to say, 'You have wit, description and philosophy—those go a good way towards the production of a novel. It is worth while for you to try the experiment.' " (GEL, II, 407.) The experiment had been worthwhile. Only John Blackwood's "want of sympathy" for the first two installments of "Janet's Repentance" had determined the new novelist to close the series. She then agreed to republish the three stories in two volumes and now wondered how the public would react to her first book.

"Amos Barton," "Mr. Gilfil's Love-Story," and "Janet's Repentance" are united by more than a common locale and an emphasis on the relations between clergymen and their flocks. All three stories equally insist on relating an unheroic existence to man's higher potentials. Their stress is largely negative: Amos Barton is drawn as a grotesquely ineffectual pastor; his predecessor, Mr. Gilfil, though far more tolerant and understanding, becomes stunted by suffering an untimely loss; Janet Dempster, brutalized by her alcoholic husband, resorts to drinking in order to escape her oppressive life. But these stories are not written by Zola. Their negations are enlisted to advance the author's ideals. Amos Barton, Caterina Gilfil, and Janet Dempster was chastened by their experiences: Amos is inspired by his wife's memory, Caterina finds life "sweet" for her husband's sake, and, in the most dramatic of the three tales, Janet discovers that her contact with the exemplary Mr. Tryan rescues her from the quicksands of anarchy and self-despair.

Yet if the three novellas are very much alike in their intentions, they are remarkably dissimilar in their form and craftsmanship. George Eliot's artificial incarnation of her ideas in "Amos Barton" betrays the story's kinship to her essays in the *Westminster Review* and sets it apart from its two sequels. By simply superimposing "glorious possibilities" (FAB, chap. 5, p. 67) on the imperfect world she had created, she compromised the very plausibility she aimed at. In "Mr. Gilfil's Love-Story," she moved away, both in setting and in mode, from the discrepancy between actual and ideal which had marred the resolution of "Amos Barton." By creating two separate orders of reality—a remote, illusory world of romance and a factual realm of existence like that portrayed in "Amos Barton"—she managed to dignify the limitations of Shepperton life far more convincingly. She returned to the mode of "Amos Barton" in "Janet's Repentance" and again was led to a sentimental exaltation of her values. But in this story the dramatic interplay between the imperfections of the society at large and the moral perfection achieved by Mr. Tryan, provided a plausible framework for the evolution of her central character. Although Janet belongs to a reality even more strangulating than that in "Amos Barton," the ideals which come to her rescue are not artificially imposed from without. Though his role strongly resembles that of the angelic Milly Barton, Mr. Tryan is a more satisfactory device to convert things "as they have been" into an exemplum of what they might become. In the short span of a year, George Eliot had mastered some of the contradictions inherent in her double aims. And while she was at work on "Janet's Repentance," she decided that she was ready for "a larger canvas" (GEL, II, 381). Her three scenes of clerical life succeeded in transforming the essayist of the *Westminster Review* and the *Leader* into the accomplished novelist who was to write *Adam Bede*.

OTHER-WORLDLINESS SATIRIZED: AMOS BARTON

The first half of "The Sad Fortunes of the Reverend Amos Barton" was published in *Blackwood's* in the same month in which the *Westminster Review* printed George Eliot's lead article, "Worldliness and Other-Worldiness: The Poet Young." Despite the difference in mode, story and essay carry quite similar implications. Each centers around the figure of a clergyman.

Both pretend to be "natural histories," the study of men under the "social conditions" which shape their lives.[2] In each case, the subject is flushed out of the past by an author who assumes the role of a scientific historian "in search of specimens." In each case, the specimen is examined with ironic amusement. Like Amos Barton, Edward Young is regarded as a curious anomaly belonging to "the species *divine*—a surprising name, considering the nature of the animal before us" ("Worldliness," p. 1). In her essay, George Eliot satirizes the "astronomical religion" which Young translates into his inflated poetry (p. 8); in her story, she treats the "geographical, chronological, exegetical mind" of Amos Barton somewhat less sardonically (FAB, chap. 2, p. 38), but indicts him for the same "impiety toward the present and the visible" of which his counterpart stands convicted ("Worldliness," p. 42).

The historical portrait of Young and the fictitious "history" of Barton's misfortunes contain identical judgments. Both men are incapable of reconciling the worldliness of their personal ambitions with the otherworldliness of their professed religious teachings. In their attempts to balance "temporalities and spiritualities," they slight the finite, temporal domain which George Eliot's positivism had taught her to regard as "real." Young writes jocosely about "our old acquaintance, *Time*" (p. 20), yet spends his own time by apostrophizing eternity and the stars; Amos Barton likewise ignores the preciousness of his own present by devoting his energies to abstract theological hairsplitting. Young professes to be deeply stirred by the "momentousness of death," but his stilted sentiments on mortality are merely calculated to impress patrons who can secure his worldly advancement. Though Barton's in-

[2] "Worldliness and Other-Worldliness: The Poet Young," *Westminster Review*, LXVII (January 1857), 1; subsequent references are given in the text. George Eliot had used the term "natural history" in the title of her 1856 review of W. H. Riehl's two social studies of German life, *Die Bürgerliche Gesellschaft* (1851) and *Land und Leute* (1855).

sincerities are less conscious, they are every bit as jarring: unable to comfort parishioners terrified at the prospect of death, he publishes the sermons they cannot understand in order to rise in the esteem of his fellow clergy. Essay and story thus attack the same object: the disregard for man's mortal life, which the author had already denounced in the person of still another clergyman, the Rev. Dr. Cumming, not long after she had concluded her translation of Ludwig Feuerbach's *Essence of Christianity* (1854).

In his *"historico-philosophical* analysis" of Christianity, Feuerbach had savagely attacked "The False or Theological Essense of Religion."[3] Seizing on the paradoxes of metaphysics, the German philosopher ingeniously exploited the contradictions inherent in a belief in "the supermundane, supernatural, and superhuman" (p. 184). In their place, he substituted the bold paradoxes of his own devising: in his system faith in God became faith in the nature of corporeal man; faith in a future life, "faith in the *true* life of the present" (p. 181). Despite his radicalism, however, Feuerbach repeatedly emphasized that his relation to religion was "not merely a negative, but a critical one"; his only object, he contended, was to separate the true from the false (p. 270). Like Feuerbach's work, which influenced her profoundly, George Eliot's early sketches are meant to be critical rather than negative. To be sure, she too wanted to demolish the theological aspects of religion. But she regarded this destruction as necessary to advance her humanist fundamentals. Like the German, she remained an idealist, but "an idealist only in the region of *practical* philosophy"; to both, a belief in the numinous "Idea" of metaphysics had to be supplanted by a forward-looking belief in the possibilities of actual life. Only a faith in man's present can lead to a "faith in the historical future" (p. xxxiv).

[3] Ludwig Feuerbach, *The Essence of Christianity*, trans. George Eliot; introductory essay by Karl Barth; foreword by H. Richard Niebuhr (New York, 1957), p. xii [Feuerbach's italics]. Subsequent references will be given in the text.

The sketches of Young and Amos Barton express George Eliot's desire to affirm such a faith. The factual world which the two men evade is endowed with a weight of its own. Both Young and Barton try to justify their evasions of that factual world through a belief in a shadowy hereafter; it remained for George Eliot to show "that in some minds the deep pathos lying in the thought of human mortality—that we are here for a little while and then vanish away" was closer to the "fountains of moral emotion than the conception of extended existence" (Worldliness," p. 34). By evoking "tears for *real* sorrow," her first story was meant to replenish these fountains (FAB, chap. 7, p. 94; italics added). As a speculative philosopher, Feuerbach had trumpeted his new creed through an impassioned presentation of his "religion of suffering." As a new novelist eager to appeal to the Christian readers of Dickens and Mrs. Gaskell, his translator was forced to proceed with far greater caution.

Amos Barton is the first of a series of clerical figures whose importance was to diminish only in George Eliot's later fiction.[4] Though comical in his unworldliness, he does not receive the same amused approval that Trollope bestowed that same year on his Dr. Harding.[5] In the eighteenth century, Fielding and Goldsmith had created clergymen whose very unworldliness betokened their superiority to their amoral surroundings. Parson Adams and Dr. Primrose (to whom some readers compared Amos Barton) trust an infinite Providence throughout their adversities: although their ill fortune occasionally makes such certainty seem quixotic or even ludicrous, the ultimate turn of events amply confirms their

[4] In *Romola*, the heroine evolves beyond the religious views of both her brother Dino and Savonarola himself; in *Felix Holt* and *Middlemarch*, despite considerable sympathy for the Rev. Rufus Lyon and the Rev. Camden Farebrother, Esther and Dorothea rise above these clerical tutors; in *Daniel Deronda*, the secular Daniel takes over the role of the Rev. Mr. Gascoigne, Gwendolen's uncle.

[5] *Barchester Towers* appeared in 1857; *The Warden*, in 1855.

steadfast belief. George Eliot, on the other hand, exploits the figure of the unworldly curate for exactly the opposite end. Barton's misfortunes—like those of Froude's ill-fated Markham Sutherland or Butler's Ernest Pontifex—merely assert the reality of a finite, material existence which no supernatural creed can surmount. Unlike Parson Adams, Amos must be brought to understand the full implications of man's mortality.[6]

To Amos Barton life at Shepperton seems static and fixed. Yet, seen from the narrator's own busy times twenty years later, Barton's era is revealed as a mere interregnum between the present and a remoter past which tried, just as vainly, to shore itself against all "human advancement." Decades before Barton's arrival, Shepperton was a placid, rural hamlet. Like the communities of Hayslope and Raveloe in *Adam Bede* and *Silas Marner*, its inhabitants were contented to be isolated from the outer world. Under the ministry of the Reverend Mr. Gilfil, the slow pace of everyday life had gone undisturbed: "The innovation of hymnbooks was as yet undreamed of; even the new Version was regarded with a melancholy tolerance, as part of the common degeneracy in a time when prices had dwindled, and a cotton gown was no longer stout enough to last a lifetime." (chap. 1, p. 6.) But historical change, though hardly perceived by the Sheppertonians, has been at work. The laws of development which Comte and Mill and Spencer regarded as invariable and universal do not bypass Shepperton. When Barton arrives, external changes have already had their impact on the village. For the new clergyman does not come "until long after Mr. Gilfil had departed this life

6 On George Eliot's relation to Fielding, see pp. 14–16, above. It is noteworthy that, in her 1857 essay, she rejects the idea that Young might have been the original of Fielding's Parson Adams; the true original, she points out sarcastically, must have had "both more Greek and more genuine simplicity" (p. 13). In her later fiction she places a greater value on quixotism: the Reverend Mr. Lyon, who does resemble Fielding's parson, is treated far more sympathetically than Amos Barton.

—until after an interval in which Evangelicalism and the Catho-
lic Question had begun to agitate the rustic mind with contro-
versial debates" (chap. 1, p. 7). At his arrival, "the hymn-book
had almost superseded the Old and New Versions." His congregation is understandably suspicious of further innovations.[7]

Mrs. Patten, "a pretty little old woman of eighty," lifts up
her withered hands in a vain gesture of protest against the "new
sort of doctrines." Puzzled by the "changes as have come about,"
she is disturbed by Barton's desire to raze the old church building
in order to build it anew (chap. 1, pp. 11, 14). Most other characters also bear the marks of time. Mr. Fitchett, a former foot-
man, now displays shrunken calves and a shock of hair that is
gray without the aid of powder. "Old stiff-jointed Mr. Tozer"
still ekes out a living through occasional gardening chores (chap.
10, p. 121). The "hard undying" Mrs. Brick presents a network
of wrinkles "as a coat of magic armor against the attacks of
winter" (chap. 2, p. 37). Old Maxum, the town's patriarch, had
once "been considered pithy and sententious in his speech; but
now the weight of ninety-five years lay heavy on his tongue as
well as on his ears" (chap. 2, p. 36). Nor are the younger characters immune to time. George Eliot's narrator makes sure to
stress that the gallant Mr. Bridmain is "decidedly becoming
gray"; he assures us, perhaps too stridently, that his prophetic eye
allows him to predict that the beauty of Bridmain's sister, the fic-

---

[7] The meticulousness with which George Eliot mapped out the chronology of the story suggests the seriousness with which she regarded her
role as novelist-historian. Barton assumes his duties "rather more than
twenty years ago" (around 1834 or 1835), although the 1834 Poor Law
had not yet come into operation. The story itself seems to be set in 1837–
1838, for the Reverend Mr. Duke condemns "the 'Pickwick Papers,' recently completed." Mr. Gilfil, we discover here, died "thirty years ago."
The decade between his tenure and Barton's curacy has been filled by an
Evangelical preacher who is probably the Mr. Parry approvingly mentioned by Mr. Hackit.

titious "Countess" Czerlaski, will also deteriorate (chap. 3, pp. 46, 48).

Time and change are the only constants in the evolutionary world that George Eliot portrays. The unaltered clock on the tower of Shepperton thus acts as a fitting emblem for the permanence of impermanence. Religion itself, like the physical structure of the church, has yielded to the mutitudinousness of modern life. Some religious rudiments, however, like the "substantial" stone tower, manage to weather the flux. The best among the Sheppertonians signify their acceptance of mutability by living lives attuned to the seasons. The Reverend Martin Cleves, the "least clerical-looking" of the motley membership of the Clerical Meeting and Book Society, is a capable farmer able to discuss the rotation of crops. Mrs. Hackit, the sharp-tongued but compassionate prototype for Mrs. Poyser in *Adam Bede*, goes so far as to regulate her costume by the calendar (chap. 6, p. 79). Yet Amos Barton, whose "time is so precious," cannot adapt his otherworldly religion to his surroundings. Impervious to the seasonal changes which punctuate his short career at Shepperton, the distracted Amos fails to make up for his "omissions" until it is too late. His story progresses from the "cold snow" of winter to the "flowers and perspiration" which mark his springtime exertions, from "summer and harvest" to the "Christmas snow" which covers his wife's fresh grave. Only after her death does he appreciate that, in George Eliot's cult of humanity, life must be spent by hallowing the present, with deference to the past and in anticipation of the future.[8]

Ironically, Amos Barton thinks of himself as one fully in tune with progress. It is he who hopes to rebuild Shepperton Church

---

[8] Amos' enforced exile from Shepperton takes place in "May again"; his one return to Milly's tomb, years later, comes appropriately "in the calm and softened light of an autumnal afternoon." As Daniel P. Deneau has pointed out, however, there are some flaws in George Eliot's timetable ("A Note on George Eliot's 'Amos Barton'—Reticence and Chronology," *Notes and Queries*, CCIV, [December 1959], 450–451).

despite the dwindling fervor of its congregation; it is he who introduces the new doctrines which puzzle Mrs. Patten and the new wedding hymns which replace those fondly remembered by Mr. Hackit. But his progressivism is a sham which hides his "bungling feebleness of achievement" (chap. 2, p. 35). His inadequacies are in direct contrast to the accomplishments of the Rev. Mr. Cleves. Whereas Mr. Cleves' working-class origins give him "hereditary sympathies with the checkered life of the people" (chap. 6, p. 87), Barton's denial of his own heritage makes him a clerical version of the upstart blinded by false expectations, so often satirized in Dickens' novels. Instead of following the example of his father, "an excellent cabinet-maker and deacon of an Independent church," Amos' imperfect training at Cambridge leads him to reject his past and to snub the "ordinary minds" of his flock (chap. 2, pp. 34, 45). While Mr. Cleves teaches through homely examples in "conversational lecture[s] on useful practical matters," Amos tries to compensate his natural inability to teach by publishing in the erudite pages of "The Pulpit" the sermons which only "trouble and confuse the Sheppertonian mind" (chap. 6, p. 87; chap. 3, p. 54). His intellectual pretensions are not only mediocre; but they lack all conviction; for the Tractarians have led him to revise some of his own Low Church principles. His revised views appeal to neither party.

But Amos' deficiencies as a clergyman merely attest to his failings as a human being. In her essay on Young, George Eliot had attacked the poet's flights of fancy as the product of a "mind in which the higher human sympathies were inactive" (p. 19). Likewise, it is Barton's dearth of feeling which lies at the core of all his failings: "For though Amos thought himself strong, he did not *feel* himself strong. Nature had given him the opinion, but not the sensation." (Chap. 2, p. 34.) His immediate predecessor, an Evangelical (like Mr. Tryan in "Janet's Repentance"), had been able to stir a certain amount of "religious excitement." Unable to move his parishioners, Amos hopes that his building program will at least enable him to counter the attraction of the local Dissenting ministers. He is therefore far more eager to catch "large fish" for his congregation than to attend to the wants of the parish paupers.

It is in a visit to the village poorhouse that he most crassly displays his insensitivity. When the ragged, hopelessly unspiritual Mrs. Brick finds her snuffbox empty, Barton not only refuses to give her a pittance to refill it, but cruelly magnifies her worldly foibles: "Ah, well! you'll soon be going where there is not more snuff. You'll be in need of mercy then. You must remember that you may have to seek for mercy and not find it, just as you're seeking for snuff." His clumsy parable produces an unintended effect: "At the first sentence of this admonition, the twinkle subsided from Mrs. Brick's eyes. The lid of her box went 'click!' and her heart was shut up at the same moment." (chap. 2, p. 40.) Totally unsympathetic to the weaknesses of others, Barton invokes his supernatural religion to cow still another offender, a seven-year-old boy who has offended the master of the workhouse: "God can burn you forever. That will be worse than being beaten." (chap. 2, p. 42.) Dissatisfied with the outcome of his "disagreeable duties," the clergyman trudges home, his heart as cold as the winter snow. But neither his wife's attention, nor the sight of his children thaws him out. He escapes into his study, settles in an easy chair, and engrosses himself in a work on the episcopacy.

Barton's religion displays the lack of charity which George Eliot had found in the creeds of Young and Cumming; his doctrines about salvation in a future world obstruct his efforts to ease the burdens of the present. But his theology is less a vehicle for intolerance than a means of avoiding the realities he fears. Like Mr. Casaubon in *Middlemarch*, this grotesque minister must nurture an illusion. In order to shield himself from his natural imperfections, he clings to the illusion of his importance as a divine. He therefore becomes an easy prey for the scheming "Countess" Czerlaski, who seeks him out only after she has been slighted by the Reverend Mr. Ely's congregation at Milby, "in spite of her assiduous church-going" (chap. 4, p. 63). Incapable of detecting the true motives of this convert, Barton accepts her indictment of his rival's preaching, even though it applies far more to his own ("It has no fervor—no heart"). Although it is evident that the former governess lacks all "taste and insight in theological teaching," he is flattered by her acuity in choosing him as her spiritual teacher. He greedily believes her when she overpraises his sermons and blushes deeply when she promises to recommend him to an imaginary aristocratic patron. In his vanity, Amos Barton fails to see that her piety is feigned. For Caroline Czerlaski's needs are not spiritual. She hopes that her cultivation of the minister will make her respectable in the eyes of Milby society: "She had serious intentions of becoming *quite* pious—without any reserves— when she had once got her carriage and settlement." (chap. 4, p. 64.)

The countess' false piety and Barton's falsified theology exemplify the misuses of religion which George Eliot had denounced in her essay on Edward Young. The countess' egoism is deliberate; Barton's, only semiconscious. Yet both are products of the same "deficient human sympathy." In her essay, George Eliot had contrasted Young's shortcomings with the positive example of William Cowper, whose work stands for "the type of that genuine love which cherishes things in proportion to their nearness" (p. 42). The deficiencies of Amos Barton and Caroline Czerlaski are emphasized by their joint disregard for their opposite, Milly Barton, the clergyman's wife. Like Cowper, Amelia Barton represents a "sublime capacity for loving" (chap. 2, p. 26).

WORLDLINESS IDEALIZED: AMELIA BARTON

Described as a "large, fair, gentle Madonna," Milly Barton is the first and most sentimentalized of George Eliot's portrayals of ideal womanhood. While Barton is grotesquely caricatured as a bald and pockmarked animal belonging to the "species divine," his wife is depicted as a semi-angelic creature who can even impart "elegance" and "distinction" to her ordinary clothes. Her attire and the gracefulness she imparts to it suggest Dorothea Brooke in the opening pages of *Middlemarch*, but George Eliot's later figure wears coarse dresses to indulge her nunlike fancies. Milly Barton's poverty, far from being a pretense, is enforced by her marriage to the impecunious curate. Dorothea's elegance-in-plainness, like her rejection of a baronet, subtly signals an incongruity in the young woman's behavior; Milly Barton's radiance-in-rags, though every bit as incongruous, is presented earnestly to convince us that there can be nobility in the commonplace. Rather self-consciously, George Eliot tries to persuade us that a creature as rare as Milly need not be destined for a finer man with "aristocratic mien"; indeed, she even asserts that Milly's perfections stem from the imperfections of her unrefined mate. Engaging the reader in a controversy, the narrator protests: "I venture to say, Mrs. Barton's nature would never have grown half so angelic if she had married the man *you* would have in *your* eye for her." (chap. 2, p. 26; italics added.) The device is clumsy. Forced into the role of matchmaker, the harassed reader may well plead that the lady protests too much.

Still, the novelist's intentions are clear. She wants to assure us that Milly's perfection is not at odds with the prosaic actuality which prevails elsewhere in the story. While Caroline Czerlaski's sham title and Barton's delusions of grandeur demonstrate their desire to evade the conditions of ordinary existence, Milly embraces that same life with open eyes:

Her body was very weary, but her heart was not heavy, in spite of Mr. Woods the butcher, and the transitory nature of shoe-leather; for her heart so overflowed with love, she felt sure she was near a fountain of love that would care for her husband and babes better than she could foresee; so she was soon asleep. But about half-past five o'clock in the morning, if there were any angels watching round her bed—and angels might be glad of such an office—they saw Mrs. Barton rise quietly, careful not to disturb the slumbering Amos. (chap. 2, p. 30.)

Milly, then, represents the "glorious possibilities" of the human nature she supposedly shares with her husband; she embodies the ideals with which George Eliot, at this early point of her career, hoped to expand the "dim and narrow existence" of men condemned to mortality. It is fitting therefore that her death should act as the catalyst which brings about Amos Barton's recognition of those aspects which his otherworldly religion has ignored. At first, the clergyman can neither believe in the finality of her death nor in the reality of his own sorrow: "It was a bad dream." At Milly's grave, however, Amos recognizes the transience which she had accepted and he had denied:

But now she was gone; the broad snow-reflected daylight was in all the rooms; the Vicarage again seemed part of the common working-day world, and Amos, for the first time, felt that he was alone—that day after day, month after month, year after year, would have to be lived through without Milly's love. Spring would come, and she would not be there; summer, and she would not be there; and he would never have her again with him by the fireside in the long evenings. The seasons all seemed irksome to his thoughts; and how dreary the sunshiny days that would be sure to come! She was gone from him; and he could never show her his love any more, never make up for omissions in the past by filling future days with tenderness. (chap. 9, p. 115.)

By dying, Amos' wife has fulfilled her role. For Milly Barton remains an abstraction. She is a passive character whose attributes are given to her so that she may teach her clergyman husband—and George Eliot's Christian readers—the painful truism that they should value life and love while they have them. Amelia's death forces Amos to consider the poverty and selfishness of his love; it allows the author to advance her own plea for reverence toward that "sacred human soul that lived so close to us, and was the divinest thing God has given us to know!" (chap. 9, p. 115.)

Milly's death also permits George Eliot to expound her Feuerbachian belief in the positive power of suffering. The same men and women who bandied "vulgar jests" about Barton and the countess who was living at his house, begin to regard their pastor in a different light: "when they saw him following the coffin, pale and haggard, he was consecrated anew by his great sorrow, and they looked at him with respectful pity." (chap. 9, p. 113.) The warmth of Mr. Cleves, who buries Milly, startles the benumbed Amos; the sudden friendliness of his parishioners thaws the "fatal frost" with which he had so far been met. Just when he believes that Shepperton is the place where he most wishes to remain, his bishop assigns him elsewhere. But the new blow marks the return of his full humanity. Amos had erected his religion as a barrier to hide his failings from the world; now that his troubles are fully exposed, they call out the "better sympathies" of the Sheppertonians. According to George Eliot's eager gloss, these sympathies are "always a source of love. Amos failed to touch the spring of goodness in his sermons, but he touched it effectually by his sorrows." (chap. 10, p. 120.)

Like Adam Bede and Silas Marner, the battered Amos profits from his misfortunes. But whereas George Eliot's later figures are allowed to remain in a rural atmosphere, he is banished to the same environment from which Silas Marner will flee. The remainder of his life will be spent "in a large manufacturing town, where his walks would lie among noisy streets and dingy alleys" (chap. 9, p. 119). It remains for Amos therefore to accept his fate, and, more important, to grasp the feelings which will make that fate bearable. Returning to the churchyard for a final farewell, he stares at the inscription on the tombstone, "Amelia, the beloved wife of Amos Barton." Aware that the "happy and unhappy past was a reality," he bursts into sobs and throws himself on his wife's grave. For the first time, his emotions have overpowered him; his tears are finally warm.

Just as Fielding upholds the living goodness of his Amelia

Booth as a model for her imperfect husband, so does George Eliot employ the pathetic death of Amelia Barton to exalt the earthly possibilities previously ignored by Amos.[9] Milly embodies the qualities extolled in the essay on Young—"all the sublime self-renunciation and sweet charities which are found in the details of ordinary life" (p. 30). She matches each of the virtues catalogued in the essay on Cumming: "The sweet charities of domestic life—the ready hand and the soothing word in sickness, the forbearance toward frailties, the prompt helpfulness in all efforts and sympathy in all joys."[10] Significantly, Milly is even endowed with an immortality of sorts: her memory hallows her husband's later life "just as of old the place was hallowed on which an angel of God had alighted" (chap. 9, p. 117). Her features are reproduced in the "sweet, grave" face of the daughter who attends Amos; her concern for what is tangible and concrete is inherited by little Dickey—the child who had cried so pathetically at his mother's deathbed becomes a self-assured engineer. The distressing picture of mutability on which the story had opened thus becomes softened. The brief passage of Milly's life makes the general flux seem slightly more bearable, though only barely less capricious. Even Amos, by now as feeble as the most superannuated of his former parishioners, has altered for the better. His head is crowned by a saintlike halo, a near-white "circlet of hair"; his glance has become "calm, and even cheerful" ("Conclusion," p. 123). Like his biblical counterpart, he has been able to turn "the shadow of death into the morning."[11] A deep distress has humanized his soul.

"Amos Barton" launched George Eliot as a novelist. As soon

[9] George Eliot intended to use a quotation from *Amelia* as a motto for the first edition of the completed *Scenes of Clerical Life* (GEL, II, 413–414).

[10] "Evangelical Teaching: Dr. Cumming," *Westminster Review*, LXIV (October 1855), 459–460.

[11] *Amos*, V, 8.

as the concluding portion had appeared, John Blackwood joyfully informed "Mr. Eliot" that the story had captivated its audience: "I could not explain the exact symptoms of popularity but to me they are literally unmistakeable." (GEL, II, 293.) And unmistakable they were. Albert Richard Smith proclaimed that the death of "sweet Milly" had made him blubber like a boy: "I did not think, at forty, I had so many tears left in me." (*ibid.*, n. 9.) Even Thackeray's eyes, according to Smith, sparkled through his spectacles as he spoke of the story. By appealing to the sentimentalism of the Victorian reading public, the new novelist had safely advanced views which—had they been stripped of their fictional garb and presented in the pages of a radical journal like the *Westminster Review*—would have alienated many a reader who shed tears over sweet Milly's fate. While some readers were led to believe that the author of "Amos Barton" must have been a clergyman himself, the more discerning perceived that he might possibly be a *"man of Science,"* whose religious views hardly corresponded with those of the established Church (GEL, II, 291). But her beliefs did not offend a public which had, after all, been taught by more orthodox novelists than herself that the true essence of Christianity was to be found in the heart of man.

Despite its contemporary success, however, "Amos Barton" stands up best as a mere prelude for the consummate achievements which lay ahead. George Eliot's first piece of "philosophic" fiction is too stark and too static a vehicle for her thought. Even John Blackwood on first reading the manuscript felt that its author fell into the error "of trying too much to explain the characters of his actors by descriptions instead of allowing them to evolve." Quite shrewdly, he reasoned that George Eliot spoiled the effect of Milly's death scene by "specifying so minutely the different children and their names." That attempt to individualize the children, he argued, could not engage the sympathies of the reader, who had gained little intimacy previously and "cannot consequently feel much interest" (GEL, II, 272).

Although Blackwood later softened his criticism in deference to Lewes' "unusually sensitive" friend, his observation remains valid.[12] For not only Milly's children but even Milly herself is insufficiently individualized. Despite her efforts to stir compassion for "commonplace troubles" and "real sorrow," George Eliot could not expect to evoke sympathy at the death of a character who fails to convince us of its reality as a flesh-and-blood figure. "Amelia, the beloved wife of Amos Barton" belongs to a world far different from that inhabited by her husband. While Amos is quite plausible as a "quintessential extract of mediocrity," his wife is too ethereal to be convincing. In her essay on Young, George Eliot had denounced the poet's personification of abstractions, as evidence of the insincerity of his feelings. True emotions, she maintained after Wordsworth, had to be attached to concrete facts: "Strong emotion can no more be directed to generalities apart from particulars, than skill in figures can be directed to arithmetic apart from numbers." (pp. 30–31.) Unfortunately that criticism can also be leveled at her own characterization of Milly Barton, where the mechanical means of disguising "generalities" as "particulars" remain conspicuous.

George Eliot's Amelia is more idealized than her namesakes in Thackeray or even Fielding. As a sketchy personification of "glorious possibilities," she becomes too obviously a device to assure us that the ideal can influence ordinary life. Less than a year before George Eliot began "Amos Barton," she had reviewed an inferior novel by Julia Kavanaugh, *Rachel Gray: A Tale Founded on Fact*, and argued that the novelist who deals with the more prosaic details of life must be "neither a caricaturist nor a rose-colour sentimentalist."[13] But in her own story, the prosaic tone of ridicule with which she describes Amos Barton awkwardly changes pitch whenever she extols the virtues of his

[12] For an opposite view, see Thomas A. Noble, *George Eliot's Scenes of Clerical Life* (New Haven, 1965), pp. 115–116.

[13] "Rachel Gray," *Leader*, VII (5 January 1856), 19.

angelic mate. Irony and indirection are dropped in favor of direct, impassioned, but disturbingly ineffectual, exhortations; "Soothing, unspeakable charm of gentle womanhood! which supersedes all acquisitions, all accomplishments" (chap. 2, p. 24). Even the unsentimental eyes of the reliable Mrs. Hackit are clouded at the mere sight of Amos' "pale" and "feeble" wife. The matter-of-fact descriptions of the congregation at the workhouse or the gathering at the Clerical Meeting and Book Society, clash with the staginess of the scene in which the dying Milly's "soft white hand" is kissed by the sobbing little Dickey with "tenderness and pity." Like the allusion to the Christmas snow which covers the grave of the mother and the newborn child, such contrivances recall the world of Dickens' Christmas tales. In "The Haunted Man" (1849), for example, Milly Swidger fulfills a function quite similar to that of Milly Barton. Both heroines are earthly angels whose ministries of love teach their men not to evade "the memory of sorrow, wrong, and trouble."[14] But the sentimentalism which permeates Dickens' tale is perfectly acceptable in a phantasy peopled by unearthly specters and animalistic Calibans. In the "real" world of Amos Barton, where pity and terror must revolve around the fatal illness of a dull curate's pregnant and overworked wife, the same sentimentality seems out of place.[15]

Not only the tone of the narrator but even his self-characterization is inconsistent. Like the Wordsworth of the *Lyrical Ballads*, who professes that his knowledge of Aristotle is secondhand,

[14] *Five Christmas Novels* (New York, 1939), p. 342.

[15] In his discussion of "Amos Barton," Mr. Noble tries to combat Joan Bennet's contention that the story's pathos rings untrue. He asserts that the deathbed scene shows "a firm grasp of reality," a sure "sense of reality," a "simple realism," a "realistic picture," a reflection of "the experience of real life" (*George Eliot's Scenes of Clerical Life*, pp. 113–115). But even his contention that "such scenes were undoubtedly acted out in thousands of Victorian homes," surely misses the point in its confusion of the logic of a created work of art with the "truth" of actual life.

George Eliot poses as a commonsensical observer in touch with the concrete verities of life. At the end of chapter five, the narrator claims to be neither "erudite or eloquent"—he cannot quote Virgil or apostrophize calumny in order to dignify Barton's plight; yet, pages earlier, he has quoted Homer in Greek and incorporated an allusion to Shakespeare in defining his subject.[16] Although these contradictions may well be semi-ironic, they do dramatize George Eliot's uneasy adoption of the double role of the natural historian who wants to compel the reader by the veracity of his subject and the novelist-moralist who hopes to reassure his audience that he is not merely retelling an actual occurrence. This duality, of which "Amos Barton" is the most prominent example, may well be responsible for those stylistic tricks which, according to W. J. Harvey, she used "as a kind of check or defense mechanism" in her early fiction.[17]

George Eliot's contention that her story was intended to counter the expectations of readers trained to prefer the ideal thus smacks of considerable self-deception. Intellectually, her monist outlook had prompted her to endorse only those ideals which could be rooted in historical fact; artistically, however, her efforts to fuse the factual and the ideal were not wholly successful. For "Amos Barton" suffers from virtually all the defects which Coleridge had detected in the lesser poems of Wordsworth. By fettering herself in the shackles of the historian, George Eliot faced the same problems encountered by her favorite poet. She is guilty of the same disproportion between occasion and thought, expression and subject, matter-of-factness and loftiness of purpose. Her aggrandizement of the "four walls" of a "loving woman's world" (chap. 7, p. 97) is almost akin to Wordsworth's tendency to compose blank verse about the chattering teeth of Harry Gill. Obviously, the "equivocation in the use of the word

[16] He claims that his task is to reproduce the manners of men whose chat "is more or less bland and disjointed." Cf. *i Henry IV*, I, iii, 1, 65.

[17] *The Art of George Eliot* (London, 1961), p. 212.

'real,' " which Coleridge found in Wordsworth's theory and practice, would plague George Eliot as well.

As a former Calvinist and as a new convert to the anthropologism of Lewes, Comte, and Feuerbach, George Eliot was doubly interested in the links between motivation and action. As a novelist, she now realized that her ethic would be most compelling if presented through the causes and effects of human action. And yet, as Blackwood had correctly noted, "Amos Barton" had been undramatic, too reliant on actionless tableaux. Not only Amos and his wife, but all the secondary characters, had functioned as passive illustrations of their creator's values; though fully delineated, they are inert exempla, closer to the essayistic pictures of Young and Cumming than to their animated prototypes in the fiction of George Eliot's predecessors. Rather than interacting with each other, the characters in "Amos Barton" are jointly acted upon by accident. Even the key role of "Countess" Czerlaski, who, by precipitating Milly's death, becomes as culpable as the egotists in George Eliot's later fiction, does not receive the attention later given to Hetty Sorrel, Rosamond Vincy, or Gwendolen Harleth.

"Amos Barton" thus left George Eliot with two immediate problems to resolve. The discrepancy between her treatments of Amos and Amelia led her to redouble her efforts to fuse the actual and the ideal; the inadequacy of her passive exempla convinced her of the need for a more dramatic exploitation of her humanist ideals. She tackled the first of these problems in "Mr. Gilfil's Love-Story," which she began to write even before "Amos Barton" was published; she turned to the second in "Janet's Repentance," the story which rounded out her three scenes of clerical life.

3. Two Uses of Melodrama: "Mr. Gilfil's Love-Story" and "Janet's Repentance"

> To see a World in a Grain of Sand
> And a Heaven in a Wild Flower
> Hold Infinity in the palm of your hand
> And Eternity in an hour.
>
> —BLAKE

> The golden moments in the stream of life rush past us, and we see
> nothing but sand; the angels come to visit us, and we only know
> them when they are gone.
>
> —"JANET'S REPENTANCE"

MR. GILFIL'S UNROMANTIC ROMANCE

The first part of "Mr. Gilfil's Love-Story" was published by
Blackwood's on March 1 of 1857, in the issue following the
one that had concluded "Amos Barton." At first glance, the two
stories would seem to belong to the same mode, to contain complementary accounts of "commonplace troubles," designed to win
the reader's sympathy. "Amos Barton" depicts the growth of a
dull man who realizes his potential for love only after the loss of
his wife; "Mr. Gilfil's Love-Story" portrays the history of a
"man so wrapt up in a woman" (GLS, chap. 1, p. 147) that he
becomes dulled by her premature death. While George Eliot's
first tale concludes with a sketch of the patriarch who has been
sanctified by the memory of Milly Barton, her second scene of
clerical life opens with a picture of old age and then retraces the

youth of the man who had once been the "loving" husband of
Caterina Gilfil. The two stories thus move in opposite directions.
"Amos Barton" progresses forward from a not too distant past
to the near present; the story of his predecessor at Shepperton
projects backwards, from an era just prior to Amos' curacy to the
latter decades of the eighteenth century. A few of the characters
introduced in "Amos Barton" appear again, though only to act as
guideposts in time: Mrs. Patten, an octogenarian during Barton's
era, turns out to have been too young to be acquainted with the
details of Mr. Gilfil's early life.[1]

The opening sketch of the Rev. Maynard Gilfil is closest in
time to the events in "Amos Barton" and the vicar's sphere of
activity belongs to the same prosaic actuality depicted in that tale.
Still, even though the old gentleman's "slipshod chat and homely
manner" resemble Barton's, his bearing suggests a "quaint yet
graceful gallantry" that his successor could not have imitated.
As a clergyman, Mr. Gilfil is all that Amos is not.[2] While Barton
tries to intimidate Mrs. Brick for her unspiritual foibles, Mr.
Gilfil tolerantly accepts the ways of Dame Fripp, a grimy old
lady who prefers the company of her pig to that of her fellow
Christians. Barton threatens young Master Fodge with eternal
damnation; Mr. Gilfil uses sugarplums to bribe a similar recusant,
Tommy Bond. Whereas Amos alienates his congregation by re-

---

[1] Amos assumes his duties in 1834 or 1835 ("rather more than twenty
years ago"); the first chapter of Mr. Gilfil's story begins with his death
in 1826 or 1827, "thirty years ago." The second chapter moves back to
the summer of 1788, just before the French Revolution, while the third
recedes to 1773. Allusions such as that to the marriage of Sir Christopher
and Lady Cheverel in 1753 remove the story a full century from the narrator's own present. For an evaluation of some of these time-shifts, see
W. J. Harvey, *The Art of George Eliot* (London, 1961), pp. 109–112.

[2] That George Eliot had planned from the first to have her two protagonists complement each other is evident in "Amos Barton": Amos, we
are told, is "quite another sort of clergyman" than his "excellent" predecessor, Mr. Gilfil.

questing funds for his building program, Gilfil's claim on his flock's veneration is never "counteracted by an exasperating claim on their pockets" (chap. 1, p. 131). Unlike his pliable successor, whose eagerness to please the "influential" countess is so ruinous to his career, Mr. Gilfil denounces the abuses of a former patron, Mr. Oldinport, who, like the old Squire in *Adam Bede*, is harsh to his tenants. The vicar's short sermons are cherished all the more for having been heard many times before. Unlike Barton's doctrinal disquisitions, they amount to little more than "an expansion of the concise thesis, that those who do wrong will find it the worse for them, and those who do well will find it the better for them" (chap. 1, p. 138). While Amos is fearful of his Dissenting rivals, Mr. Gilfil is far more influential than the Rev. Mr. Pickard of the Independent Meeting. He sets his parishioners at ease by addressing them in their own dialect; yet his familiarity does not compromise the respect due to his position. Amos Barton's suffering as a man eventually causes the Sheppertonians to forgive his ineffectuality as a clergyman; in Mr. Gilfil's case, however, man and office are bound up in his personality, the distinction between the two being, "as yet, quite foreign to the mind of a good Sheppertonian Churchman" (chap. 1, p. 137).

The introductory sketch of Mr. Gilfil's activities at Shepperton thus clearly suggests the values which his successor ought to have inherited. As a clergyman who belongs to "the course of nature," Mr. Gilfil resembles the Rev. Mr. Cleves of "Amos Barton"; as a human being endowed with a distinctly feminine "strain of maternal tenderness," he recalls the exemplary Milly Barton (chap. 19, p. 13).[3] But the picture of his earthy benevolence is deliber-

---

[3] "In the love of a brave and faithful man there is always a strain of maternal tenderness; he gives out again those beams of protecting fondness which were shed on him as he lay on his mother's knee." It is noteworthy that the clergyman's surname should be a matronymic, "gille fil" or "fil gille" being the equivalent of "son of Jill" (Charles Wareing Bardsley, *English Surnames, Their Sources and Significations* [London, 1884], pp.

ately limited to the opening chapter; his portrayal is free from the rapturous exclamations which accompany the portrayal of Milly. For Mr. Gilfil's story contains more than a foil to Amos Barton's insufficiencies. George Eliot's first novella had ended with its protagonist's exile. Though Shepperton life had been ordinary, it had become "sanctified" for Amos by his attachment to Milly's grave. His banishment to a still more prosaic environment of "noisy streets and dingy alleys," though harsh, seemed just; only by confronting more adverse physical conditions, without Milly's support and protection, could Amos hallow her memory. "Mr. Gilfil's Love-Story," however, introduces a figure who inhabits and accepts the world from which Barton is banished, but is himself an outcast from still another "reality." Like Milly, Mr. Gilfil lends meaning to a Shepperton life denoted by "markets and tollgates and dirty bank-notes" (chap. 1, p. 131). But he has belonged to a sphere of existence totally unknown to her. His acceptance of actuality, unlike hers or that of the chastened Amos, is a far more bitter compromise.

In "Amos Barton," George Eliot had tried to impress pathos on the ordinary circumstances of Barton's life by exalting the figure of his wife. In "Mr. Gilfil's Love-Story," however, she stresses the ordinariness of the old minister, even though he embodies all the virtues of her previous heroine. The shift is calculated. The portrait of Milly relies on sheer assertion: the author asks us to accept a curate's myopic wife as a sublime Madonna; she exhorts us to believe that the lady in frayed gowns is superior

---

73, 553). According to Feuerbach, it is Christ and those living in Christ who represent "the womanly sentiment of God" (*The Essence of Christianity*, trans. George Eliot [New York, 1957], p. 71). The absence of a patronymic and the lack of any allusion to Gilfil's father may also suggest reasons for Sir Christopher's interest in his ward. Daniel Deronda, also raised by an aristocrat, suspects that Sir Hugo is his natural father. At any rate, George Eliot balances the "feminine" surname with a virile Christian name; the Germanic Maynard ("mein-hart") carries connotations of bravery and firmness.

to any Clarissa ever desired by a hero of "aristocratic mien." The opening portrait of Mr. Gilfil, on the other hand, relies on understatement and concealed irony: only as his story unfolds do we discover to our amazement that the kind, but common, old man before us possesses an extraordinary past in which he has wooed and won an exotic bride who was betrayed by a genteel Lovelace.

Resorting to the device already used in "Amos Barton," the author pretends to confront the accusations of her imaginary lady readers. The refined ladies have been offended by the story's prosaic details. They have expected a tale with romantic interest; instead, the author has presented them with an old, slightly eccentric, gin-drinking country parson: "you may as well ask us to interest ourselves in the romance of a tallow-chandler," they protest haughtily (chap. 1, p. 141). George Eliot's narrator quickly meets their challenge. Romance, he asserts with Wordsworthian zeal, can easily be hewn out of the reality of everyday life. To the lady readers, his portrait may seem too placid and commonplace; but, to him, it carries a universal drama: "I, at least, hardly ever look at a bent old man, or a wizened old woman, but I see also, with my mind's eye, that Past of which they are the shrunken remnant, and the unfinished romance of rosy cheeks and bright eyes seems sometimes of feeble interest and significance, compared with that drama of hope and love which has long ago reached its catastrophe." (chap. 1, pp. 141–142.)

George Eliot's drift is plain. Her lady readers have been deceived by their own unimaginativeness: the gnarled features of Mr. Gilfil do not at all exclude "a vast amount of antecedent romance." This romance, invisible to those who are insensitive to the drama of time, must now be extracted from the annals of the past. It must be presented, not by the chronicler of "Amos Barton," but by an imaginative dramatist whose "mind's eye" can range beyond the known actuality of Shepperton life.

"Mr. Gilfil's Love-Story," then, deliberately reverses the mode and manner of "Amos Barton." It exposes, rather than glosses over, the earlier contradictions evident in George Eliot's brand of realism. Amos' memory of his "sweet" wife is meant to soften the impact of his painful future. Mr. Gilfil's remembrance of a lost romantic world amidst his present life in Shepperton only sharpens his and our pain by calling attention to the same gap which Milly Barton's image was meant to obliterate. In her first story, the four walls of Milly's home—"a loving woman's world" —made too narrow a stage for George Eliot's insistence on universal love in the face of mutability and suffering. In "Mr. Gilfil's Love-Story," however, the locked chamber in the old clergyman's house acts as but a "visible symbol" of a drama enacted entirely outside the confines of Shepperton life. The intended loftiness of her drama is no longer constrained by George Eliot's medium. By drawing on the correlatives of the Gothic novel and Romantic poetry, she went beyond the limitations inherent in her previous mode of presentation. Whereas Barton's domestic pathos was restricted by the realities of a quasi-contemporary, middle-class life, the tragic story of Gilfil's love is projected into the hazy and aristocratic "days of cocked-hats and pigtails." Cheverel Manor, the palatial residence of Sir Christopher and Lady Cheverel, furnishes a setting which Shepperton cannot provide. In it, "the passion and the poetry" of Maynard Gilfil's early life can flicker undisturbed.[4]

Gilfil's love for Caterina Sarti and the girl's own passion for Captain Anthony Wybrow, Sir Christopher's nephew and heir, take place amidst an atmosphere totally different from that which dominates the opening of the story. The dingy vicarage of Shep-

---

[4] The few discussions of this tale have missed this intention. For example, Thomas A. Noble praises the opening chapter for continuing "the simple manner" of "Amos Barton," but sees the rest as an inexplicable incursion into romance (*George Eliot's Scenes of Clerical Life* [New Haven, 1965], p. 125). He explains the shift to Cheverel Manor as fulfilling a desire "to be absolutely faithful to what must have been one of the most impressive of remembered childhood scenes, Arbury Hall" (p. 126).

perton gives way to a backdrop made up of corridors studded with statuary and coats of armor, of lofty halls ornamented with Italian paintings and portraits by Sir Joshua Reynolds, of cultivated landscapes worthy of "some English Watteau." Even the quarters of Sir Christopher's servants partake of the refinements of aristocratic life. Though resembling the Sheppertonians in speech and manner, the housekeeper and her friends converse in a room casually adorned with the blackened visage of a Renaissance Madonna and a likeness of Sir Francis Bacon. For Cheverel Manor is a monument to Sir Christopher's taste. Anticipating by a decade the Romantic reaction against "the insipid imitation of the Palladian style" still current at the time, the baronet restores his mansion to its full Gothic splendor. Disregarding mere utility, he displays "some of that sublime spirit which distinguishes art from luxury, and worships beauty apart from self-indulgence" (chap. 4, p. 193).

Yet Sir Christopher is guilty of some self-indulgence in his transplantation of Caterina, the daughter of an Italian musician. Like old Earnshaw in *Wuthering Heights*, who takes the dark and alien Heathcliff into his home, the baronet does not suspect that the dark-eyed child he brings with him from Italy will cause future sorrows. Much "too English and aristocratic to think of anything so romantic," neither he nor Lady Cheverel have any notion of adopting this foreign orphan as their daughter: "No! the child would be brought up at Cheverel Manor as a *protégée*, to be ultimately useful, perhaps, in sorting worsteds, keeping accounts, reading aloud, and otherwise supplying the place of spectacles when her ladyship's eyes should wax dim." (chap. 3, p. 181.) Tina, however, soon sees life through different spectacles. Her new setting affects her development. Just as the manor, restored by Italian craftsmen, grows from ugliness into beauty, so does she grow from a "yellow bantling" into the accomplished creature whose spirited ways and melodious voice delight her benefactors. But unlike them, Tina becomes a full-blown Ro-

mantic. Willfully, she tries to convert the well tended and orderly gardens of Cheverel Manor into a reflection of her own inner
turmoil. Pressing her head against the cold pane of her window,
Caterina, like Emily Brontë's Catherine Earnshaw, identifies herself with all that is turbulent in nature: the "hurrying clouds"
and "tossing motions" of the trees appeal to her; "the shiver-
ing grass makes her quake with sympathetic cold" (chap. 5,
p. 220–221).

Sir Christopher's stately manor thus provides Tina with an
atmosphere eminently suited for romance. The shift from Mr.
Gilfil's and Amos Barton's prosaic Shepperton to the splendid setting which acts as a stimulus for this Romantic's emotions resembles that shift in time and tone which, in *Wuthering Heights*,
separates Lockwood from the passionate Earnshaw children and
the young Heathcliff. Caterina's actions, like those of Brontë's
Catherine, are always marked by excess. If Brontë's heroine prefers Heathcliff to the mild Edgar Linton, so does Tina reject the
gentle Maynard. But the man she loves, Captain Wybrow, is
hardly a Heathcliffian figure. Betrayed by Wybrow, Tina paces
up and down with histrionic exaggeration—"her hands clinched,
her eyes gleaming fiercely and wandering uneasily as if in search
of something on which she might throw herself like a tigress"
(chap. 12, p. 268–269). Pointedly George Eliot relates the
"terrible" struggles in the girl's breast to those occurring simultaneously, but on a far grander scale, across the Channel in the
dawn of the French Revolution. The parallel becomes palpable
when Tina resolves to revenge herself on the aristocrat who has
deceived her. Compared to a "pale meteor," a dragonfly wheel-
ing in its flight, she rushes to meet Captain Wybrow. The fiery
temperament which has already set her apart from the unsentimental Lady Cheverel as much as from the phlegmatic English
servants, boils over at last. Transformed into a Medea breathing
revenge, the child who had been incapable of harming the
smallest animals, now clutches an unsheathed dagger and boldly

dreams, "in the madness of her passion, that she can kill the man whose very voice unnerves her" (chap. 13, p. 280).

But the dreaming Tina does not attain the heights of a tragic heroine. The dagger intended for Anthony Wybrow's chest will be carefully restored to its former place, unused and bloodless, by the prudent Maynard Gilfil. Wybrow does die; yet he perishes without bombast or violence, not as the prey of an enraged avenger, but as a cardiac—the literal victim of his enfeebled heart. Suddenly, we realize that we have been deliberately deluded. The melodrama which George Eliot has pretended to build up to this climax is nonexistent, itself but an empty dream. The author who had sentimentalized Milly Barton has created Tina in order to expose the same "unhealthy sentimentalism" which George Henry Lewes had detected in the *Sturm und Drang* movement of German Romanticism.[5] Like the lady readers who were warned by the author, we have, through Tina, been misled into falsifying experience. The ladies' genteel bias prevented them from seeing that romance could exist amidst the aspects of ordinary life; our own expectations have blinded us to the ordinary life existing beneath the veneer of romance.[6]

For despite its refinements, Sir Christopher's pleasure dome is affected by the same universal laws which shattered the abode of that other master builder, Amos Barton. Like Tennyson's "Palace of Art," the temple of taste which the baronet has erected is no refuge from mutability and suffering. Earlier, Sir Christopher had relished the thought that "Cheverel Manor would be inherited by a grand-nephew, whom he might even yet live to see a

---

[5] George Eliot approvingly quotes Lewes on the "morbid symptoms" of Werther's era in her review of his *Life of Goethe* (*Leader*, VI [3 November 1855], 1058).

[6] A reader who ought not to have remained in this trap is Mr. Noble, who wonders why George Eliot might have wanted to depict the melodramatic actions of unreal aristocrats when "farm folk" had always been so much more "real" to her (p. 127).

fine young fellow with at least the down on his chin. Why not? one is still young at sixty" (chap. 5, pp. 205–206). Insensible to Christina's secret anguish, he had jovially tried to coax her into marrying Gilfil through still another projection into the future: "I shall get old and tiresome, and there will be Anthony's children putting your nose out of joint." (chap. 13, p. 273.) Now, in the face of his nephew's death and Tina's disappearance, Sir Christopher's own carefully built world has forever been put out of joint. The well-meaning nobleman finds himself curiously altered by the reality he has shut out in the past: "a single day and night of grief had aged the fine old man. The lines in his brow and about his mouth were deepened; his complexion looked dull and withered; there was a swollen ridge under his eyes; and the eyes themselves, which used to cast so keen a glance on the present, had the vacant expression which tells that vision is no longer a sense, but a memory." (chap. 18, p. 3.)

Sir Christopher has been crushed by time. The pre-Romantic visionary has shrunk into a creature reflecting the reduced Romantic attitudes of his Victorian creator: only through "memory" can man still transcend the limits of mortality. No longer an isolated and decorative backdrop, the surroundings of Cheverel Manor have likewise become part of a larger scheme. Watteau has been replaced by Turner. The narrator's earlier hints about the deceptive loveliness of the seasons now gain an added meaning:

The inexorable ticking of the clock is like the throb of pain to sensations made keen by a sickening fear. And so it is with the great clockwork of nature. Daisies and buttercups give way to the brown waving grasses, tinged with the warm red sorrel; the waving grasses are swept away, and the meadows lie like emeralds set in the bushy hedgerows; the tawny-tipped corn begins to bow with the weight of the full ear; the reapers are bending amongst it, and it soon stands in sheaves; then, presently, the patches of yellow stubble lie side by side with streaks of dark-red earth, which the plough is turning up in preparation for the new-threshed seed. And this passage from beauty to beauty, which to the happy is like the flow of a melody, measures for many a human heart the approach of foreseen anguish—seems hurrying on the moment when the shadow of dread will be followed up by the reality of despair. (chap. 5, p. 203.)

No earthly gardens are immune to the cycles of time. To Blake and Wordsworth, daisies and buttercups could yield a soothing vision of eternity; even Keats could freeze the transient seasons into momentary permanence. But Tina, like the romantic Fausta of Arnold's poem "Resignation" or like Tennyson's Lady of Shalott, is forced to recognize that man finds little solace from the "unmoved and terrible beauty" of the natural world. At best, she must learn her own insignificance; her troubles seem petty when dwarfed by the "mighty torrent" of change which affects the stars, the tides, and the destinies of nations (chap. 5, p. 222).

And yet it is this transitory world, the "hard, familiar realities" that Tina has ignored in her life at Cheverel Manor, which also induce her regeneration. Sir Christopher's palace is first replaced by the humble cottage of the coachman who has married Tina's former nursemaid, Dorcas, and then by the modest parsonage of Mr. Gilfil's brother-in-law, the Rev. Arthur Heron. Led to Foxholm Parsonage by Gilfil, Tina finds "a nest of comfort, without any of the stateliness that would carry a suggestion of Cheverel Manor" (chap. 20, p. 28). Her new surroundings are not picturesque. But their very ordinariness provides stability and comfort: "Contented speckled hens, industriously scratching for the rarely-found corn, may sometimes do more for a sick heart than a grove of nightingales; there is something irresistibly calming in the unsentimental cheeriness of topknotted pullets, unpetted sheep-dogs, and patient cart-horses enjoying a drink of muddy water." (chap. 20, pp. 27–28.)

Amidst a pastoral environment similar to that later expanded in *Adam Bede*, under the care of Mr. Gilfil and "his mild gentle sister," Tina acquires a new set of values. She learns what the clergyman has already known, that "every new day and night of joy or sorrow is a new ground, a new consecration, for the love that is nourished by memories as well as hopes" (chap. 19, p. 23). Gradually, her infatuation for Captain Wybrow fades away and a new and genuine bond is formed in its stead. One day, singing a passage from Gluck's *Orfeo* that had delighted Sir Christopher and his nephew only a few months before, Tina penetrates its full meaning for the first time. Experience has made her wise: "*Ho perduto il bel sembiante.*" She has forever lost the illusory paradise of Cheverel Manor; her innocence has yielded to the knowledge of good and evil. The "untroubled home" she had cherished exists no more. Still, like Maggie Tulliver, Tina can also find strength in the memories of a past she has lost. For if Cheverel Manor contained unreal aspirations, it also harbors—like Dorlcote Mill in the later novel—the ineradicable memories of childhood.[7] The tune from *Orfeo* therefore brings back a surge of feeling, a rebirth of love: "The long happy days of childhood and girlhood recovered all their rightful predominance over the short interval of sin and sorrow." (chap. 20, p. 30.) Weeping with joy, Tina nestles against Maynard Gilfil. Sir Christopher's decorative songbird has become a woman at last.

Tina's wedding journey takes her on a "circuitous route" to Shepperton, where Mr. Gilfil has been installed as a vicar (chap. 21, p. 34). But her marriage is short-lived. She dies in childbirth —as does Milly Barton, in the same vicarage room, a generation later. George Eliot's own tale has been "circuitous." We have moved from Shepperton to the deceptively romantic Cheverel Manor only to return once again to the opening picture of a gnarled old gentleman, "the Mr. Gilfil of those late Shepperton days." In *Wuthering Heights*, Catherine dies on giving birth to

[7] "Among all the many kinds of first love, that which begins in childish companionship is the strongest and most enduring" (chap. 4, p. 197). The few paragraphs on Tina's and Maynard's childhood romps almost read like a thumbnail sketch for the relationship in the first third of *The Mill on the Floss*.

Edgar Linton's child; but the second Cathy, whose humane Linton blood tempers that of the Earnshaws, finds the fulfillment denied to her romantic mother. In "Mr. Gilfil's Love-Story," however, the humane Mr. Gilfil remains a childless widower. We have tasted romance, but the romance has been expended only to affirm the harsh realities of a time-bound world:

Rich brown locks, passionate love, and deep early sorrow, strangely different as they seem from the scanty white hairs, the apathetic content, and the unexpectant quiescence of old age, are but part of the same life's journey; as the bright Italian plains, with the sweet *Addio* of their beckoning maidens, are part of the same day's travel that brings us to the other side of the mountain, between the sombre rocky walls and among the guttural voices of the Valais. (Epilogue, p. 36.)

The analogy is appropriate. For Mr. Gilfil must spend his days on the other side of the mountain, banished to a realm of retrospection and regret.

Writing to George Henry Lewes, John Blackwood remonstrated that he "should have liked a larger gleam of sunshine before poor Tina passed away." The story's ending, he felt, strikes "rather too drearily upon the heart" (GEL, II, 323, 322). George Eliot promised Blackwood an epilogue, but insisted that the very nature of a conclusion could at best be "a negation" (GEL, II, 324). Her epilogue only confirms this claim. Whereas the epilogue of "Amos Barton" has the task of softening the calamities visited on the curate's head, that of "Mr. Gilfil's Love-Story," by calling attention to Maynard Gilfil's undeserved fate, only reaffirms the painful nature of a world in which happiness is brief and romance lies hidden. Though able to bear the reality which had destroyed the frail Caterina, Mr. Gilfil must suffer for his own romantic sensibility. Like Tina, he is a sentimentalist. If she endows the landscape with her own states of mind, he, too, falsely identifies the "somber sky" and the pool's black depths with his "murdered hopes" (chap. 17, p. 299). While she exaggerates both her love and her mourning for Wybrow, he, in turn, magnifies her into something she is not. Although his wife's death presumably increases his tolerance for human frailty, her memory does not act upon him as the memory of Milly acts on Amos Barton. He tries to arrest time by preserving Tina's chamber; the locked room's drawn blinds and thick curtains block the daylight which mocks the short-lived "poetry" of his life. His ritual is directly opposite from that of Emily Brontë's tormented lover, Heathcliff. Heathcliff's soul eventually escapes at night through the opened window. Mr. Gilfil barely allows old Martha, his housekeeper, to open "the Gothic casement of the oriel window" for a quarterly airing. There is no supernatural reality, no haunted moor, on the other side of the glass.

If Tina is identified with the fragile Eurydice of *Orfeo*, Maynard Gilfil cannot aspire to become an Orpheus and follow his beloved into a realm of shadows. Although a Christian minister, he remains as bound to the material world as Amos Barton. Yet his reversal seems far more capricious and undeserved than that of the grotesque Amos. Though sketched out by nature as a strong and noble tree, the blighted clergyman must assume the character of a "poor lopped oak." What might have been "a grand tree expanding into liberal shade, is but a whimsical misshapen trunk" (Epilogue, p. 37). George Eliot's very diction betrays her reservations about the temporal order whose inescapability she asserts. For all its skillful interpenetration of two separate orders of experience, a pattern she was to employ again in *Silas Marner* and her later novels, "Mr. Gilfil's Love-Story" ends on a note far more negative than that of "Amos Barton." Both stories attack those who would escape the limitations of ordinary existence: Amos Barton's Christianity and Tina's Romanticism are checked by the realities of the temporal world. But by subordinating Tina's story to that of a man condemned to remain in that temporal world, George Eliot was guilty of a revealing change in emphasis. The same ambivalence which she was able to exploit on a far more magnificent scale fifteen years later in *Middlemarch* informs her second work of fiction.

Like Dorothea Brooke, Mr. Gilfil is a cygnet prevented from becoming a swan. For this benevolent clergyman is demeaned by the very "worldliness" that George Eliot tried to dignify. In the sheltered parks of Cheverel Manor, Sir Christopher's ward could have grown into a noble tree or an elegant swan. Yet the extraordinary world of Sir Christopher was created by George Eliot only to affirm the power of the ordinary. In their *Lyrical Ballads*, Coleridge and Wordsworth had hoped to balance two separate worlds of the imagination. The one's interest in "characters supernatural, or at least romantic" would compensate the other's attention to characters such "as will be found in every village and its vicinity."[8] In "Mr. Gilfil's Love-Story," the realm of "Christabel" yields to that of "Michael," yet a "Michael" devoid of Wordsworth's confident trust in a beneficent cosmic order.

THE CONTEST FOR JANET DEMPSTER

In May 1857, George Eliot promised John Blackwood the first part of her third novella. Aware that Mr. Gilfil's tale had developed into a "very melancholy story," she had earlier expressed her longing to be "merrier again" (GEL, II, 310). Led to assume that her new "scene" would therefore be on a brighter theme, Blackwood was soon to be disappointed. The brutality of Lawyer Dempster, the alcoholism of his harassed wife, the crudities of the town of Milby, were painted more harshly than anything in "Amos Barton" or "Mr. Gilfil." Seen through the mocking eyes of the Milbyites, the Rev. Edward Tryan, whose clerical life the story had begun to unfold, seemed far less ideal a figure than even Mr. Cleves or Maynard Gilfil had been. Blackwood felt entitled to remonstrate: "When are you going

[8] S. T. Coleridge, *Biographia Literaria*, chap. 14.

to give us a really good active working clergyman, neither absurdly evangelical nor absurdly High Church?" (GEL, II, 345.)

Blackwood's accusation is as telling as George Eliot's prompt reply. Pointing out that he had misread the intentions of her story, she hinted that her presentation of Mr. Tryan actually was to be along the very lines that he had demanded: "Mr. Tryan will carry the reader's sympathy. It is through him that Janet is brought to repentance." At the same time she defended her harsh portrayal of the same Milby society whose intolerance toward "Countess" Czerlaski had been briefly satirized in the fourth chapter of "Amos Barton": "Everything is softened from fact, so far as art is permitted to soften and yet to remain essentially true. The real town was more vicious than my Milby; the real Dempster was far more disgusting than mine; the real Janet alas! had a far sadder end than mine, who will melt from the reader's sight in purity, happiness and beauty." (GEL, II, 347.)

It is easy to see how, on the incomplete evidence of the four initial chapters of "Janet's Repentance," Blackwood could have missed George Eliot's intention to leave her readers fortified with a "belief in goodness" (GEL, 348). For the new work opens on an oppressive note, unlike the previous two tales. In "Amos Barton" and "Mr. Gilfil's Love-Story," George Eliot had deployed her irony against those who would deny the limitations of actual life. Through the stories of Amos, Sir Christopher, and Tina, she had undermined the expectations of readers desirous of "the ideal in fiction." In "Janet's Repentance," however, there is a significant reversal. Now, the satire is directed not so much against those who ignore the imperfections of human existence as against imperfection itself—the mediocrity of a world that denies all ideals.

The town of Milby represents that mediocrity. Shepperton, Milby's rural neighbor, acts as a setting for attainable values.

Although not idyllic, located as it was "on the other side of the mountain" from the Happy Valley once inhabited by Tina and Maynard Gilfil, it represented an environment in which a limited perfection was possible. But George Eliot had chafed at these limitations. The elegiac note struck at the end of "Mr. Gilfil's Love-Story" shows her dissatisfaction with the commonplace world to which she had relegated her characters. Hence, while Shepperton had at least allowed a compromise between the ideal and the actual, Milby, a large "dingy looking" market town, only magnifies the defects of the reality which had thwarted the full development of Maynard Gilfil. Like St. Ogg's, Treby Magna, or Middlemarch, Milby embodies George Eliot's revulsion at the imperfect and erratic universe to which she had been forced to consign her idealism. The Sheppertonians of Mr. Gilfil's day had responded to his homely benevolence; they had supported a fellow sufferer even during the "degeneracy" of Amos Barton's time. The Milbyites, who live in the same "degenerate times" as Amos (JR, chap. 9, p. 152), are far more insensible to goodness. Led by the immoral Lawyer Dempster, they spurn, taunt, and defame the idealistic religion of the town's new Evangelical minister.[9]

"Janet's Repentance" thus opens on a note of hostility. And the hostility of the Milbyites towards Mr. Tryan's efforts is matched by the author's hostility towards them. No longer wasting her satire on imaginary lady readers, George Eliot mocks the "pungent irony" and "incisive satire" by which the Milbyites belittle Mr. Tryan and his followers (chap. 5, p. 108). Her repeated allusions to the town's "sarcastic parish demagogues," to

[9] The story is set "more than a quarter of a century ago"; an allusion to the Rev. Mr. Parry as "the new clergyman that's just come to Shepperton" (chap. 11, pp. 177–178), places the events a few years before Barton's curacy. Some of the characters introduced in the earlier tale, such as Mr. Pilgrim, the doctor, or Mrs. Landor, the attorney's wife, re-appear in this third "scene."

the "satirical turn" of its young men and the feeble "powers of sarcasm" of its young ladies, to the lampooning playbill which exemplifies the "keenest edge of Milby wit," and to the vindictiveness of its doctors are all meant to illustrate the deliberate obstructionism of a society unable to extricate itself from stultification.[10] Even the kindhearted Janet Dempster partakes of this mood. She buys Mr. Tryan's sermons in order to ridicule them; she helps her husband with his savage lampoon of the clergyman. Her burlesque is designed to please Dempster, although she does herself "like to laugh at the Tryanites" (chap. 7, p. 126). But the playbill only contributes to the town's general hatred and negativism: "Mr. Dempster's sarcasms were not merely visible on the walls; they were reflected in the derisive glances, and audible in the jeering voices of the crowd." (chap. 9, pp. 154–155.)

Janet's tone, like that of her creator, will alter considerably: "too much given to satire" in the early parts of her story, she will become an earnest convert to Mr. Tryan's belief in Infinite Love. For "Janet's Repentance" depicts a contest between opposites. If Dempster's Milby magnifies the crippling reality shown in the epilogue of "Mr. Gilfil's Love-Story," Mr. Tryan's religion is an expansion of the "glorious possibilities" previously attributed to Amelia Barton. Displaying a symmetry and balance found in neither of her previous two scenes of clerical life, George Eliot creates an active combat that can almost be read as a schematized allegory for her own divided state of mind. Like Janet herself, the author is an unbeliever who knows that, "I can't leave this world and go to another. There may be no pity for me there, as there is none here." (chap. 14, p. 194.) The "daylight" of reason (which Mr. Gilfil had shut out from the room in which he preserved the relics of his romantic past) only sickens Janet's sense "with the dreary persistence of definite mea-

[10] The very opening of the novella is a vehement denial: " 'No!' said Lawyer Dempster, in a loud, rasping, oratorical tone. . . ."

surable reality" (chap. 16, p. 194); the romantic forms pressed on her imagination by night are "false, fitful, exaggerated," as deceptive as the melodrama of Caterina Sarti. But like her heroine, George Eliot refuses to admit that life may be nothing more than a "sun-dried, barren tract."[11] Just as Carlyle's Teufelsdröckh must go beyond the Everlasting No, so must Janet be brought to deny negativism. To hallow "all the commonplace reality that surrounded her," she must first dispel the "oppressive distinctness" of the details of a "weary life to be lived from day to day" (chap. 16, p. 211).

Janet's plight lends credibility to the otherwise artificial tug-of-war in which she is subjected. Pulling on one side is Robert Dempster, her husband; tugging on the other, is Edward Tryan, her spiritual teacher. Dempster is Satanic; he is identified with "old Harry" and "old Nick."[12] Tryan is angelic; his brushed-up hair looks "almost like an aureole." Even in death Dempster vows defiantly, "I know the law," but the laws he relies on are perishable and corrupt. Mr. Tryan, on the other hand, "knew suffering," and for George Eliot his recognition of the universality of human pain involves a recognition of all that is divine and imperishable. Dempster's "devilish glance" reflects the "theologi-

---

[11] The sight of a child "often stirred in Janet's mind a sense of the childlessness which had made a fatal blank in her life" (chap. 26, p. 301). The parallel to George Eliot's situation is hard to miss. The illegality of her union with Lewes prevented her from bearing children, although, like the barren Nancy Cass in *Silas Marner*, she wanted motherhood. Her statement about Janet applies to herself: "if Janet had been a mother, she might have been saved from much sin, and therefore from much of her sorrow" (chap. 13, p. 186). Like Janet or Romola, Marian Evans had to content herself with being the loving "Mutter" of another's offspring. Mothers who deny or betray their children recur throughout her fiction; the motif has an obvious personal significance that goes beyond the themes of her novels.

[12] Compare Mr. Tulliver's allusions to Lawyer Wakem in *The Mill on the Floss* or the Raveloers' view of *Silas Marner*.

cal hatred" of Milby at large, as well as his excessive fondness for the "demon" alcohol. The "hectic brightness" of Mr. Tryan, however, recalls Milton's rosy seraphs; it is a token of the love on which his "self-renouncing faith" is built, as well as a premonition of his impending death from tuberculosis (chap. 19, p. 237). The names of both men stress this conflict. The lawyer is the "dempster"[13] who wants to doom his wife to the spiritual death of his own existence. He casts Janet out of his house without her clothes. Mr. Tryan, however, who is ridiculed as "Mr. Try-it-on" in his rival's squib, welcomes Janet to his house when she wears the new attire provided by her neighbor. The minister introduces her to an existence in which "all things are become new"; unclothed by her husband's lack of charity, she is now "clothed upon" by new spiritual garments.[14]

The fates of both men are explicitly counterpointed. Each dies attended by Janet, but their death scenes are as antagonistic as their lives. Dempster expires in a coma, unable to recognize his wife's forgiveness: "her lips touched a corpse" (chap. 24, p. 278). Mr. Tryan dies fully assured that his teachings will survive; the chaste kiss that his disciple bestows on his "wasted dying" lips is a "sacred kiss of promise" (chap. 26, p. 314). Janet has successfully moved from the negative actuality represented by her husband to the new life offered by her saintly master. Far more than Mr. Gilfil, she can face the future with "resigned memory." If Tina's memory was responsible for Mr. Gilfil's rustication, the memory of Mr. Tryan makes the older Janet more "noble-looking" than she had been. Like the beatified

[13] See Scott's *Heart of Mid-Lothian*, note XIII on "Doomster, or Dempster, of Court" as "the pronouncer of doom or sentence." The significance of this and other names in the story is not touched upon in Daniel P. Deneau's discussion of the metaphoric texture of "Janet's Repentance" in "Imagery in *Scenes of Clerical Life*," *Victorian News-Letter*, 28 (Fall 1965), 18–22.

[14] II Cor. 5 : 17; 5 : 4.

Amos, comforted in his old age by Patty, Janet, too, becomes surrounded by the children of her adopted daughter.

"Janet's Repentance" is as sentimental and schematic a tale as "Amos Barton"; its melodrama, unlike that of "Mr. Gilfil's Love-Story," is conducted in earnest. Still, the story is saved from the mawkishness that marred the characterization of Amelia Barton. Furthermore, it squarely faces the dilemma left unresolved in "Mr. Gilfil's Love-Story." In that tale George Eliot had been forced to go outside the ordinary world to affirm the meaning of a life restricted by "worldliness." The creation of Cheverel Manor had allowed her to employ the artistic correlatives of the very Romanticism she set out to deny. The return to the "degenerate times" of Milby, however, did not permit her to use this device. As in *The Mill on the Floss* later on, she tried to bring the extraordinary into contact with an existence marked by "dreary prose." In "Janet's Repentence," she solved this problem by exposing the unusual Mr. Tryan to a heroine enmeshed in the mediocrity of Milby.

Though as angelic as Amelia Barton, Mr. Tryan is not at all enveloped by his ordinary surroundings. Like Gilfil, he is an outsider whose suffering has been experienced elsewhere. But whereas Mr. Gilfil's abortive romance paralyzed and debased him, Tryan's own romantic past has set him in motion. Gilfil yields to the rusticity of Shepperton; Tryan remains apart from Milby —he is in, but not of, its reality. While Gilfil adopts the slipshod manners of the Sheppertonians, Tryan has the stature required for an Aristotelian tragic figure. In rank, education, and humanity he excels the university-trained lawyer whose false interpretation of the word "Presbyter" is readily accepted by his uneducated followers. Gilfil conceals his exotic past—the story of Caterina's betrayal by Wybrow must be unearthed by an imaginative narrator who relies on his "mind's eye" to reconstruct the past. But Tryan deliberately tells Janet of his betrayal of the young woman he drove to perdition. The melodramatic account of his discovery of Lucy's "dead painted" face is utterly devoid of the irony which marks Caterina's discovery of Captain Wybrow. It is a stock piece of romance inserted in a "realistic" tale in order to convince the reader that, unlike the sinless Gilfil, this ideal clergyman has been a noble sinner.[15]

Gilfil's desolation over Tina's death is all the more painful because of his blamelessness; at the most, he is guilty of having loved unwisely, of refusing to admit to himself—as Adam Bede would do with Hetty—that he converted his beloved into something she was not. Crushed by his disappointment, the clergyman is almost Job-like in his fate. Not so Mr. Tryan, for it is his admitted guilt which prompts Janet's teacher to embrace a creed of universal suffering. Gilfil's stunned acceptance of an imperfect world in which good men suffer unjustly encumbers his further growth; Mr. Tryan's ready acknowledgment of his imperfections is essential to his enlarged sympathies. His recognition converts him into an active missionary who chooses to accept "the vulgar, the commonplace, and the ugly, whenever the highest duty seemed to lie among them" (chap. 11, p. 171). The difference is notable. Caterina's wretched husband must adopt a

---

[15] That this little melodrama was at variance with the "realism" which George Eliot, under Lewes' influence, had espoused in "Amos Barton" is evident from his remarks to Blackwood, who had apparently objected to the episode: "What you say about the hacknied [sic] nature of the clergyman's story is perfectly true; and it appears all the more hacknied because the rest of the tale is so entirely original; but the vaguer such a story, the *more* hacknied it would necessarily appear; details give an air of reality, and I wish G.E. had been more detailed." (GEL, II, 378.) One wonders whether Lewes dared to transmit this slight objection to the sensitive "G.E." If so, she took little heed. She resorted to similar thumbnail romances in the "realistic" *Felix Holt* and *Middlemarch*, where she rendered the stories of Esther Lyon's mother and Lydgate's experience with the French actress Laure. In later works like *Romola* or *Daniel Deronda* which relied on a mixture of romance and "realism," she felt even more free to insert highly melodramatic (though hardly "hacknied") episodes.

pagan stoicism; Janet's Christ-like mentor teaches another how to bear Milby's "griping worldliness." His influence is diffusive. If Janet learns to imitate his precepts, she can in turn become an example for the Milbyites.

To fulfill his task, Mr. Tryan must first admit his own failings as a worldling. Feuerbach had claimed that the "essence" of Christianity was precisely such a recognition of "human weakness." Christ's voluntary martyrdom had been preceded by his recognition of the universal plight affecting all those who, like himself, were mortal. Contrasting Stoicism to his own version of Christianity, the German philosopher compared (as Mill and Pater did in later years) the death scenes of Socrates and Jesus: "While Socrates empties the cup of poison with unshaken soul, Christ exclaims: 'If it be possible, let this cup pass from me.' Christ is in this respect the self-confession of human sensibility."[16] It is only through such a "self-confession" of his vulnerability as a human being that Mr. Tryan can become Janet's confessor. The man who has led one woman to poison herself can now rescue another woman from the venomous reality of Milby. Although he is himself an exemplary martyr who deliberately inflicts privations on himself, the clergyman must convince Janet that his religion of suffering does not demand absolute perfection. Like Feuerbach's version of Jesus, his Christ "does not condemn you to wak alone without stumbling. He does not tell you, as your fellow-men do, that you must first merit his Love" (chap. 18, p. 230). Mr. Tryan informs Janet of what Amos Barton had to experience in his own flesh: that an awareness of the plight of mortal men burdened by time is enough to qualify her as a follower of the human Christ.

Auguste Comte's *Catechisme Positive* was being translated by Richard Congreve, who later became George Eliot's friend,

[16] Ludwig Feuerbach, *The Essence of Christianity*, pp. 60–61. See also, Bernard J. Paris, *Experiments in Life: George Eliot's Quest for Values* (Detroit, 1965), pp. 98–100.

around the same time that she was working on "Janet's Repentance." In it, the Frenchman expounded his religion of humanity through the "systematic conversations" of a woman with a "priest" of the new secular faith.[17] Though ostensibly a minister belonging to "the Evangelical school of his own day," Mr. Tryan is of course also a spokesman for George Eliot's modern humanist "essence." Like Comte, the novelist sees herself as a "philosophical" and "practical" servant of Humanity who, "in the name of the Past and of the Future," wants to impress direction on this world.[18] But the clergyman's interaction with Janet is not limited to a purely essayistic exposition of George Eliot's views. It is his predicament as a sufferer who belongs to, yet rises above, Dempster's mundane present that is meant to steer us and Janet toward the "purity, happiness, and beauty" that the novelist alludes to in her letter to Blackwood.

To the modern reader, less sympathetic to conversion stories than the Victorians, George Eliot's mixture of satire and hagiography may well seem disturbing. Some of the incongruities of her previous two attempts at reconciling the ordinary with the extraordinary still remain in "Janet's Repentance." Though neatly balanced, the contrast between a brutal wife-beater who dies of delirium tremens and a consumptive saint with a romantic past is too gross. Janet's own attraction to the demon alcohol, "the long-accustomed stimulus," her hesitant fingering of the "dangerous keys" which unlock her husband's liquor cabinet, would seem to belong more properly to the temperance tracts which George Eliot and Lewes found so ridiculous[19] than to an allegory about

---

[17] The English translation was published in 1858; its full title was *The Catechism of Positivism, or, Summary Expositions of the Universal Religion. In Thirteen Systematic Conversations Between a Woman and a Priest of Humanity.*

[18] *Ibid.*, p. 1.

[19] "The Physiological Errors of Teetotalism," George Henry Lewes' attack on W. B. Carpenter's *The Philosophy of Temperance*, appeared in the *Westminster Review* which preceded that in which George Eliot at-

man's predicament in a godless universe. The unnecessary pathos interjected as Dempster beats his wife ("The blow falls—another—and another. Surely the mother hears that cry—'O Robert! pity! pity!' ") smacks of the cheap melodrama of the Victorian stage. Nonetheless, George Eliot does manage to narrow the gap so obvious in her earlier two tales. Dempster's "rasping voice" and nefarious behavior may well have shocked the staid John Blackwood. Yet the lawless lawyer is more than a stage villain; his kindness to his mother and his rare outbursts of affection for his wife suggest that he is capable of better emotions.

For George Eliot hints that her creed of sympathy is applicable to all men. If Dempster is corrupt, he must also be capable, at least potentially, of the redemption undergone by his wife: "In the man whose childhood has known caresses there is always a fibre of memory that can be touched to gentle issues, and Mr. Dempster, whom you have hitherto seen only as the orator of the Red Lion, and the drunken tyrant of a dreary midnight home, was the first-born darling son of a fair little mother." (chap. 7, p. 122.) The blackguard whose iniquity we have witnessed is not irreclaimable. Just as Mr. Tryan is a paragon of virtue with an infamous past, so is Dempster a wrongdoer who has only suppressed the innate goodness which, according to the author, "tries to get the upper hand in us whenever it seems to have the slightest chance." In George Eliot's relativist outlook, absolute evil, like absolute virtue, is not allowed—Swift must be balanced by Rousseau.

Thus, some of the sentimentalism spent on Tryan is extended to the Yahoo lawyer who is nevertheless kind to his "little Mamsey." Conversely, the satiric treatment of Dempster and his followers is also applied to the Tryanites. The clergyman's faithful

---

tacked the writings of the Rev. John Cumming. There are some interesting similarities between the two essays, which rely on their authors' knowledge and application of Continental scholarship to discredit moralities which they regard as uninformed and provincial.

supporters are not devoid of self-interest. It is no coincidence that the most ardent among them are all spinsters. The Misses Linnet worship the handsome minister because of his attractiveness and his eligibility as a bachelor; Milby's bluestocking, Miss Pratt, makes him the object of her most impassioned verses, "Forward, young wrestler for the Truth." Even Mr. Tryan's character is not immune to George Eliot's irony. Just as the self-sacrificing Dinah Morris in *Adam Bede* is contrasted to the practical Mrs. Poyser, so is Mr. Tryan compared to Mr. Jerome, whose sensible offer of a horse he rejects in his obsessive desire for martyrdom. Although the story falls short of the balance achieved in *Adam Bede* and perfected in *Silas Marner*, there definitely is a similar attempt at equipoise. Painted in black and white, Dempster and Tryan blend into the gray reality which Janet learns to accept. And it is Janet who makes that reality seem authentic. Her conversion is more gradual than Amos' abrupt change of heart; her predicament, much more compelling than that of Mr. Gilfil.

"Janet's Repentance" thus achieves in a limited fashion what George Eliot's first two stories failed to accomplish; it depicts a time-bound world in which transcending ideals are still possible. Though it repeats the elements in "Amos Barton," it corrects their imbalance and disproportion. The town of Milby, rather than the single figure of Amos, is now the object of the author's satire; Janet and the contrite Milbyites who follow the casket of a near-saint, rather than the mourners of Milly Barton, dramatize the novelist's creed; the death of a genuinely "ideal character," and not that of an overworked housewife, exemplifies the basic values of that creed. Like Amelia and Caterina, the minister dies to teach us the "sad weakness" that "the thought of a man's death hallows him anew to us; as if life were not sacred too" (chap. 11, p. 176).

All three *Scenes of Clerical Life* rely on this melancholy truism. The deaths of Captain Wybrow and Lawyer Dempster act as ironic reminders of man's vulnerability to time; the ambitions of both, their past promises and expectations, come to naught. But death also reminds man of his duty to sanctify the present: "the angels come to visit us, and we only know them when they are gone" (chap. 5, p. 109). Milly Barton and Mr. Tryan are two such angels in human form; their deaths are meant to bring about a purification. Even Caterina Gilfil's premature death is intended to produce a wider sympathy for her husband; pity, but also fear, are to be extracted from a "drama of hope and love" long since buried by layers of time. Yet the death of Edward Tryan has the widest effect; there is a greater sense of catharsis and a feeling of completion and rededication. Unlike the deaths of Amelia and Caterina, his end marks a triumph over his temporal self. The clergyman who was afraid of losing "so much time," of leaving "nothing done at all," becomes the most adequate vehicle for that "awe and pity" which George Eliot wanted to stimulate in her three novellas.

This awe and pity, however, are not those of tragedy. Tryan's death is that of a martyr; it is exemplary and pathetic rather than dramatic. The story's dramatic movement is provided by Janet's inner conversion and not by her passive observation of another's Christ-like passion. The matured Janet comes to admit that the world she has deprecated is not devoid of love and purpose. But her conversion is still rendered sentimentally, still marked by those teardrops which according to Feuerbach, "mirror the nature of the Christian's God."[20] George Eliot was now ready for the larger canvas of *Adam Bede*. In it she tried to justify the tragedy of man's fall without resorting to the sentimentality of her three *Scenes of Clerical Life*. Amos Barton, Maynard Gilfil, and Janet Dempster accept their fates through the tearful deaths of others; Adam Bede learns how to bear his lot directly through his own experience. Although he, too, is affected by extraneous events such as his father's death and Hetty's degradation, in his

[20] Feuerbach, *The Essence of Christianity*, p. 61.

strength and self-reliance he seems less passive than George Eliot's previous three protagonists. Like Mr. Tryan, the son of Thias the carpenter emulates the second Adam; yet unlike Mr. Tryan, he is allowed to live.

George Eliot had learned much from her experimentations in the *Scenes of Clerical Life*. In the course of writing her three novellas she had significantly shifted her initial objectives. Though they were planned after the model of Balzac's "scènes de la vie de province,"[21] her stories had moved from the scientific "étude" of Barton's grotesque ministry to an attack on the shortsightedness of those who would filter out imperishable essences through their "scientific lenses" (chap. 11, p. 169). George Eliot was no longer the rationalist of the *Westminster Review*. "Janet's Repentance" is replete with sarcastic allusions to the "ingenious philosophers of our own day," those Benthamites prescribing felicity according to "arithmetical proportions" (chap. 22, p. 252). The "philosophic doctors," the narrator claims, see the world only in material terms. But there are hidden processes which are "mysterious," incalculable: "Ideas are often poor ghosts; our sunfilled eyes cannot discern them . . . But sometimes they are made flesh" (chap. 19, p. 236). "Janet's Repentance" thus illustrates a curious reversal. The satirical naturalist who had presented both the poet Young and Amos Barton as inferior "animals" belong-

---

[21] In a review written only five months before she began "Amos Barton," George Eliot recommended *La Folle du Logis* by Leon Gozlan to the admirers of *Scènes de la Vie de Province*. Her description of Gozlan's book applies equally well to "Amos Barton": "It is an entomological tragi-comedy which has many parodies in human society—parodies which Balzac, of all artists, best loved to describe; witness his incomparable *Curé de Tours*" ("Story of a Blue-Bottle," *Leader*, VI [26 April 1856], 401). In "Brother Jacob," which, like "Amos Barton," relies on the grotesque aspirations of its protagonist, she again alludes to Balzac. Her familiarity with the French novelist, evident throughout her letters, seems to have been due to the influence of Lewes, who had written two articles on Balzac.

ing to the "species divine" is no longer in evidence. Instead, the narrator of "Janet's Repentance" turns on an imaginary critic of Mr. Tryan's Evangelical faith, a critic who, surprisingly enough, employs the same vocabulary as the narrator of "Amos Barton." From his "bird's-eye station" this myopic critic stereotypes Mr. Tryan: "Not a remarkable specimen; the anatomy and habits of his species have been determined long ago." But the critic is immediately accused of presumption by the narrator: "Our subtlest analysis of schools and sects must miss the essential truth unless it be lit up by the love that sees in all forms of human thought and work, the life and death struggles of separate human beings." (chap. 10, pp. 165–166.)

With "Janet's Repentance" George Eliot began a self-dialogue which acquired far richer overtones in the novels to follow. In a modest fashion, she had already found a way to be artistically true to the double aims of her "realism." Yet she remained dissatisfied with the reality of Milby. The actual world —which, as she told Blackwood, was so much more vicious than in her story—still weighed upon her. It is significant that in *Adam Bede* she should leave Milby and return to a remoter past, a Wordsworthian realm of unpetted sheep dogs, speckled hens, and patient cart-horses such as had surrounded Tina's brief regeneration, in order to ease Adam's plight.

In 1857, the year in which George Eliot rounded out her three scenes of clerical life, Herman Melville published *The Confidence Man: His Masquerade*. In that obscure fantasy he mocked the secular optimism which in America and in Europe had supplanted the waning religions of the past. The old faith in a Divine Chronometer had been replaced by a belief in the human horologe. But the new belief had altered the shape of the universe; it denied evil; it deliberately ignored the distinct possibility that beyond the veil masking men's existence there might simply be nothing at all. Melville, in the words of a perceptive commentator, regarded the new optimism as but "a confidence-game played, as it were, by mankind on itself."[22] Like Melville, George Eliot could no longer believe in a Divine Chronometer. But unlike him, she shrank from the full terror of accounting for the nature of evil in a universe without design. Melville exploited the terror of disorder in his fiction; he played with the ambiguities of life and mocked the "confidence" of those who projected their own wishes on the universe. George Eliot wanted to temper her own fear of a "measurable reality" which seemed anarchic and without purpose; to do so, she measured life by a human horologe. "Janet's Repentance" was her first successful attempt in this direction. But despite the story's forceful ending, the author betrayed her lack of confidence. She had not dispelled her horror over Milby. And, like Janet, she was too honest to keep up "the old pretence of being happy and satisfied."

[22] Ernest Tuveson, "The Creed of the Confidence Man," *ELH*, XXXIII (June 1966), 269.

4. Pastoralism and the Justification of Suffering: *Adam Bede*

"O goodness infinite, goodness immense!
That all this good of evil shall produce
And evil turn to good . . ."
  —*Paradise Lost*, XII, 469–471

  "But I've that opinion of you, that you'll rise above it all, and
be a man again; and there may good come out of this that we don't
see."

  "Good come out of it!" said Adam, passionately. "That doesn't
alter th' evil."

—*Adam Bede*

To approach *Adam Bede* by way of *Scenes of Clerical Life* is to appreciate the extent to which George Eliot profited from the composition of those three experimental novellas. *Adam Bede* reiterates all the elements found in the *Scenes*; it shares the same intentions and embodies a similar creed. Both books try to validate existence in a finite, time-bound world; both reflect their author's desire to be faithful to the empirical standards of veracity she had adopted and to the moral values she hoped to vindicate. Yet to arrive at *Adam Bede* from "Amos Barton" or "Janet's Repentance" is to move from ingenious pieces of machinery to the near perfection of realized art.

The three *Scenes of Clerical Life* are shaped by what Coleridge called Fancy: they are terse, mechanical, and diagrammatic,

pressing together the disparate realities of naturalism and romance. *Adam Bede*, on the other hand, mediates between the
concrete and the universal; it is shaped by that imaginative faculty which "dissolves, diffuses, dissipates, in order to recreate" out
of the forms of actuality the analogue of an ideal world.[1] In her
Scenes, George Eliot relied on an external logic in order to advance her moral purpose. All three stories were built around accidents: the accidental deaths of Amelia Barton, Tina Gilfil,
Robert Dempster, and the Rev. Edward Tryan were enlisted to
endow the fortuitous universe of Victorian science with a semblance of moral design. In "Janet's Repentance," the saintly Mr.
Tryan must die in order to "ennoble" the anarchical existence
represented by Milby; yet in order to sanctify that existence he
has to belong to a different order of reality, to be endowed with
a romantic past enacted outside the dreary, quasi-contemporary
realm to which Janet is bound. In *Adam Bede*, however, the re-
moteness of Loamshire's pastoral world permits the author to
create a domain where, to borrow E. M. Forster's fine phrase,
morality can exercise its own logic. Like Mr. Tryan, Adam Bede
eventually becomes a personification of Feuerbach's Suffering
Jesus.[2] But, whereas Mr. Tryan is a stranger forced upon Milby,
Adam is inextricably a part of his hazy surroundings.

Henry James was the first to note the "autumn haze" that
seems to set apart George Eliot's pastoral novels. In their "Eden-
like peace and loveliness," (AB, chap. 4, p. 73) the undulating
slopes of Loamshire recall the landscape which surrounded Cheverel Manor in "Mr. Gilfil's Love-Story." But the artificial gardens of Sir Christopher were rejected by the Victorian "realist"
who insisted on the ordinariness of all life. In *Adam Bede*, how-

[1] *Biographia Literaria*, chap. 13.

[2] See Bernard J. Paris, *Experiments in Life: George Eliot's Quest for
Values* (Detroit, 1965), pp. 98–100, 103–106, and my *Religious Human-
ism and the Victorian Novel: George Eliot, Walter Pater, and Samuel
Butler* (Princeton, 1965), pp. 52–59.

ever, Eden—or its earthly approximation—is the chief locale.
Not Loamshire, but the Stonyshire which Dinah Morris will re-
nounce, is harsh, barren, and inhospitable.[3] While Tina Gilfil
was not allowed to survive in the makeshift Arcadia of Foxholm
Parsonage and while Janet Dempster was forced to remain in
the hostile Milby, Dinah joins Adam in the fertile valley where
she will bear his children. Adam's initial vision of a paradisiac
existence with Hetty is as rudely jolted as Mr. Gilfil's expectation
of happiness with Tina; but Adam's life with a second Eve allows him to become a Loamshire patriarch whose children will be
fruitful and multiply. It is Hetty and Arthur who must thread
their solitary way outside of Eden.

Adam Bede combines the Romantic correlatives of "Mr. Gilfil's Love-Story" and the Christian archetypes of "Janet's Repentance." Far more boldly than before, George Eliot now
availed herself of artistic forms used by both her Romantic and
Christian predecessors, in order to justify man's lot in the finite
world. In its skillful treatment of reality, vision, and knowledge,
Adam Bede displays her reliance on those Romantic poets and
novelists who had likewise tried to find the ideal in the factual.
What is more, in its attempt to justify man's banishment to a
temporal world, George Eliot's first full-length novel reveals
her highly imaginative appropriation of *Paradise Lost* for her
own philosophical purposes.

From Milby to Loamshire

Loamshire with its autumn haze is as important a vehicle for
George Eliot's ideals as any single character in her previous three
novellas. When in "Janet's Repentance" we first see Mr. Tryan,
he is already a saint whose life of guilt and suffering has been

[3] For a perceptive discussion of the symbolic relationship between the
two counties, see George R. Creeger, "An Interpretation of *Adam Bede*,"
ELH, XXIII (September 1956), 218–238.

enacted in a different setting. In *Adam Bede*, however, George Eliot creates a complete setting in which the naturalistic and the emblematic coexist. Adam, the son of the fallible carpenter Thias, can eventually be sanctified as a secular manifestation of Dinah Morris' suffering Son of God. But Adam's transformation is almost as gradual and imperceptible as the motions of rural life around him. The sheep grazing in the "amphitheatre of green hills," where Dinah Morris tells about the drama of Christ's passion, seem arrested; their movements can be perceived only "by memory, not detected by sight" (chap. 2, p. 22). Dinah's voice is just as invisible. But, like that of the singer in "Yarrow Unvisited" or that described in "Wordsworth's short poem on the Power of Sound" that had once delighted Dinah's creator (GEL, I, 68), it gives the visible landscape a fuller meaning. To penetrate the essence of this world requires an act of imaginative participation not called for by the three *Scenes of Clerical Life*. We come as strangers to Loamshire, are teased by the lushness of its visual detail, and then are suddenly asked to perceive the essentials which these details hide. Like the outsider who stops to listen to Dinah Morris' "mellow treble voice" on the darkening village green, we must *hear* as well as *see*. Like that observer, we soon become shocked into recognizing a higher rhythm not discernible to the naked eye.[4]

In his *Biographia Literaria*, Coleridge had tried to explain his own similar sense of surprise on first hearing Wordsworth recite a poem which gave a startling new dimension to its stark and simple subject matter. The "unusual impression" made on him by "Guilt and Sorrow" caused Coleridge to mark its author's "imaginative faculty in modifying the objects observed" and led him to muse his friend's "original gift of spreading the tone, the

---

[4] Cf. George Eliot's far more sentimental and clumsier suggestion of such an invisible rhythm in "Amos Barton," when the dying Milly cries "Music— music—didn't you hear it?" But Amos is deaf to this angelic music.

atmosphere, and with it the depth and height of the ideal world around forms, incidents, and situations, of which, for the common view, custom had bedimmed all lustre."[5] It was this faculty of bestowing novelty on admitted truths which, in the same chapter, led Coleridge to identify Wordsworth's genius with Milton's own "imaginative mind," and set the stage for his subsequent differentiation between Fancy and the Imagination.

Coleridge's observation is of interest to the student of *Adam Bede* for more reasons than one. First, as I have intimated, it is in this novel that George Eliot first demonstrates her Wordsworthian ability to modify the ordinary objects she observes. Her creation of an atmosphere such as Coleridge speaks of was to be repeated in the first half of *The Mill on the Floss* and in *Silas Marner*, a tale which she claimed only Wordsworth could have appreciated and which, like *Adam Bede*, is prefaced by an epigraph drawn from Wordsworth's poetry. In its profusion of details, *Adam Bede* has the same sensuous immediacy of "Tintern Abbey" or the early portions of *The Prelude*; in its arrangements of these details, it reflects the same yearning to draw the intimations of an invisible moral order from the visible physical world.[6]

Moreover, Wordsworth is deliberately woven into the fabric of George Eliot's novel. *Adam Bede* is set in 1799, a year after the publication of *Lyrical Ballads*. In the fifth chapter, Arthur Donnithorne tells his godmother, Mrs. Irwine, that he has just received a volume of poems from London. The circumstances are noteworthy. Mrs. Irwine has just declared that a mere glance at outward forms can reveal their inner character. Relying on a somewhat homely metaphor, the old lady compares men to food:

[5] *Biographia Literaria*, chap. 4; Coleridge's italics.

[6] Thomas Pinney's "George Eliot's Reading of Wordsworth: The Record," *VNL*, No. 24 (Fall 1963), pp. 20–22, documents her familiarity with Wordsworth's work; Pinney's "The Authority of the Past in George Eliot's Novels" (*NCF*, XXI [September 1966], 131–147), while not strictly about George Eliot's debt to Wordsworth, suggests some interesting links between her use and Wordsworth's belief in "Memory."

"I don't want to know people that look ugly and disagreeable, any more than I want to taste dishes that look disagreeable. If they make me shudder at the first glance, I say, take them away. An ugly, piggish, or fishy eye, now, makes me feel quite ill; it's like a bad smell" (chap. 5, pp. 93–94). The allusion to eyes, presumably, reminds Arthur of *Lyrical Ballads*:

"Talking of eyes," said Captain Donnithorne, "that reminds me that I've got a book I meant to bring you, godmamma. It came down in a parcel from London the other day. I know you are fond of queer, wizard-like stories. It's a volume of poems, 'Lyrical Ballads:' most of them seem to be twaddling stuff; but the first is in a different style— 'The Ancient Mariner' is the title. I can hardly make head or tail of it as a story, but it's a strange, striking thing. I'll send it over to you; and there are some other books that *you* may like to see, Irwine—pamphlets about Antinomianism and Evangelicalism, whatever they may be. I can't think what the fellow means by sending such things to me. I've written to him, to desire that from henceforth he will send me no book or pamphlet on anything that ends in *ism*." (chap. 5, p. 94.)

Arthur's bewilderment over Coleridge's "striking" poem is as telling as his dismissal of Wordsworth's contributions. For, like his godmother, he is grounded by the logic of the sensory world. He discerns the universal appeal of "The Ancient Mariner," but cannot quite grasp the meaning of a poem that is not a story. On the other hand, he all too readily rejects Wordsworth's treatment of ordinary reality as being "twaddling stuff" taken out of the everyday world. His lack of interest in religion is also self-indicting; like the imaginary critic in "Janet's Repentance" who belittled Mr. Tryan's Evangelicalism, he cannot go beneath sectarian squabbles. In fact, a few pages earlier, Arthur has shown a similar superficiality in his assessment of Dinah Morris the Methodist: there is "something rather striking" about her, he admits, using the same adjective; yet she seems ordinary—she "looks" as quiet and inoffensive as a mouse.

As the creation of a post-Romantic author who fully understands the similarities in intention of Wordsworth's natural and Coleridge's supernatural poems, Arthur clearly will have much to learn. For those early poems about betrayal, guilt, and redemption through sorrow do have a distinct bearing on his and Hetty's lot. Though she will be praised for her beauty by Arthur's godmamma, Hetty, like Martha Ray in Wordsworth's "The Thorn," will become a child-murderess who wears a scarlet coat.[7] And like Stephen Hill, Arthur Donnithorne will help create "a thorny thicket of sin and sorrow" (chap. 15, p. 236): "O Guilty Father—would that death/Had saved him from that breach of faith" (ll. 131–132). Hetty later considers drowning her child in a ditch or pond; but then she buries it in a hole under a nut tree and covers the ready-made grave with grass. The analogy to Wordsworth's poem is plain: "Some say she drowned it in a pond / Which is a little step beyond: / But all and each agree, / The little Babe was buried there, / Beneath that hill of moss so fair" (ll. 204–209). The Hetty who later admits that the child "was like a heavy weight hanging round my neck" (chap. 45, p. 249) resembles the Ancient Mariner and Martha Ray in that she is forced to enact an exemplary role. Her story is designed to make Arthur and Adam into sadder but wiser men. The young squire has clearly underestimated the qualities of Wordsworth's imagination.

But Coleridge's remarks on the nature of the imagination have a further bearing on *Adam Bede*—his identification of Wordsworth with Milton is too valuable to be ignored. Milton's eighteenth-century imitators, poets like the Edward Young whose

---

[7] "The Thorn," line 168; Martha's attire also matches the moss which is "spotted red." In *Adam Bede*, Hetty's red coat is mentioned at least thrice (chaps. 35, 38, 43); and her surname, Sorrel, is the name of a reddish plant. It is curious that in a two-page essay in which he traces all the instances of "thorn imagery" in the novel, Clyde De L. Ryals should have missed the analogy to Wordsworth's poem: "The Thorn Imagery in *Adam Bede*," *VNL*, No. 22 (Fall 1962), pp. 12–13.

Night-Thoughts George Eliot had savagely attacked, mechanically emulated his outward style; but reinterpretation of his goals was left to the Romantics, who saw in him a precursor whose powerful imagination had led him to create a realm of essences in order to validate human existence in the finite world. Milton the sufferer and outcast, Milton the lover of liberty, Milton the poet who had coined the word *sensuous*, became in the eyes of Coleridge, Wordsworth, Keats, and Shelley a model for their own exertions, Shakespeare's sublime compeer.

George Eliot's own relation to Milton has yet to be fully assessed.[8] Her letters are studded with references to "my demigod Milton" (GEL, V, 238). In all the phases of her career—as a pious Evangelical enthusiast, as an essayist and agnostic thinker, as a novelist, and as the author of the blank-verse epic *The Spanish Gypsy*—she drew on her close familiarity with Milton's work. In her 1855 review of Thomas Keightley's biography of the poet, she dwells on Milton's doctrines about divorce in terms which definitely pertain to her own personal situation at the time.[9] In that essay, she also hints that her predecessor's "materialistic view of the human soul" need not be incompatible with that of a Victorian agnostic.[10] Above all, Milton remained for her, as for Coleridge, the great "philosophic" poet who in *Paradise Lost* had justified man's lot in the temporal world. Her own belief in

[8] Though valuable as a study of Milton's reputation in the Victorian era, James G. Nelson's *The Sublime Puritan: Milton and the Victorians* (Madison, 1963), does not examine the imaginative assimilations of Milton's work by any major nineteenth-century writer other than Tennyson.

[9] "Life and Opinions of Milton," *Leader*, VI (4 August 1855), 750; see *Essays of George Eliot*, ed. Thomas Pinney (London, 1963), p. 154. She also reviewed Keightley's study in the "Belles Lettres" section of the *Westminster Review*, LXIV (October 1855), 601–604, where she defended Milton's "true principle in education" by arguing that his desire to cultivate "reason" as much as "imagination and memory" foundered only because of the immaturity of seventeenth-century science.

[10] Pinney, *Essays*, p. 155.

scientific veracity did not allow her to create a supernatural world of essences; yet in her way she shared Milton's purpose. The epic strain that was to find its most complex embodiment in *Middlemarch* is introduced in *Adam Bede*. In its subject matter, in its treatment of vision and knowledge, in its temporal ironies, and even in the nature of its reconciliation, *Adam Bede* displays George Eliot's intimate understanding of Milton's great poem.

THE FUTILITY OF FORESIGHT:
ADAM BEDE AND PARADISE LOST

The mere notion that *Adam Bede* is in any sense comparable to *Paradise Lost* would seem at first glance to run counter to the aims George Eliot professes in the seventeenth chapter of her novel. There, in the oft-quoted paragraphs on "this rare, precious quality of truthfulness" that her narrator admires in the paintings of the Dutch masters, George Eliot intimates that "cloud-borne angels," sibyls, and heroic warriors are to be excluded from her art. "There are few prophets in the world; few sublimely beautiful women; few heroes. I can't afford to give all my love and reverence to such rarities." Thus, rather than showing tragic suffering or "world-stirring actions," her Wordsworthian canvas will present only "commonplace things," in order to make men see "how kindly the light of heaven falls on them" (pp. 268–271). Although these statements do considerably amplify the "realistic" creed first voiced in "Amos Barton," there is still the same satiric treatment of an "idealistic friend," the same mockery of "that lofty order of minds who pant after the ideal" (pp. 269, 277).

Yet George Eliot's own idealism is far more in evidence in *Adam Bede* than in "Amos Barton." Like Amos, Adam is the son of a workingman who sets himself apart from his fellow men; but, whereas the ungainly Amos was inferior to his rustic parishioners, Adam is preeminent—in his "tall stalwartness" he

looms far above every one of his Loamshire compatriots. Even
though the novelist declares that she cannot create heroes, she
does admit only two chapters later that Adam "was not an average man" (chap. 19, p. 320). Like the dalesmen of Cumberland
whom Wordsworth had idealized in his "Guide to the Lakes,"
Adam draws strength from his consciousness of the uninterrupted
centuries that lie behind his race. His suffering will consequently
be far more "world-stirring" than that of poor Amos Barton or
Mr. Gilfil.

Again, though George Eliot claims that there are few prophets in the actual world, Dinah Morris belongs to these elect; she
is a rarity treated most reverentially. Just as Tertius Lydgate in
Middlemarch will recognize Dorothea as a select spirit, so does
the chastened Arthur Donnithorne profess that he "could worship that woman" (chap. 49, p. 275).[11] Dinah's liquid eyes are
those of a visionary; they are not the "dull gray eyes" which
George Eliot had defended in "Amos Barton." Her "treble
voice" speaks of experiences far deeper than those which could
be uttered by "a voice of quite ordinary tones" ("Amos Barton,"
chap. 5, p. 67). Even Rector Irwine, whose imperfections have
presumably provoked the author's defense of her "realism," is
superior by far to all but one of the previous clerical figures. The
rector is an aloof but kindly aristocrat who wears a powdered
wig, reads and quotes Aeschylus, and is called "Dauphin" by his
regal mother. In bearing, humanity, and understanding, he is
above the future squire: even the "superior refinement of his
face was much more striking than that of Arthur's" (chap. 24,
p. 402). Yet Arthur is also elevated by his role. In the third
chapter, George Eliot disparages those readers who "weep over
the loftier sorrows" of "heroes riding fiery horses, themselves
ridden by still more fiery passions" (p. 53). Nonetheless, Arthur

[11] Cf. Lydgate's observation that Dorothea seems to want only a chair
"from which she can look down with those clear eyes at the poor mortals
who pray to her" (M, chap. 76, p. 361). Dorothea is likened to St.
Theresa; Dinah, to St. Catherine.

becomes such a figure. Spurring his "hot" horse in order to save Hetty from the gallows, the young man looks "as if his eyes were glazed by madness" (chap. 47, p. 263). The description of his eyes resembles that of Tina's expression as she rushes to avenge herself on her seducer. But Captain Wybrow was a mere stage prop used to undermine the girl's histrionics; Captain Donnithorne's melodramatic ride is to be taken seriously. As the instrument of Adam's and our understanding of universal sorrow, he must be loftier than a mere figure out of a Dutch painting.

The main characters in *Adam Bede*, then, are given a far greater stature than was possible in the domestic stories in *Scenes of Clerical Life*. But although they are protagonists in a wider ranging drama,[12] their size is hardly akin to those epic colossi whose actions range over Milton's Heaven, Earth, and Hell. In *Paradise Lost*, Milton invokes God's Celestial Light to implant him with inward eyes by which he may "see and tell / Of things invisible to mortal sight" (III, 51–55). In order to show "how kindly the light of heaven falls" on ordinary life, George Eliot overwhelms us with visual details that are deliberately commonplace. Whereas the opening portion of *Paradise Lost* introduces a timeless, numinous realm never before seen by men, the opening paragraphs of *Adam Bede* display the workshop of a carpenter exactly "as it appeared on the eighteenth of June, in the year of our Lord 1799." Our sense of sight is supported by the senses of touch, smell, and sound: we are invited to feel the warmth of the afternoon sun, to breathe the odor of pinewood planks, to hear Adam's "strong barytone" above the "sound of plane and hammer." The sun of which Adam sings will accompany his movements throughout the novel. We are in a temporal world. The date and precise hour of each event is given by a novelist who, like Fielding, poses as a "judicious historian." Clocks tick

---

[12] The main movement of the novel takes place in five books, corresponding to the five acts of a play (the sixth book, dealing with Adam's marriage to Dinah, was an afterthought not contemplated in the original design).

throughout the narrative: in the opening chapter, a stroke of six by the church clock causes the workers to lay down their tools; in the epilogue, Dinah tells us that she has measured the hours by the watch which Arthur has left her. The novel ends as it began, on a note of time: "Come in, Adam, and rest; it has been a hard day for thee."[13]

The hymn sung by Adam in the opening chapter recalls those hosannas to the celestial bodies so devoutly intoned by Adam and Eve in Eden. The craftsman who has finished his day's labor is self-satisfied:

> Let all thy converse be sincere,
> Thy conscience as the noonday clear;
> For God's all-seeing eye surveys
> Thy secret thoughts, thy works and ways.

But God's all-seeing eye does *not* regulate the temporal Eden to which this Adam belongs. Despite its "Eden-like peace," Loam-shire is the creation of a Victorian unbeliever. Though Dinah Morris justifies each of her actions by the "leading of Providence" (chap. 3, p. 49), "Nature"—that awesome "dramatist" so frequently personified by the narrator—is the actual power which determines the destinies of all characters. For Dinah's creator no longer believes in the providential scheme which Fielding or Scott, her models among her forerunners, or even her contemporary, Dickens, embodied in their fiction. This Adam's confidence will therefore be shaken even more severely than that of his counterpart in *Paradise Lost*. Adam Bede's trust resembles Arthur Donnithorne's smug belief that, despite his past actions,

---

[13] For three excellent complementary discussions of the treatment of time in the novel, see Dorothy Van Ghent, "On *Adam Bede*," *The English Novel: Form and Function* (New York, 1953), pp. 171–181; Maurice Hussey, "Structure and Imagery in *Adam Bede*," NCF, X (September 1955), 115–129; and W. J. Harvey, "The Treatment of Time in Adam Bede," *Anglia*, LXXV (1957), 429–440.

he can avoid pain: "he was really such a good fellow at bottom, Providence would not treat him harshly" (chap. 29, p. 40). Like Milton's fallen pair, Arthur and Hetty will have to see their false projections come to naught. They—and that other couple, Adam and Dinah—will have to accept the limitations of the temporal world without the assurance of Milton's eschatology.

Nothing would seem to be further from Milton's timeless, spatially unlimited world. But the invisible realm of *Paradise Lost* is, after all, enlisted to justify an unheroic temporal existence very much like that which George Eliot attempts to dignify. In Milton's epic, the poet turns to a visionary past only to illuminate man's confinement to his fitful present. He gladdens the eyes of the fallen Adam with a sight even "more wonderful / Than that which by creation first brought forth / Light out of darkness!" (XII, 471–473). George Eliot creates a mythical past for a similar purpose. Although she turns back a mere sixty years from that "atheistic Half-Century" which Carlyle had inveighed against in *Past and Present* (1843),[14] she too wants to establish an atmosphere in which she can justify man's resignation to a temporal order. Taken from Wordsworth's *The Excursion*, her novel's epigraph describes aims which are also Miltonic:

> so that ye may have
> Clear images before your gladdened eyes
> Of Nature's unambitious underwood,
> And flowers that prosper in the shade. And when
> I speak of such among the flock as swerved
> Or fell, those only shall be singled out
> Upon whose lapse, or error, something more
> Than brotherly forgiveness may attend. (VI, 651–658)

Carlyle ended *Past and Present* with an epic apostrophe to England's workingmen: "Chaos is dark, deep as Hell; let light be,

[14] Ed. Richard D. Altick (Boston, 1965), Book IV, chap. 6, pp. 293–294.

and there is instead a green flowery World. O, it is great, and there is no other greatness" (Book IV, chap. 8). By placing a master craftsman in such a green and flowery world, by telling of the lapse and error of those who fell, George Eliot tried to light up her own acceptance of an existence darkened by the materialism of Victorian science.

In Eden, even before his fall, Milton's Adam had to learn that vision was not to be trusted. "Experience," not Fancy, was held out as the proper guide:

> That which before us lies in daily life
> Is the prime Wisdom; what is more, is fume,
> Or emptiness, or fond impertinence . . . (VIII, 193–195)

After the Fall, this same lesson is all the more painfully impressed on Adam. Given a partial preview of the fate of his descendants, he cries out against the gift of foresight:

> O Visions ill foreseen! better had I
> Liv'd ignorant of future, so had borne
> My part of evil only, each day's lot
> Anough to bear . . . (XI, 763–765)

Adam's despair is unfounded, of course. We know, and he will soon learn, of a new covenant following the Flood and the redemption made possible by Christ, the second Adam. What is more, his "evil" is inseparable from the suffering his descendants will endure. But though his deductions are false, his emphasis is partly correct:

> Let no man seek
> Henceforth to be foretold what shall befall
> Him or his Children, evil may be sure,
> Which neither his foreknowing can prevent,
> And he the future evil shall no less
> In apprehension than in substance feel
> Grievous to bear . . . (XI, 770–776)

In his grim determinism, Milton's Adam leaves no room for man's ability to avoid evil; he does not yet understand the redemption made possible by Christ. Ironically, he has become our inferior. For, whereas before poet and reader had to be "illumined" with celestial light in order to behold "past, present, future," now their historical hindsight is sufficient for them to detect the error of Adam's projection. The unfallen Adam had been warned not to inquire too deeply into the nature of the heavenly motions; the fallen Adam, shrunken in stature, must share the curbs placed on the motions of all mortal men. He does not yet know, as the Son does, that his exile from Eden can bring forth fruits "of more pleasing savor" than those "which his hand manuring all the Trees / Of Paradise could have produc't" (XI, 26–29). Faith, rather than knowledge, will give meaning to the uncertain future of his descendants.

Despite its unheroic setting, George Eliot's *Adam Bede* re-enforces Milton's epic theme. Instructed by Michael, Milton's Adam learns to recognize "goodness infinite" ordering the future—"That all this good of evil shall produce / And evil turn to good." Adam Bede, too, learns to recognize that "there may good come out of this that we don't see." In *Paradise Lost*, we have the paradox of a visionary poet who exhorts us and Adam to admit that all vision is "fume" or "fond impertinence"; in *Adam Bede*, we have the contradiction inherent in the philosophical stance of a materialist who yearns for truths unperceived by scientific lenses. If Loamshire is primarily ruled by the causal laws which affect all matter, it is also a semilegendary domain where man can occasionally break out of his bondage to time and space. Hetty Sorrel is too absorbed by the visible and tangible, but Dinah, by closing her eyes, has developed the faculty of feeling "more intensely the presence of a Love and Sympathy deeper and more tender than was breathed from the earth and sky" (chap. 15, p. 235). Dinah's subjectivism is not treated with the irony directed at Tina Sarti's. For the imaginative force of her sympathy allows her to penetrate truths undetected by the sharp-eyed rustics who are solely guided by the texture of the visible world.

Even though George Eliot does not share Dinah's belief in an otherworldly Divine Presence, she does very much partake of the young preacher's fervent desire to impose love and purpose on an actuality which displays a "strange deadness to the Word" (chap. 8, p. 134). The original germ for the novel apparently grew from her desire to contrast the lovelessness of Hetty Sorrel, a child of nature, to the altruism of the "Methody," whom she modeled on her aunt Mrs. Samuel Evans.[15] This opposition is quite similar to that between Lawyer Dempster's anarchic Milby and Mr. Tryan's belief in the transcendence of Love. Dinah's religion, like Mr. Tryan's, corresponds to Feuerbach's Christocentric religion of suffering. For both, love and sympathy are always identified with the "visible manifestations of Jesus" (chap. 2, p. 40). Although George Eliot's Feuerbachian creed is devoid of Milton's teleology, there are some noteworthy parallels between her humanism and his more orthodox faith.[16] In *Paradise Lost*, it is the promised sacrifice of Jesus the man which leads to the work's apotheosis: Adam and Eve's acceptance of exile is conditioned by the anticipation of a second paradise on earth, a "far happier place / Than this of Eden" (XII, 464–465). In *Adam Bede*, it is Adam's own eventual identification with Dinah's suffering Christ which likewise gives direction to his and her lives.

Like Milton, Dinah possesses the Puritan gift of seeing the immaterial in a "literal way" (chap. 3, p. 53). She forces her hearers to visualize the sorrow of a being who is as actual and alive to her as the saintly Mr. Wesley whom she saw as a child:

[15] Cf. "History of 'Adam Bede,' " GEL, II, 502–503.

[16] It was the human embodiment of Christ, not the insubstantial Son of God, that captured Milton's imagination. In *Paradise Regained* it is His mortality which makes Jesus heroic: the fallible human being who faithfully resists temptation is closer to Samson or Moses (with whom Adam Bede identifies) than to the shining godhead who drives out Satan's armies.

"Ah! wouldn't you love such a man if you saw him—if he was here in this village?" (chap. 2, p. 35.) In recreating Christ's passion on the Cross, Dinah appeals to her listeners' sense of sight: " 'See!' she exclaimed . . . 'see where our blessed Lord stands and weeps' . . . 'See the print of the nails on his dear hands and feet . . .' " For Dinah wants her audience to behold "that great agony in the garden" which lies beyond their placid surroundings (chap. 2, p. 40). Like the novelist herself, she wants men to grasp their relation to the universals that exist outside the range of their sensuous perception. Later in the novel, George Eliot superimposes "an image of a great agony—the agony of the Cross" on the deceptive tranquility of the natural world (chap. 35, p. 112). While Dinah's preaching is overheard by a traveler whose presuppositions are shaken by her words, the author urges an imaginary observer to consider the crucifixes she has herself seen in the landscape of foreign countries: "if there came a traveller to this world who knew nothing of the story of man's life upon it, this image of agony would seem to him strangely out of place in the midst of this joyous nature." And yet, the narrator insists, this artificial image would be as "true" as that of its natural surroundings: "No wonder man's religion has so much sorrow in it; no wonder he needs a Suffering God" (chap. 35, p. 112).

At least one critic has dwelt on the abundant allusions to sight and perception which run through *Adam Bede*.[17] We have already discussed how Mrs. Irwine, whose "excellent sight" is praised by the old squire, prides herself on her ability to judge internal character from external appearances. The old lady vows that she will never "risk a single prophecy on Arthur until I see the woman he falls in love with" (chap. 16, p. 255). But when she does see Hetty, she not only fails to recognize her as Arthur's beloved, but also misjudges her character. By praising the pretty

---

[17] See Reva Stump, *Movement and Vision in George Eliot's Novels* (Seattle, 1959), pp. 8–35, ff. Unfortunately, her treatment of "moral vision" is imprecise; it consists of examining image patterns for their own sake.

girl for her dark eyes, Arthur's godmother is as blind as his grand-father, whose nearsighted eyes cannot make out faraway images (chap. 25, p. 412). Again and again, the characters are depicted in terms of their vision. Adam's desire for a wider scope of action is evident in his remark that he would not like to live in the low-lands where "you can see nothing of a distance"—an opinion shared by Dinah. Hetty's narrowness, on the other hand, is con-veyed by her irritation over the distorted close-up of her reflected face.

For George Eliot, as for Milton or the Romantic poets, seeing is a metaphor for knowing. Although the narrator repeatedly ex-horts us to "see," "behold," and "look" at the tangible objects before us, he also warns us that the mirror of his own mind does more than reflect actuality (chap. 17, p. 265). If this narrator identifies himself as a historian, he also intimates in the opening sentence of the book that, like a vatic poet or sorcerer, he can use his ink "for a mirror" which refracts "far-reaching visions of the past." The eyes of all characters are deliberately contrasted. Adam's, Lisbeth's and Mrs. Poyser's are repeatedly described as "keen." All three characters have accurate insight into the ma-terial and the substantial. Dinah, on the other hand, fixes her eyes on intangibles. There is "no keenness" in "the liquid look which tells that the mind is full of what it has to give out, rather than impressed by external objects" (chap. 2, p. 29). Yet it is Dinah whose "sympathetic divination" correctly foresees Hetty's plight. While the girl is contemplating her reflection, Dinah's closed eyes penetrate the future in store for her cousin: "her imagination had created a thorny thicket of sin and sorrow, in which she saw the poor thing struggling torn and bleeding, look-ing with tears for rescue and finding none" (chap. 15, p. 236).

Two modes of perception, then, are depicted in the novel. Both will be synthesized by the union of Adam and Dinah. Adam, "keen in the region of knowledge," must recognize that there is also a knowledge based on intuition. Dinah, farsighted in spiritual matters, must accommodate herself to Adam's and Mrs. Poyser's empirical view of reality. For Dinah resists the physical verities acknowledged by her perspicacious aunt: "if you loved your neighbour no better nor you do yourself, Dinah, it's little enough" (chap. 18, pp. 286–287). The young woman's devotion to the image of Jesus is almost nunlike. She can visualize abstractions, yet is afraid of the sensual. Dinah tells her listeners that they would love a man such as Christ, could they discern him among them. But when the manly Adam declares his love for her, she shies away from him and flees to the isolation of Stonyshire. Ironically, this virginal resident of Snowfield, not only bears the name of a biblical figure deflowered by a gentile,[18] but also is associated with the "large moon," which acts both as a symbol for her imagination and as the emblem of Diana the chaste.

Despite her visionary powers, Dinah is rendered ineffectual by her rootlessness and fastidiousness. As a preacher, she hopes to counter "the hard looks of the men, who seemed to have their eyes no more filled with the sight of the Sabbath morning than if they had been dumb oxen that never looked up to the sky" (chap. 8, p. 133). But she fails with the skeptical Loamshire peasants because, unlike them, she has not looked down sufficiently at the earth. Though Bessy Cranage is moved by her sermon, the girl soon reverts to her former ways; though Lisbeth derives a "vague sense of goodness and love" from her ministrations, she sees Dinah above all as an eligible mate for her favorite son. Un-

---

[18] To Victorian agnostics like Frederic Harrison, George Eliot's Comteist friend, the biblical story of Dinah's rape and her brothers' treachery (Genesis, 34) in itself refuted those who cited the Bible as a moral authority: "Maurice, Coleridge, Carlyle, and F. Newman, in different ways and often without intending it, would fill me with horror and shame at the many passages of Scripture and many dogmas which I felt to be profoundly repugnant to morality and even to human nature. I never can forget poor dear old Maurice stammering through the story of Dinah, when that horrible chapter of Genesis came to be read in its turn" (*The Creed of a Layman: Apologia Pro Fide Mea* [New York, 1907], pp. 17–18).

like Adam or Arthur, Dinah grasps Hetty's character; unlike Rector Irwine, she foresees the girl's disgrace. But her warnings are as futile as the rector's delicate words to Arthur. Mr. Irwine refuses to live among his parishioners; though for different reasons, Dinah also isolates herself. She is absent during Hetty's trouble, cannot be reached by the "lonely wanderer," and returns only after the course of events can no longer be averted. She tries to soothe the fallen Hetty by appealing to the visible Christ: "Come, mighty Saviour! let the dead hear thy voice; let the eyes of the blind be opened" (chap. 45, p. 246). But her appeal does not greatly move Hetty. It cannot, in Adam's words, "alter th'evil." For Dinah's intuition cannot prevent the full force of George Eliot's deterministic Nature, a power severer even than Milton's Hebraic God. By anchoring herself in the village of Hayslope, Dinah acknowledges the mandates of a world where prophecy must be replaced by memory. In *Adam Bede*, even more than in *Paradise Lost*, it is hindsight, not foresight, which must yield the higher meaning.

THE VALUE OF HINDSIGHT: ADAM'S FORTUNATE FALL

In *Adam Bede*, as in the *Scenes of Clerical Life*, the past imparts meaning to the uncertainties of the present and the future. Though Mrs. Poyser intimidates her servant with a "Dantean picture of her future" and later causes little Tommy to fear "the dreadful picture she had made of the possible future" (chap. 6, p. 109; chap. 20, p. 344), her dire predictions are always founded on past experience. Adam Bede, likewise, on catching his "imagination leaping forward" checks his tendency to make "arrangements for an uncertain future." Experience and tradition have given him principles which he regards as "knowledge to be acted on" (chap. 19, p. 316). He is therefore unlike Mr. Craig, the gardener, whose "calkilations" lead him to make weather forecasts as faulty as those made by the astronomer in

Rasselas. More important, Adam is unlike Arthur and Hetty whose irresponsibility leads them to deny the "tyrannous memories" of the past (chap. 29, p. 32). Yet he will nonetheless be drawn into the tragedy created by Hetty.

Like Milton's Eve, Hetty wants to cast her past life behind her; but her "narrow bit of an imagination" only leads her to make "ill-defined pictures" of the future (chap. 15, p. 230). Whereas Dinah's sympathetic intuition is based on her awareness of biblical history, Hetty's mind has never adopted "a single Christian idea or Christian feeling" (chap. 37, p. 144). She is guided only by her current sensual responses. In *Paradise Lost,* Eve's appetite is aroused "by the smell / So savory of that Fruit" as she approaches the Tree of Knowledge (IX, 740–741). Similarly, Hetty is stimulated by the "sweet languid odours of the garden at the Chase" where she will lose her innocence (chap. 13, 202). Eve wants to be immortal, to rise in station. She fancies herself heightened "through expectation high / Of knowledge, nor was God-head from her thought" (IX, 789–790). Hetty, who will later crave "the means of living as long as possible" (chap. 37, p. 139), also flutters between "memory and dubious expectation" as she passes the gates of the forbidden Fir-Tree Grove (chap. 13, p. 200):

That was the foreground of Hetty's picture; behind it lay a bright hazy something—days that were not to be as the other days of her life had been. It was as if she had been wooed by a river-god, who might at any time take her to his wondrous halls below a watery heaven. (chap. 13, p. 202.)

Eve indulges in a pagan worship of the tree of which she has eaten. Arthur mythologizes the wood in which he seduces Hetty as a "sacred grove" immune to time:

His arm is stealing round the waist again, it is tightening its clasp; he is bending his face nearer and nearer to the round cheek, his lips are meeting those pouting child-lips, and for a long moment time has vanished.

He may be a shepherd in Arcadia for aught he knows, he may be the first youth kissing the first maiden, he may be Eros himself, sipping the lips of Psyche—it is all one. (chap. 13, p. 204.)

But Hetty is not a Keatsian goddess; the stasis of this garden is but a figment of Arthur's imagination. The novelist's mythological references are every bit as ironic as those Milton uses to describe Adam and Eve's lovemaking after the Fall. If Adam and Eve soon feel ashamed in their nakedness, Arthur, too, becomes uncomfortable, suddenly conscious that "something bitter had begun to mingle itself with the fountain of sweets." Adam and Eve are reminded of God's rule; Arthur is reminded of time. He pulls out his watch and wonders "how late it is." He hopes that his watch is too fast. It is later than he thinks.

In *Paradise Lost*, man's loss of innocence is momentous: all Nature groans, and time is born. In *Adam Bede*, the repercussions are less earthshaking. Still, Hetty's crime will alter the world around her; Loamshire life will never be the same. Social bonds are to be broken: Adam Bede and Martin Poyser will find, contrary to their own predictions, that the young squire has made their bread bitter to them. The bonds of family and friendship are violated: the Poysers feel disgraced by their niece, and the rector regrets his blind trust in Arthur. The microcosm George Eliot has created becomes as disturbed as Milton's gigantic universe. The fall of Adam and Eve leads to the murder of Abel, their son; Arthur must share the blame for the murder of his child. In each case, error could have been avoided and "tomorrow would have been a life hardly conscious of a yesterday" (chap. 12, pp. 193–194). Yet, both authors want characters and readers to be conscious of this yesterday, if truth is to come out of error and faith out of despair.

Hetty's crime forces Adam to reconsider his confident belief in an ordered world. He questions "if there's a just God" at all (chap. 41, p. 203). An idealized portrait of Robert Evans, George Eliot's father, he is more sinned against than sinning.

But, like Milton's more culpable Adam, he too must overcome despair by recognizing the paradox of a fortunate fall. For Milton, this recognition is based on Adam's understanding of the mercy promised by Christ; for George Eliot, it is predicated on Adam's acceptance of the creed of love which Ludwig Feuerbach had attributed to his Man of Sorrows. Milton's Son of God identifies himself with Adam on recognizing the "contrition in his heart" (XI, 27); similarly, Adam Bede is elevated as soon as his heart leads his imagination. In *The Essence of Christianity*, Feuerbach had asserted:

Christianity is distinguished from other religions by this, that in other religions the heart and imagination are divided, in Christianity they coincide. Here the imagination does not wander, left to itself; it follows the leadings of the heart; it describes a circle, whose center is feeling . . . in brief, it has, at least generally, a practical concentric tendency, not a vagrant, merely poetic one . . . With the Orientals, with the Greeks, imagination, untroubled by the wants of the heart, revelled in the enjoyment of earthly splendour and glory; in Christianity it descended from the palace of the gods into the abode of poverty, where only want rules,—it humbled itself under the sway of the heart.[19]

It is in the "abode of poverty," his narrow chamber at Stoniton, that Adam Bede becomes capable of joining the heart and imagination in the fashion of Feuerbach's Christ. Hetty's trial has forced him to "look back on all the previous years as if they had been a dim sleepy existence" (chap. 42, p. 209). So far, he has shown the "practical" imagination Feuerbach describes: " 'There's nothing but what's bearable as long as a man can work,' he said to himself: 'the natur o'things doesn't change, though it seems as if one's life was nothing but change. The square o'four is sixteen, and you must lengthen your lever in proportion to your weight' " (chap. 11, p. 171). But Adam had lacked "fellow-feeling with weakness that errs in spite of fore-

[19] *The Essence of Christianity*, trans. George Eliot (New York, 1957), pp. 148–149.

seen consequences" (chap. 19, p. 316). Sure of his own course, he had been intolerant of his father's failings. Rejecting his mother's solicitous offers of food, he had worked on the coffin that Thias was to have finished, rigidly fixing his thoughts on "the sad present and probably sad future." But Adam had been unaware of that future's immediacy; only after he found his drowned father the next morning did his memory check his former harshness: "Adam's mind rushed back over the past in a flood of relenting and pity" (chap. 4, p. 76).

Now, at Stoniton, with a watch before him, "as if he were counting his long minutes," Adam rejects the food proffered by Bartle Massey. The "brave active man" feels himself like a Samson blinded by Delilah, powerless to contemplate "irremediable evil." His father's death so far only has taught him the "alphabet" of the lesson he is about to learn, namely, that men must share the outward consequences of the errors committed by others, as well as their "inward suffering" (chap. 19, p. 316). At first, Adam is conscious only of his own helplessness. Soon, however, he sees his own lot in relation to that of others through Bartle's vivid description of Hetty's misery, her uncle's shame, and the rector's charity. His imagination finally follows the leadings of the heart: "We hand folks over to God's mercy, and show none ourselves. I used to be hard sometimes: I'll never be hard again. I'll go, Mr. Massey—I'll go with you." By accepting the cup of wine and the loaf of bread pushed on him by the schoolteacher who is himself a sufferer, Adam becomes a celebrant in George Eliot's religion of humanity. The new Adam and "the Adam Bede of former days" have at last become one (chap. 42, p. 214).

Adam still must forgive Hetty and her seducer in order to signify his new-found compassion. But he has been initiated "into a new state." It is Arthur who now must be made sadder and wiser. Possessed of the "vagrant" fancy that George Eliot, like Feuerbach, dislikes, he must be confronted with the "concentric tendency" that will end the wanderings of his mind. Adam has been renovated through his acceptance of the yoke of suffering; Arthur, however, informed of his grandfather's death, envisions a "renovated life" without sorrow. He bursts out of his room and gallops to Loamshire, yielding to his habitual tendency of "speculating what might happen in the future" (chap. 16, p. 259). With consummate irony, George Eliot follows the new squire on his ride from Liverpool. His thoughts are as panoramic as the countryside; though "not quite at ease about the past" (chap. 44, p. 228), Arthur confidently charts a future without Hetty.

Anticipating a new meeting with the girl, Arthur orders his thoughts. He assures himself of his present chastening and contemplates his possible reactions on seeing Hetty once again: "It was the exaggerating effect of imagination that made his heart still beat a little more quickly at the thought of her. When he saw the little thing again as she really was, as Adam's wife, at work quite prosaically in her new home, he should perhaps wonder at the possibility of his past feelings. Thank heaven it had turned out so well" (chap. 44, p. 230). Arthur's precarious manipulation of the future recalls his rationalization on deserting Hetty: "She would owe the advantage of his care for her in future years to the sorrow she had incurred now. *So* good comes out of evil. Such is the beautiful arrangement of things!" (chap. 29, p. 36). But his airy anticipations are dashed to pieces when a second letter informs him of Hetty's trial. Only now does he see her "as she really was." And, more important, he is also forced to see himself correctly for the first time. On his way to Hayslope, he had hoped that "his real life was beginning." His real life *has* begun, but it is a life that will be spent in recollection, shaded by guilt. The disparager of Wordsworth has become one of the outcasts of *Lyrical Ballads*.

For George Eliot, as for Wordsworth, memory lends meaning to the present. But the temporal ironies of *Adam Bede* are closer to Milton than to Wordsworth. Just as Satan's magnificent taunts are completely undermined by our having witnessed, beforehand, the very outcome of the archangel's defiance, so are Arthur's intentions to "show the Loamshire people what a fine country gentleman he was" presented only after we have already been apprised of their futility. The distortion in time allows the reader to exercise hindsight, to perceive that the characters cannot halt the sequence of events which they have unleashed. In chapter thirty-nine, "The Tidings," the novelist plays with the incompleteness of both Adam's and the rector's knowledge. A messenger is speaking to Mr. Irwine, and Adam is asked to wait. Staring absently "at the clock on the opposite wall," he becomes engrossed in his own thoughts: "he could not care about other people's business" (chap. 39, pp. 175, 176). Yet their business proves to be his very own. The rector has just been informed of Hetty's pregnancy, crime, and capture; he is pained to think that Adam is about to confess having fathered Hetty's child. Adam, however, thinking that Hetty has joined Arthur, has come to identify her seducer. Skillfully, George Eliot plays with each man's ignorance of what the other man knows. Adam's allusion to Arthur staggers Mr. Irwine: "No, Adam, no—don't say it, for God's sake!" Yet Adam completes his révelation. The rector, now in possession of the total truth we have already suspected, makes his own revelation: Hetty has been seized for child-murder. Adam's disbelief echoes that of the clergyman: "It isn't possible. She never had a child" (chap. 39, pp. 178, 181). Adam is forced to review his past relationship with his intended bride, to reject his false interpretation of her motives in wanting to marry him. The rector likewise must recall his earlier fastidiousness in intruding on Arthur's secret: "He saw the whole history now by that terrible illumination which the present sheds back upon the past" (chap. 39, p. 180). Adam becomes bent on revenge against Arthur; but Mr. Irwine knows what has to be done: "there are others to think of, and act for, besides yourself . . . I expect it from your strength of mind, Adam—from your sense of duty to God and man—that you will try to act as long as action can be of any use" (p. 185).

The rector's words introduce the somewhat melancholy creed that Adam and Dinah will ultimately adopt. Pain must be transformed into sympathy, and sympathy into action. Adam likes to read about Moses in the Old Testament because, as he puts it, "He carried a hard business well through, and died when other folks were going to reap the fruits: a man must have courage to look at life so, and think what'll come of it after he's dead and gone" (chap. 50, p. 298).[20] Even Dinah the spiritualist knows that men can "live only a moment at a time" (chap. 3, p. 51). Adam and Dinah come to bear an "easy yoke" with "steadfast patience."[21] They learn "to strengthen each other in all labour, to rest on each other in all sorrow, to minister to each other in all pain, to be one with each other in silent unspeakable memories at the moment of the last parting" (chap. 54, p. 369). Labor, sorrow, pain, and death: Adam and Dinah must be allowed to retain their earthly paradise, for in George Eliot's view there can be no "happier life" such as that vouchsafed, in another world, to the couple which Milton had banned east of Eden.

Adam thus finds a way of bridging past and future through his Carlylean gospel of work. *Past and Present* ends with a poetic salvo:

> The future hides in it
> Good hap and sorrow;
> We press still thorow,
> Nought that abides in it
> Daunting us,—onward.

Adam the carpenter also presses onward. He is not a historical figure like those magnified in *On Heroes*; his actions are less

---

[20] Cf. George Eliot's Miltonic poem "The Death of Moses," which ends: "He has no tomb, / He dwells not with you dead, but lives as Law."
[21] The words belong to a hymn by John Wesley which Dinah sings.

imposing than those of Tennyson's forward-looking Ulysses. Yet he is celebrated for his Puritan belief in salvation through work: like Carlyle's ineloquent "man of practice" or the Telemachus who civilizes the Ithacans, he brings stability and direction to the social order. Adam promises Arthur that he will carry out the improvements which the squire had wanted to introduce: "It's all I've got to think of now—to do my work well, and make the world a bit better place for them as can enjoy it" (chap. 48, p. 277). Arthur—a follower of the "undivine Ignavia," Idleness—has not been a "valiant Abdiel, found faithful still."²² In *Adam Bede*, as in *Past and Present*, it is up to the man of practice whose heart is "full of sorrow, of unspoken sadness, seriousness,"²³ to regenerate the flowery world that others must vacate.

THE DILEMMA OF HETTY SORREL

The determined Adam becomes the vehicle for the novelist's attempt to reconcile the discrepant realities of a material and a moral order. In a chapter entitled "The Reconciliation of Realism and Moralism," Bernard J. Paris states that George Eliot demanded that all her characters view reality scientifically but that, at the same time, she recognized that a purely objective view of reality could provide no morality or sense of purpose. Hence, though rejecting "the subjective approach as a means of arriving at truth," she also regarded it as "the only way of comprehending the significance of human values." Mr. Paris continues: "Her procedure is to view the cosmos first objectively,

²² *Past and Present*, Book IV, chap. 6, p. 279. Carlyle's condemnation of the landed gentry who seek others to do their work, is echoed by George Eliot's treatment of Arthur. She sent Jane Welsh Carlyle a copy of *Adam Bede*, hoping unsuccessfully to give "the philosopher" the same sort of pleasure she had from the beginning of *Sartor Resartus* (GEL, III, 23).

²³ *Ibid.*, Book III, chap. 5, p. 161.

as it is presented by science, and then, without losing sight of its true nature, to seek its moral implications."[24]

Mr. Paris' statement about George Eliot's general intentions certainly applies to *Adam Bede*, where she tried, far more arduously than in her three *Scenes of Clerical Life*, to create a "cosmos" containing both natural and moral laws. Yet intentions are not necessarily achievements: *Adam Bede* is hardly free from the serious difficulties which this philosophical novelist met throughout her career in her desire to be faithful to two essentially opposed criteria of truth. Though far less crude than in her *Scenes*, these difficulties are quite palpable in her first full-length novel. The combination of "realism" and moralism did not come as easily as Mr. Paris' statement would suggest; George Eliot herself complained in the novel's seventeenth chapter that "Falsehood is so easy, truth so difficult." In *Adam Bede*, that "falsity, which despite one's best efforts, there is reason to dread," manifests itself in two ways: in the narrator's ambivalence towards the "Nature" whose sway and power he interprets and in the disproportionate castigation of Hetty Sorrel. It is in her characterization of the latter that George Eliot seriously infringes on the artistic "quality of truthfulness" that she maintains so superbly through most of the novel.

Adam Bede is ruled by a power as absolute as Milton's God. "Nature," the narrator informs us, knits men together "by muscle and bone, and divides us by the subtler web of our brains; blends yearning and repulsion; and ties our heartstrings to beings that jar us at every moment" (chap. 4, p. 55). This Nature stamps the personality of all men (chap. 12, p. 186) and "has a language of her own, which she uses with strict veracity" (chap. 15, p. 228). Those who dare to "extract the very opposite of her real meaning" (p. 229) will suffer for their mistakes; even those who submit to her buffets soon learn, as small children do,

---

[24] Paris, *Experiments in Life*, pp. 242–244.

"not to expect that our hurts will be made much of" (chap. 27, p. 5). Though equally harsh and demanding, Milton's God had been just; moreover, His justice was tempered by the Son's mercy. By comparison, the exacting Nature whose ways George Eliot's narrator tries to justify seems capricious and indifferent. It shows as little awareness of love as that power which Tennyson had depicted in the earlier portions of *In Memoriam.*

The novelist's trust in love and goodness consequently becomes a check, a defense, against this unperturbed temporal power. Like Dinah, the narrator must plead that we trust intuitions: "I am of the opinion that love is a great and beautiful thing too; and if you agree with me, the smallest signs of it will not be chips and sawdust to you: they will rather be like those little words, 'light' and 'music,' stirring the long-winding fibres of your memory, and enriching your present with your most precious past" (chap. 50, p. 311). But Nature herself yields few such signs. She remains unsentimental. As in "Mr. Gilfil's Love-Story," the landscape is unmoved by the "blighting sorrow" that can befall man. It reveals no omens to those who would be guided by it: "For if it be true that Nature at certain moments seems charged with a presentiment of one individual lot, must it not also be true that she seems unmindful, unconscious of another?" (chap. 27, p. 4.)

It is noteworthy that, in the novel's scheme, these opposing moods of a two-faceted Nature should correspond exactly to the figures of Dinah and Hetty. Dinah, capable of "presentiment," always cares for the lot of her fellow men; Hetty remains so "unmindful" and "unconscious" of others that, in her instinct to survive, she rids herself of her own child as soon as it is born. Both are incomplete halves. In chapter fifteen, where George Eliot contrasts the two women, she comes close to explicitly allegorizing them by calling them "higher" and "lower nature," respectively (p. 240). Dinah, she implies, can be made whole again "by a good deal of hard experience"; but

Hetty must remain undeveloped and incomplete. Dinah can give up "the art of vision" and readjust her sights by taking Hetty's place in Adam's material world. Hetty, however, will remain blind. Throughout the novel, the girl whom Arthur idealizes as Psyche is uncomprehending and devoid of soul. Dinah's "treble tones"—like Milly Barton's deathbed perception of angelic music —are meant to signify the awareness of a higher rhythm than that which punctuates the purely physical world. Hetty, on the other hand, is noted for her "limited range of music." Her cousin's "sweet clear voice" is irritating to her, "mingling with her own peevish vexation like music with jangling chains" (p. 238). Far more than Arthur, Hetty is chained to the sensory world.

Beyond her brief confession to Dinah, there is no evidence that Hetty ever understands the full import of her actions. Even the donkey-like Bessy Cranage, that other recusant who is so slow and unresponsive, is declared to be Hetty's superior "in the matter of feeling" (chap. 5, p. 415). Arthur's rationalizations are always treated with ironic understanding; he is tolerated as a well meaning, if foolish, young man. But Hetty is indicted from the start; even her initial innocence, we are told, has a "false air" about it (chap. 7, p. 122). The hardness which Mrs. Poyser has noticed in her niece comes to the fore during Hetty's flight: "A hard and even fierce look had come in the eyes, though their lashes were as long as ever, and they had all their dark brightness. And the cheek was never dimpled with smiles now. It was the same rounded pouting, childish prettiness, but with all love and belief in love departed from it—the sadder for its beauty, like that wondrous Medusa-face, with the passionate, passionless lips" (chap. 37, p. 145). Unlike Caterina or Maggie Tulliver, Hetty learns nothing from her flight. The author's pretended pity for this seventeen-year old child introduces the only discordant notes in the novel: only a few lines after the narrator has professed that his "heart bleeds for her as I see her toiling along on weary feet," George Eliot makes sure to remind us that Hetty's "objectless" pilgrimage is still "apart from all love." The girl clings to life instinctively, "only as the hunted wounded brute clings to it" (p. 153).

Yet Hetty is denied even the good instincts of a beast. Though repeatedly linked to animals throughout the novel, these associations are never in her favor. Arthur pretends to go to the Hall Farm in order "to look at the whelps Poyser is keeping for me" (chap. 5, p. 90), though he really wants to see his tenant's niece. She, by not keeping his own "whelp," will later belie Arthur's intention to bring about a "better practice of husbandry" (chap. 24, p. 400). The birth of a litter of "unnecessary babbies" to Bartle Massey's bitch Vixen, causes her misogynist master to inveigh against the uselessness of all the human laws devised to deal with women ever since Eve's fall. Yet the laws which Vixen follows are natural: she is as tender to her pups as to the master who has rescued her from drowning; her "conscience" is "all run to milk" (chap. 2, pp. 359, 370). Hetty, however, is devoid of conscience. She is so narcissistic that she denies the most basic instincts of motherhood; she kisses her own limbs before giving birth to her child and then promptly looks for a spot to drown the unwanted "babby." After the infant dies of exposure and starvation, she is found by a peasant, with a "big piece of bread on her lap" (chap. 43, p. 222).

Some critics still insist, after the manner of Leslie Stephen, that Hetty is "thoroughly charming."[25] If so, her charm is the perverse result of George Eliot's excessive efforts to denigrate her

[25] *George Eliot* (London, 1902), p. 76. Robert Speaight regards Hetty as "the *femme moyenne sensuelle* at her most attractive" and finds "no judgment in George Eliot's tracing of her fortunes" (*George Eliot* [London, 1954], p. 45). Gerald Bullett detects no differences between the author's attitudes towards Arthur and Hetty; theirs, he says, is "an idyll of first love, presented with delicacy and understanding" (*George Eliot* [London, 1947], p. 175).

character. For her creator has made this unnatural child of nature far too repulsive. The only explanations advanced to account for the homely Marian Evans' treatment of beautiful Hetty Sorrel have been biographical surmises: "It is almost as though Hetty's very prettiness is scored up as a bad mark against her."[26] It is true that, as the landlady in Windsor remarks, "It 'ud have been a good deal better for her if she'd been uglier and had more conduct" (chap. 36, p. 134). But ugliness is not necessarily a safeguard against misconduct. Some other critics have surmised, that George Eliot used this pretty, but dumb, creature to chastise herself for her own sexual lapses.[27] Yet Hetty's beauty also serves a far more explicit function: the narrator repeatedly suggests that the girl's loveliness is analogous to that of her physical surroundings. Loamshire needs the "image of a great agony" to stir men into superior feelings that can find no ready source in nature. Hetty, whose surname corresponds to the plant which in "Mr. Gilfil's Love-Story" had been a part of the natural cycle so impervious to Tina's suffering,[28] is forced by her creator to wear a crown of thorns. Unlike Dinah, she has refused to "vibrate in the least under a touch that fills others with a tremulous rapture of quivering agony" (chap. 9, p. 141). She must be made to suffer.

The motives for George Eliot's inclemency are hardly to be found in any personal resentment against her creation's beauty. The beautiful egoists of her later novels, figures like Esther

[26] Walter Allen, *George Eliot* (New York and Toronto, 1964), p. 102. Joseph Warren Beach is more explicit: "This great bluestocking . . . this scholar with a face like a horse" cannot sympathize with a creature "so pretty as Hetty Sorrel" (*The Twentieth-Century Novel: Studies in Technique* [New York, 1960], p. 19).

[27] Cf. V. S. Pritchett, *The Living Novel* (New York, 1957), p. 92: "George Eliot was punishing herself and Hetty has to suffer for the 'sins' George Eliot had committed, and for which, to her perhaps unconscious dismay, she herself was never punished."

[28] Cf. pp. 68–69, above.

Lyon or Gwendolen Harleth, respond like Arthur Donnithorne
to the moral vision with which they are confronted. Even the unresponsive Rosamond Lydgate in *Middlemarch* (who, like Hetty,
is responsible for losing a child) is not castigated so severely as
the "hardhearted hussy" whom Mrs. Poyser likens to a fruit "wi'
a hard stone inside it." The reasons for George Eliot's fierceness
are to be found elsewhere. At one point in the story, Rector
Irwine asks Arthur if it is "some danger of your own that you
are considering in this philosophical, general way?" (chap. 16, p.
258). The same question might be asked of the novelist. The
"general way" in which she disposes of Hetty's "lower nature"
reveals that, far from being reconciled, her moralism and the
"realism" with which she beholds an amoral natural order still
are in conflict.

In the urban setting of "Janet's Repentance," George Eliot
had tried to overcome the moral blindness of Milby by playing
Lawyer Dempster against Mr. Tryan. In the rural world of
Adam Bede, Hetty's resistance to the love represented by Dinah's
"higher nature" epitomizes the novelist's fear of the indifference
of the natural order. Poor Hetty is made to stand for all that is
inhuman in "Nature." Her characterization is almost totally
devoid of those touches which the novelist had used to soften
Dempster's malevolence: Mrs. Poyser's children delight in the
birds they encounter on their walks, but "Hetty could not be got
to give any heed to these things" (chap. 18, p. 289). Adam
identifies his exertions with those of the worker-ants, but Hetty
is impassive, "not caring to know the difficulties of ant-life"
(chap. 20, p. 333). Instead, she is destructive, careless: she
plucks "leaves from filbert-trees" and tears them up in her hand
(chap. 30, p. 49). In the chapter which George Eliot significantly entitles "Hetty's World," she strongly hints that this
world is devoid of soul.

In "Janet's Repentance," George Eliot had identified Dempster's unreceptiveness with the negativism of an entire town.

Hetty, however, stands apart from the Loamshire rustics. She is too frail a target for her creator's Miltonic artillery. Whereas Gwendolen Harleth can stand for an entire social order in need of purpose, Hetty's "world" is, after all, merely that of her tiny dairy. George Eliot's wrath at this Perdita-like "queen of curds and creams" seems disproportionate. The expiation she allows to Arthur is denied to a creature who is made to seem far more culpable than the original Eve had been. In *Romola*, the unthinking Tessa, seduced by Tito Melema, is left unscathed; it is Tito, a more malignant Arthur Donnithorne, who in the course of the novel alters his shape from archangel to fiendish "Satanasso." In *Adam Bede*, however, Hetty almost becomes Eve and Serpent rolled into one. Bartle Massey claims at one point that only in Paradise was man exempt from the treachery of woman, "though you see what mischief she did as soon as she'd an opportunity" (chap. 21, p. 361). Yet the first Eve's "mischief" seems slighter than Hetty Sorrel's; left unprotected by Adam, deluded by Satan, she showed nobility in her disgrace. In *her* disgrace, however, Hetty merely wants Dinah to remove her fears. Whereas the God of *Paradise Lost* refused to create "another Eve" for the equally guilty Adam, the novelist of *Adam Bede* conveniently places Dinah in Hetty's stead.

The contrast between Dinah and Hetty is indebted to that between Jeanie and Effie Deans in Scott's *The Heart of Mid-Lothian*, a novel which also contains deliberate links to Wordsworth's "The Thorn."[29] Scott, too, professes to be a "realist" in the role of historian. But he is less interested in chastising the "lower nature" of Effie Deans than in vindicating the beliefs

[29] In Scott's novel, Madge Wildfire becomes deranged, like Martha Ray, after the loss of her child; it is she who steals Effie's son. When Jeanie finds her, Madge sits on "a variegated hillock of wild flowers and moss, such as the poet of Grasmere has described in his verses on the Thorn" (*The Heart of Mid-Lothian*, ed. John H. Raleigh [Boston, 1966], p. 298).

of her spirited sister. It is Jeanie's actions which are at the center of his book. If Hetty's pilgrimage is one of despair, Jeanie's is one of trust. Dinah's powers of presentiment cannot prevent the "thorny thicket" which George Eliot weaves for Hetty; though rescued from human justice, Hetty is executed by her moralistic creator. Jeanie Deans, however, successfully defies the laws of probability to save her sister. Though she is "no heroine of romance," Scott admits that there is nonetheless "something of romance in Jeanie's venturous resolution" (chap. 27). Her resolution substantiates her belief—and the author's—in a justice higher than those of the fallible Scottish courts.

Scott's belief in such justice allows him to be kindlier to Effie than George Eliot can afford to be to Hetty Sorrel. Hetty dreams of becoming a lady by marrying her seducer. Yet the novelist denounces her presumption; not only Adam but even Arthur deserves a better lot. Effie Deans, on the other hand, becomes Lady Staunton; her sister is surprised to see the refinements she has acquired. Although Effie loses both her husband and her child, she lives on, aware of her faults. Hetty's own understanding matters little to George Eliot. Her "lower nature" remains an obstacle in the way of the novelist's desire to demonstrate the rationality of universal love in a universe no longer ordered by a providential dispensation. Not until *Silas Marner*, where she, like Scott, would allow the illogic of the fairy tale, would George Eliot be able to dispense justice in her fictional world.

The only link between Hetty and the other characters in the novel is provided by the common denominator of suffering. In *Adam Bede*, as in the poems about guilt and sorrow in the *Lyrical Ballads* or in Emily Brontë's *Wuthering Heights*, the recognition of sorrow triggers an awareness of a higher order of reality. Like Martha Ray, the Ancient Mariner, and Heathcliff, Hetty must face the terror of isolation, the "horror of this cold, and darkness, and solitude—out of all human reach" (chap. 37, p. 147). In "The Thorn," the implications of Martha's story are impressed upon a Gulliver-like "captain of a small trading vessel"; the agonies of the Ancient Mariner and Heathcliff are sufficient to disrupt the complacency of their witnesses—the Wedding Guest and Lockwood, the city dweller. In *Adam Bede*, likewise, the death of Hetty's child and the girl's trial widens the understanding of all major characters, if not Hetty's own. It is the acceptance of Adam—a Wedding Guest turned titular hero—which chiefly concerns George Eliot. Yet Dinah, the Poysers, Rector Irwine, must also readjust their aims; the solitude first experienced by Hetty and then by the outcast Arthur leads them to regroup and close their ranks. The gaps left by the two exiles are filled: Adam carries out Arthur's improvements, and Dinah takes Hetty's place. To a greater extent than in "Amos Barton" or "Janet's Repentance," there is a sense of completion and restoration. Suffering *has* yielded purpose; though not as Arthur intended, good *has* come out of evil.

George Eliot's predecessors had used the stereotype of the guilty sufferer to imply the existence of an essentially benevolent universe. Martha Ray's suffering and the Ancient Mariner's expiation suggest that they have committed infractions against an order which is essentially harmonious; Heathcliff's Satanism is belied by the wholesome relation which springs up in the next generation of lovers; even Effie Deans's skeptical view of earthly and divine justice is undermined by her sister's unflagging faith in a reasonable Providence which sorts out error from truth. In all these cases, the tribulations merely confirm the existence of a purposeful design. George Eliot likewise means to chasten her Adam into giving his assent to a universe which she—like Wordsworth, Coleridge, Brontë, and Scott—wants to infuse with the intuition of love. But her predecessors had relied on an aura of the supernatural to validate this intuition: even the unsentimental Jeanie Deans embarks on a pilgrimage in which the various stages correspond to those encountered by Bunyan's Christian. The supernatural spirits of "The Ancient Mariner," the shaking earth which refuses to yield up Martha's buried child, Lock-wood's surrealistic dreams, and the fantasies of the demented Madge Wildfire create atmospheres in which we can suspend our disbelief and envision an order beyond the ordinary reality represented by the Wedding Guest, the sea captain and the vil-lagers, Lockwood and Nelly Dean, and the unimaginative courts of Scotland.

In *Adam Bede* George Eliot repeatedly hints that there is such a higher order behind the visible, temporal world of Loamshire. Yet the autumn haze which envelops her pastoral world hides only a recognition of the universality of human misery. The narrator of "The Thorn" ends his account by recollecting Martha's piercing cry: "Oh misery! oh misery! / Oh woe is me! oh misery!" The cry, like the thorn, attests to the existence of a reality more extraordinary than that grasped by the fact-finding villagers. In *Adam Bede*, on the other hand, this same cry of misery must by itself compel men to love each other. Despite her Miltonic efforts, George Eliot could not bring her-self to impress mind and conscience on an order that remained unmindful and unconscious to higher feeling.

In "Janet's Repentance," the novelist had already expressed her revulsion over this material order: "When our life is a con-tinuous trial, the moments of respite seem only to substitute the heaviness of dread for the heaviness of actual suffering: the cur-tain of cloud seems parted an instant only that we may measure all its horror as it hangs low, black and imminent, in contrast with the transient brightness" (chap. 5, pp. 112–113). In *Adam Bede*, both Dinah and Hetty must recognize that they are living in "this solid world of brick and stone." Dinah must give up her yearning for transcendence; Hetty must abandon her dreamy tendency to see "all things through a soft, liquid veil" (chap. 9, p. 146). It is significant that immediately after the publication of *Adam Bede* George Eliot should turn to the ro-mantic horror tale of "The Lifted Veil." In that fantasy she examined the trances of a seer unable to bear the heavy world of actuality. Gifted with powers of foresight far stronger than those of Dinah Morris, Latimer unveils terrors unsuspected by Dinah or Adam. George Eliot's "mental phases" were far from over. Clearly this Victorian "realist" had not yet reconciled her acceptance of objective truth with her reservations about her right to imagine a reality that might also be true to a better world.

5. Escape Through Fantasy:
"The Lifted Veil"

Lift not the painted veil which those who live
Call Life: though unreal shapes be pictured there,
And it but mimic all we would believe
With colours idly spread,—behind, lurk Fear
And Hope, twin Destinies; who ever weave
Their shadows, o'er the chasm, sightless and drear.
I knew one who had lifted it—he sought,
For his heart was tender, things to love,
But found them not, alas! nor was there aught
The world contains, the which he could approve.
Through the unheeding many did he move,
A splendour among shadows, a bright blot
Among this gloomy scene, a Spirit that strove
For truth, and like the Preacher found it not.
—SHELLEY, "SONNET" (1818)

[H]orror was my familiar, and this new revelation was only like
an old pain recurring with new circumstances.
—"THE LIFTED VEIL" (1859)

Six months after the publication of *Adam Bede* there appeared
in the July 1859 issue of *Blackwood's* an anonymous horror tale
entitled "The Lifted Veil." By this time the second impression
of *Adam Bede* was under way, and, despite her previous hesita-
tions and against the advice of her publisher, George Eliot di-
vulged the secret of its authorship. To her elation, the writer,
who could now openly sign "Marian Evans Lewes" in her letters
to John Blackwood, found that her book's popularity was not

greatly affected by this revelation.[1] Busily at work on her next novel, she wrote in October of 1859 to an old Swiss acquaintance, François D'Albert Durade, in order to apprise him of her recent success:[2] "I have turned out to be an artist—not, as you are, with the pencil and pallet, but with words. I have written a novel which people say has stirred them very deeply—and *not a few* people, but almost all reading England. It was published in February last, and already 14,000 copies have been sold. The title is 'Adam Bede'; and 'George Eliot,' the name on the title page, is my *nom de plume*. I had previously written another work of fiction called, 'Scenes of Clerical Life,' which had a great *literary* success, but not a great *popular* success, such as 'Adam Bede' [h]as had. Both are now published by Tauchnitz in his series of English novels." (GEL, III, 186.)

It is noteworthy in this exuberant account of her good fortunes that the new novelist who had captured "almost all reading England" should suppress any reference to "The Lifted Veil." Indeed, almost until the very end of her career, both she and John Blackwood thought it best not to acknowledge the authorship of that strange tale about a diseased visionary cursed with the power of seeing beyond the "veil" of reality. On arranging for

[1] The sales of *Adam Bede* were only slightly impaired. A provincial lady vowed that she would prove from internal evidence that the novel was written by a woman of loose morals; and Major Blackwood, always more pessimistic than his brother John, predicted that the "circulation in families" of the novelist's future works might drop considerably. But the harassment expected by George Eliot and Lewes never materialized. See GEL, III, 221n, 221.

[2] Durade, at whose house in Geneva Marian Evans had lodged from October 1849 to March 1850, had painted her portrait; the narrator of "The Lifted Veil" also poses for "the portrait-painters, who are thick as weeds in Geneva." D'Albert Durade later translated five of George Eliot's novels into French and may, as Professor Haight points out, "have suggested some traits for Philip Wakem, the shy, deformed young lover of Maggie Tulliver," who is also a painter (GEL, I, lxiv).

an edition of her works in 1866, Blackwood advised against including the story "in the recognized series of your works. I remember the Lifted Veil was published when Adam Bede was in the full blaze of fame, and I thought it better not to accept Lewes' kind offer to put your name to it in the Magazine" (GEL, IV, 322). In 1873, it was George Eliot's turn to refuse permission to reprint it in an anthology of the best stories from *Blackwood's*. Not until its inclusion in the Cabinet Edition of her works, in 1877, was this unreal tale finally acknowledged as being the work of England's foremost "realist." Soon after, a French painter, H. É. Blanchon, exhibited a lurid composition depicting the one scene which Blackwood had once pleaded, unsuccessfully, that George Eliot omit.[3]

In 1859, however, few readers other than Blackwood or Lewes were aware that "The Lifted Veil" was by the author of *Adam Bede*. And, had not her publisher reported that "the Bedesman" showed definite promise of "coming in a winner" in that year's great literary derby (GEL, II, 28), it is doubtful that George Eliot would even have ventured to submit her fantasy tale for public scrutiny. Since then, except for a brief article in 1962 stressing its modernity,[4] little critical attention has been devoted to the story's intrinsic meaning or to its place in the development of George Eliot's ideas and art. With a curious disregard for this supernatural tale's important English antecedents and its American or Continental counterparts, most students of George Eliot have dismissed "The Lifted Veil" contemptuously as being "mixed up with too much 'spook stuff' to make the piece of more than passing interest."[5]

[3] The painting, "La Transfusion du Sang," depicted the moment when the resuscitated Mrs. Archer accuses her mistress. George Eliot commented caustically: "Perhaps that hits the dominant French taste more than anything else of mine" (GEL, VII, 163).

[4] Elliot L. Rubinstein, "A Forgotten Tale By George Eliot," *NCF*, XVII (September 1962), 175–183.

[5] Jerome Thale, *The Novels of George Eliot* (New York, 1959), p.

A Tale Nearly Anonymous

George Eliot's own reticence about "The Lifted Veil" has unquestionably contributed to its neglect. Her first allusion to the story came on March 31, 1859, and was unusually self-deprecatory: she told Blackwood that she had written "a slight story of an outré kind—not a *jeu d'esprit*, but a *jeu de melancolie*, which I could send you in a few days for your acceptance or rejection as a brief magazine story—of one number only. I think nothing of it, but my private critic says it is very striking and original" (GEL, III, 41). After Blackwood's brief reassurances, she promised to have it ready "in a few days" (GEL, III, 44), but not until April 29 did she send him the manuscript with the curt comment, "herewith the dismal story" (GEL, III, 60). Lewes had meanwhile readied Blackwood for a slight shock: "You must prepare for a surprise with the new story G.E. is writing. It is *totally* unlike anything he has written yet. The novel [*The Mill on the Floss*] will be a companion picture to Adam Bede; but this story is of an imaginative philosophical kind, quite new and piquant. As usual he is unwilling to believe that anyone will see anything in it." (GEL, III, 55.)

"G.E." was correct. For Blackwood saw little in the tale beyond evidence of the same morbidness which he had deplored in "Janet's Repentance." Still, he accepted it for publication and worded his answer as diplomatically as he could: "It is a very striking story, full of thought and most beautifully written. I wish the theme had been a happier one, and I think you must

---

13. Had the story been written by Hawthorne, Poe, Melville, or James (it bears comparison particularly to Hawthorne's "The Minister's Black Veil"), or even by Pushkin, Gautier, or Mérimée, it would undoubtedly by now have a sizable body of commentary by American and English critics. It seems to be more popular in other countries, where perhaps the image of George Eliot as a mere copyist of ordinary English life has never been as deep-rooted a prejudice. There is, for instance, a Japanese critical edition of the tale, though none exists in England or America.

have been worrying and disturbing yourself about something when you wrote. Still, others are not so fond of sweets as I am, and no judge can read The Lifted Veil without deep admiration." (GEL, III, 67.) Blackwood's perception that the story quite possibly embodied some highly personal preoccupations was hardly destined to elicit any revelations from his correspondent. It was only many years later, on asking her permission to reprint it in the anthology, that he unintentionally drew from her a comment about its aims. By telling her that he still found it a "striking although horribly painful story" (GEL, V, 379), Blackwood may well have stirred George Eliot into defending a tale she had once professed to think nothing of:

I care for the idea which it embodies and which justifies its painfulness. A motto which I wrote on it yesterday[6] perhaps is a sufficient indication of that idea:—

    "Give me no light, great heaven, but such as turns

    To energy of human fellowship;

    No powers save the growing heritage

    That makes completer manhood."

But it will be well to put the story in harness with some other productions of mine, and not send it forth in its dismal loneliness. There are many things in it which I would willingly say over again, and I shall never put in any other form. The question is not in the least one of money, but of care for the best effect of writing, which often depends on circumstances much as pictures depend on light and juxtaposition. (GEL, V, 380.)

Although "The Lifted Veil" was eventually sandwiched in the Cabinet Edition between *Silas Marner* and "Brother Jacob" (George Eliot's only other short story), the "light and juxtaposition" it demands must be afforded by *Adam Bede* and *The Mill on the Floss*. George Eliot insisted that her fiction be regarded as "successive mental phases" in her development as an

---

[6] The motto was used as an epigraph for the story in the Cabinet Edition.

artist. Therefore her incursion into a mode so utterly at odds with the "realism" she had previously expounded deserves closer scrutiny. Her movement from the pastoral mode of *Adam Bede*, set in the semi-idyllic past of eighteenth-century Loamshire, to the "tragedy" of Sister Maggie, set in the era when Mr. Deane's harnessed steam threatens to undermine the old rural order, is far more comprehensible if we regard "The Lifted Veil" as a short, but highly revealing, intermediate "phase" between the two novels. Unlike the fiction immediately before and after it, "The Lifted Veil" is nearly contemporary; its narrator ends his account on the day of his death, September 20, 1850. In its proximity to the author's own present, the story differs significantly from all of George Eliot's rural novels, resembling *Daniel Deronda*, which also is set in the near-present, on the Continent as well as in England.

The composition of "The Lifted Veil" could easily have overlapped with George Eliot's work on either the concluding portions of *Adam Bede* or the opening chapters of *The Mill*. She finished *Adam* at Richmond on November 16, 1858, after laboring on it during her stay on the Continent from April to August of that year. In "The Lifted Veil" she clearly draws on her European visit. The localities visited by Latimer, the story's narrator—Munich, Vienna, Prague, and Dresden—before his return to England in the second half of the story, correspond exactly to the itinerary of George Eliot and Lewes after their departure from Munich. And the crucial description of the Jewish cemetery at Prague, which ends the first half of the story, contains details factually recorded by the two tourists in their journals.[7]

Since "The Lifted Veil" draws on some of the external details of George Eliot's European visit, it also may reflect the inner turmoil she seems to have experienced during her three-month so-

[7] See GEL, II, 469, note.

journ in Munich. Her sensibilities heightened by the composition of *Adam Bede*, George Eliot regarded Munich with mistrust: gauche allegorical paintings, insensible Bavarian beer drinkers, eminent German scientists like Liebig and von Siebold, provided impressions which could hardly have been transferred into the pastoral novel she was then writing.[8] Loamshire had been invented to assert the restorative powers of love in a world marked by toil and suffering. Though mythical, its reality was carved out of the solid Warwickshire life George Eliot had known and yet abandoned. Her German surroundings could only have accentuated her sense of isolation from that native reality and led her to question the power of her art. How "true" was Loamshire? In her novel, George Eliot stressed her reluctance to falsify experience, her desire to maintain "this precious quality of truthfulness." Yet in the distant rural world which supported Adam and his second Eve she had created a reality as it ought to be or might have been and not as it was.[9] Munich she found to be devoid of the communal spirit she had celebrated in her novel. The city, she claimed, lacked the organic sense of "community" she had detected in the medieval remnants of Nürnberg. Accordingly, the jovial Lewes speculated, "Who knows but some day we may have a Nürnberg novel, as the product?" (GEL, II, 449.) Instead, George Eliot only seemed to have stored up a darker mood, a vision revived months later in England, when her sister's death brought to the fore again her deep sense of desolation.

[8] There is one significant exception in chapter 35 of *Adam Bede*, where she contrasts Loamshire to those rural scenes in "foreign countries" where man-made crucifixes stand amidst the natural landscape.

[9] Cf. George Eliot's later remarks about *Adam Bede*: "As to my indebtedness to facts of locale, and personal history of a small kind, connected with Staffordshire and Derbyshire—you may imagine of what kind it is, when I tell you that I never remained in either of those counties more than a few days together, and of only two visits have I more than a shadowy, interrupted recollection." (GEL, III, 176.)

When Lewes abruptly left Munich for a week's visit to Switzerland, she felt miserable and lonely. Her dependence on him became as painfully evident during this short absence as it was to be many years later upon his death: "I suffered a great deal in thinking of the possibilities that might prevent him from coming," she wrote in her journal after his safe return (GEL, II, 467). Uncertain of her own future, at work on a novel in which she asserted that temporal man should prefer his limited vision, the unusual image of a seer capable of foreseeing his destiny might then have impressed itself for the first time in her imagination. In Munich she alternately complained about "the inconvenience of climate," felt at odds with a society as stolid as Milby or St. Ogg's, and claimed to be without energy to write to her few friends in England (GEL, II, 460, 464). Even Lewes' scientific activities, which she normally would have shared with zeal and interest, may have jarred her overexcited mind. The revivification experiment at the end of "The Lifted Veil" (which probably owes more to Mary Shelley's *Frankenstein* and other Gothic romances than, as Blackwood later intimated, to Lewes' "experiments on some confounded animalcule" [GEL, III, 67]) may well have been stimulated by those "wonders" which the delighted Lewes observed in the dissecting rooms of the Munich Academy (GEL, II, 454). The travelers at last left southern Germany "with ungrateful alacrity" (and the still unfinished manuscript of *Adam Bede*). Lewes probably spoke more for his partner than for himself when he claimed to carry away "no pleasant memories" (GEL, II, 465). Ahead—as in Latimer's journey—lay Vienna, Prague, Dresden, and, beyond, an uncertain future in England.

Yet, though the impetus for the first—the "Continental"—half of "The Lifted Veil" stems from George Eliot's stay in southern Germany, the composition of both halves of the tale could not have been undertaken until some time between the tourists' return to Richmond in September 1858 and their possession of Holly Lodge at Wandsworth on February 6, 1859. Three days before she sent the completed story to Blackwood— April 28, 1859—George Eliot recorded in her journal: "Finished a story—'The ⟨Hidden⟩ Lifted Veil'—which I began one morning at Richmond as a resource when my head was too stupid for more important work" (GEL, III, 60). This more "important work" was either *Adam Bede* or, more likely, the projected companion piece she speaks of in her next paragraph: "Resumed my new novel, of which I am going to rewrite the first two chapters. I shall call it provisionally 'The Tullivers,' for the sake of a title *quelconque*, or perhaps 'St. Ogg's on the Floss.' "[10]

It is therefore quite possible that the first portion of the tale— with its emphasis on a romantic *isolato* whose gift of vision sets him apart from his fellow mortals, but finds no outlet in art— was stimulated by George Eliot's isolation in Munich, but not begun till she was at Richmond, during a period in which she was wracked by doubts that she would ever again be capable of producing a work as "true" as *Adam Bede*.[11] The second portion could then have been finished at Wandsworth as a "*jeu de mélancolie*," designed to clear the air for the work on "The Tullivers," which she had projected since January 12, 1859. More important, however, both halves of the story hide or "veil" highly personal preoccupations, some of which also were to enter *The Mill on the Floss*, commonly regarded as George Eliot's most autobiographical work. Only a month before she first mentioned "The Lifted Veil" to Blackwood, the novelist became "weary and ailing and thinking of a sister who is slowly dying" (GEL, III, 24). Though the sisters had remained on friendly

---

[10] J. W. Cross, *George Eliot's Life as Related in Her Letters and Journals* (Edinburgh and London, 1885), II, 103.

[11] "Shall I ever write another book as true as 'Adam Bede'? The weight of the future presses on me, and makes itself felt even more than the deep satisfaction of the past and present." (*Ibid.*, II, 101.)

terms for some time after Marian's elopement with Lewes, Chrissey (Mrs. Edward Clarke) finally had followed brother Isaac's example by breaking off relations in 1857; but upon becoming aware of her fatal illness, she had written to seek forgiveness. George Eliot had welcomed this return of "a naturally just and affectionate mind," apparently hoping that the restoration of sisterly love would also pave the way for a reconciliation with Isaac, whose "external influence" she correctly blamed for Chrissey's previous silence. She wanted to banish "the idea of alienation" altogether, to resume only those bonds of affection which had once united the Evans family: "The past is abolished from my mind—I only want her to feel that I love her and care for her" (GEL, III, 26). Yet her sister's death blasted whatever expectations she might have had for a gradual reconciliation with a brother even more intransigent than Tom Tulliver was to be.

"The Lifted Veil" can be read on several related planes. On one, it is a highly private work in which the stable and sane commentator whom we have falsely come to regard as equivalent to George Eliot herself, is replaced by the morbid narrator, Latimer, a projection as much a part of Marian Evans as that sage public voice we hear in *Middlemarch*. Latimer, the "I" of this tale, enacts some of George Eliot's innermost doubts and feelings of guilt. Just as the self who is Maggie Tulliver was destined from the beginning to drown in the flooding waters of the Floss, so this young man—who, unlike Maggie, cannot even find solace in his childhood memories of rural England—is predetermined to die an extraordinary death. The date of his death, September 20, 1850, may even have held a private meaning for his creator. If so, that meaning remains a secret, for her journal for that year has been destroyed. Yet some clues remain. Latimer's father, so unlike his feminine, sickly, artistic son, is thoroughly British: "a firm, unbending, intensely orderly man, in root and stem a banker, but with a flourishing graft of the active landholder, aspiring to county influence: one of those people who are always like themselves from day to day, who are uninfluenced by the weather, and neither know melancholy nor high spirits" (LV, chap. 1, p. 281). Robert Evans, who fitted this description, had died in 1849. It was in 1850, upon her return from Geneva and after visits to Isaac and Chrissey, that Marian Evans, more and more compelled to find an outlet for her unique powers of intellect, concluded that she no longer had any "motive for living" among her provincial kin. Melchisedec, she vowed with bitter irony, was "the only happy man," for of him it was said that he was without father, without mother, without descent, having neither beginning of days nor end of life (GEL, I, 356). Later that year, in November, she left Warwickshire for London, to become the "infidel *esprit*" of the *Westminster Review*. Her past self died in that year (possibly, in her mind, on September 20th); yet it would be revived in her later fiction in figures as disparate as the rebellious Maggie and the detached, satirical Mary Garth of *Middlemarch*.

Whatever its exact origins in George Eliot's personal life, "The Lifted Veil" clearly holds a special position in her canon as a novelist. In its terrifying presentation of "our alienation, our repulsion from each other" (chap. 2, p. 324), this anonymously published story yields a nihilistic vision which its author would never have expressed as relentlessly in her acknowledged fiction. By resorting to a mode as fantastic as that of Coleridge's "Ancient Mariner" or Mrs. Shelley's *Frankenstein*, George Eliot gave prominence to anxieties which she had barely allowed to surface in the stories of Janet Dempster and Adam Bede. Yet, though it relies on the irrational mode of the fantasy tale, "The Lifted Veil" nonetheless displays the conscious effort to master all that is anarchic and irrational which is so characteristic of George Eliot's art. In *Adam Bede*, the novelist punished Hetty Sorrel to assuage her own apprehension over an erratic and amoral universe; in "The Lifted Veil," where the idealistic narrator uncovers an even more frightening vision of cosmic evil and meaninglessness, she likewise tries to conquer the nihilism to which Latimer succumbs by blaming him for excessive despair. In its intensity, however, Latimer's disillusionment is all too convincing. Like Maggie Tulliver, this character is less a victim of his own faults than of his creator's uncertainties and deep misgivings about the reality she hoped to vindicate. In the discussion which follows, I shall first focus on the horror dramatized by the allegory of "The Lifted Veil" in order to proceed then to George Eliot's more conscious attempts to subdue the doubts she had unveiled.

PRIVATE ALLEGORY: THE UNVEILING OF HORROR

Like Mary Shelley's *Frankenstein*, which had been composed during its author's sojourn in Switzerland in 1816, "The Lifted Veil" is a fantasy which partly stems from a highly imaginative Englishwoman's metamorphosis of an alien European environment. George Eliot had been in Europe on two occasions before her 1858 stay in Munich. Both of the earlier visits had led to important turning points in her life. After returning from Geneva in 1850 (a visit on which she clearly draws in "The Lifted Veil"), she decided to cut the ties of her provincial past and become a member of London's intelligentsia. Her second European residence marked an even more momentous in its severance: in July 1854 Marian Evans and Lewes eloped to Germany, fully aware of the probable repercussions of their decision. Two years later Lewes encouraged Marian to write fiction. The moderate success of *Scenes of Clerical Life* promised, just as her editorial work on the *Westminster* had, a new way toward her intellectual fulfillment. Thus, unlike Mary Shelley, George Eliot was already at work on a full-scale novel—an English novel—when a Continental environment again intruded on her imagination.

From Munich, George Eliot had written to Sara Hennell, who had recently lost her mother: "All the serious relations of life become so much more real to one—pleasure seems so slight a thing, and sorrow and duty and endurance so great" (GEL, II, 465). In *Adam Bede*, the serious-minded Adam comes to share this insight; he and Dinah impose meaning and direction on the potentially anarchic existence represented by Hetty and Arthur. Yet Hetty, even more than Arthur, bears the brunt of her creator's desire to justify the purposiveness recognized by Adam and Dinah. Though Hetty becomes the vehicle for Adam's and Dinah's understanding, she also is removed from their order of experience. Uncomprehending and childlike, this English country lass must face terrors unknown to the other characters: "the horror of this cold, and darkness, and solitude—out of all human reach" (AB, chap. 37, p. 147). Killed offstage, Hetty must pay for her lovelessness: her place is taken by one who trusts in the pulsations of "Love" even among the dreary blankness of Stonyshire.

In *Adam Bede*, Hetty's vision of horror is not allowed to disturb the novel's positive ending. In "The Lifted Veil," however, the horror informs the entire tale. Its vehicle is not an uncomprehending country girl, but a curiously un-English, Continentally educated visionary who resembles Dinah Morris, rather than Hetty, both in his idealism and his ability to foresee the future. Unlike Hetty, Latimer is essentially guiltless. He is betrayed by his blonde wife and by his extraordinary capacities of insight and foresight—faculties developed, significantly enough, during his sojourn in Europe. Whereas the animalistic Hetty never understands the implications of her own deed, the imaginative Latimer deliberately underscores the most terrible implications of the story he narrates in his own voice.

Adam Bede had relied on the correlatives of Milton and Wordsworth; "The Lifted Veil" harks back to a somewhat different tradition. Like *Frankenstein*, the story uses a mixture of European and English settings. But, while Mary Shelley's romance ranges from the Swiss Alps and a "solitary isle" in Scotland to Russia and a British vessel bound for the arctic North,

George Eliot's horror story is neatly apportioned between the opposing atmospheres of the Continent and England. In *Frankenstein*, the heterogeneous backgrounds of the two main characters are deliberately fused: Walton the English narrator, a seafarer nourished on "The Ancient Mariner," finds that his hunger for higher knowledge unites him to the Genevese scientist Victor Frankenstein. Gradually, as in Conrad's "The Secret Sharer," the two dissimilar men identify with each other; together they defy the arctic chills in order to hunt down Frankenstein's creature. The affection both men deny the monster nonetheless binds them together. Eventually, English caution triumphs over foreign yearning for a higher consciousness. It is in England significantly, that Frankenstein decides not to duplicate his monster; it is the English Walton (named after the prudent Puritan angler) who finally turns to safer waters and thus avoids the self-destruction that consumes both Frankenstein and his monster. The scientist (whose creature has read *Paradise Lost*) echoes Raphael's warning to Milton's Adam: "Seek happiness in tranquillity and avoid ambition."[12] Like George Eliot's Adam Bede, Walton presumably will find his tranquility in ordinary English life: "But I journey towards England, and I may there find consolation" (chap. 24, p. 207). The disastrous, self-annihilating Prometheanism of his Swiss counterpart has destroyed innocent lives; concerned with the safety of his crew, Walton turns his ship back from the cracking ice to the sanity and limitations of normal existence. He shall, as he promised, "kill no albatross" (Letter 2, p. 20). The monster and his creator, who dared to emulate God,

[12] Mary Shelley, *Frankenstein*, ed. Harold Bloom (New York, 1965), chap. 24, p. 206; subsequent references are given in the text. After rebuking Adam for aspiring to know truths reserved for God's omniscience, Raphael enjoins him: "Be strong, live happy, and love, but first of all / Him whom to love is to obey . . ." (*Paradise Lost*, VIII, 633–634); the same advice is repeated by Michael after the Fall: "only add / Deeds to thy knowledge answerable, add Faith, / Add Virtue, Patience, Temperance, add Love, / By name to come call'd Charity" (XII, 581–584).

are left behind. In Milton's allegorical scheme, Walton has accepted the reduced visionary scope that Adam acknowledges after his fall; in Romantic terminology, Walton has rejected the quest for a Coleridgean transcendence, Blakean emanation, or Shelleyean epipsyche. In Freudian parlance, his ego has withstood the allurements of irrational opposites; id (the monster) and superego (Frankenstein's aspirations) have been mutually destructive. Walton alone survives.

Despite its far more fantastic setting, the conclusion of *Frankenstein* resembles the resolution of *Adam Bede*, where George Eliot wants to stress Adam's acceptance of ordinary existence by disposing of the excesses represented by the libidinous Hetty and by Dinah's yearning for a suprarational transcendence. But for Latimer such a compromise with reality is impossible. Like Walton an Englishman by birth, he too is a poet manqué who possesses "the poet's sensibility without his voice" (LV, chap. 1, p. 284). Yet, unlike Walton, Latimer cannot simply turn from poetry to the study of physical science. Sent to Switzerland to be educated (like Dorothea in *Middlemarch*), he soon shrinks from his scientific studies and identifies instead with Continental prototypes like Rousseau and Novalis. Although, like Walton, he does befriend a scientist, Charles Meunier (whose later ability to confer life to cadavers clearly resembles Frankenstein's achievement), the bond between the men differs considerably from that which had joined Walton and Frankenstein. Latimer and Meunier have not experienced familial affection; they do not share a desire for higher knowledge. Instead, they are attracted to each other only by loneliness and their rejection by others. They are to be separated again when Latimer's powers—bestowed on him capriciously against his will, not developed consciously as were Walton's or Frankenstein's—first manifest themselves. Latimer is alone. While his predecessor in Mrs. Shelley's romance writes his strange story to a beloved and happily married English sister, Latimer records his adventures solipsistically, merely for the sake of unburdening himself. His readers are unknown to him; he expects little or no sympathy from them while he is alive: "I have never fully unbosomed myself to any human being; I have never been encouraged to trust much in the sympathy of my fellow-men. But we have all a chance of meeting with some pity, some tenderness, some charity, when we are dead" (chap. I, pp. 278–279).

Latimer's pessimism is justified. Even before his gift of vision allows him to penetrate the heart of darkness lurking in the actual world, he has been spurned by his English family and friends. Describing himself as a "shrinking, romantic, passionate youth" whose mind is too "full of German lyrics," he finds himself in deep antipathy with his conservative British father and his broad-chested, fox-hunting elder brother Alfred, a Philistine whose "self-complacent soul" is reminiscent of Tom Tulliver's in *The Mill* and Arthur Donnithorne's in *Adam Bede*. The arctic cold which Walton resists successfully in the faraway North, Latimer finds in England itself. Sitting in his isolated room, he foresees his death by suffocation and ponders the "icy unanswering gaze" which has met his yearning for love, even his longing "for brotherly recognition," and which will meet him again in death (chap. I, p. 279). In retrospect, his childhood seems happier to him than it actually was; for then, at least, he had still not fathomed the selfishness and puerility of other minds. But Europe, too, reveals only horrors. For it is there that he first develops his dire gift of vision. The "barren worldliness" which he later glimpses in the soul of his future wife, first is revealed through a vision of Europe's historical past. At Geneva, after an illness, Latimer experiences what he innocently regards as a "happy change," the removal of "some dull obstruction" (chap. I, p. 289). A casual allusion to Prague, a city he has never seen, forces on his mind a curious landscape. The long descriptive passage bears quotation in its entirety:

My father was called away before he had finished his sentence, and he left my mind resting on the word *Prague*, with a strange sense that a new and wondrous scene was breaking upon me: a city under the broad sunshine of a long-past century arrested in its course—unrefreshed for ages by the dews of night, or the rushing raincloud; scorching the dusty, weary, time-eaten grandeur of a people doomed to live on in the stale repetition of memories, like deposed and superannuated kings in their regal gold-inwoven tatters. The city looked so thirsty that the broad river seemed to me a sheet of metal; and the blackened statues, as I passed under their blank gaze, along the unending bridge, with their ancient garments and their saintly crowns, seemed to me the real inhabitants of this place, while the busy, trivial men and women, hurrying to and fro, were a swarm of ephemeral visitants infesting it for a day. It is such grim, stony beings as these, I thought, who are the fathers of ancient faded children, in those tanned time-fretted dwellings that crowd the steep before me; who pay their court in the worn and crumbling pomp of the palace which stretches its monotonous length on the height; who worship wearily in the stifling air of the churches, urged by no fear or hope, but compelled by their doom to be ever old and undying, to live on in the rigidity of habit, as they live on in perpetual mid-day, without the repose of night or the new birth of morning. (chap. 1, p. 287.)

At first Latimer exults in his unexpected powers of vision: "was it the poet's nature in me, hitherto only a troubled, yearning sensibility, now manifesting itself suddenly as a spontaneous creation? Surely it was in this way that Homer saw the plain of Troy, that Dante saw the abodes of the departed, that Milton saw the earthward flight of the Tempter" (chap. 1, pp. 288–289). Yet, like fallen Troy, the Inferno, or Satan's Pandemonium, this visionary landscape carries terrifying implications still unfathomed by Latimer. Coleridge's "sunny pleasure-dome with caves of ice," though also ominous, is at least beautiful and tempting; this city, where eternal sunshine beats down on frozen men, is repulsive. Sterile, dead, irretrievable, it is a past composed of "the stale repetition of memories," at odds with George Eliot's usual emphasis on those temporal props by which "the world of memory and thought / Exists and is sustained."[13]

In "Janet's Repentance," Janet Dempster overcame her de-

[13] *The Prelude*, VII, 464–465.

spair over the "sun-dried, barren tract" of her present. In later
novels such as *Romola* or *Middlemarch*, the dusty and parched
past will be identified with antiquarian figures like the blind
Bardo or Mr. Casaubon and will be carefully disassociated from
figures like Romola, Dorothea, or Caleb Garth who animate the
past by channeling its currents into the present and the future.
Yet, in "The Lifted Veil" this city of the dead, so similar to the
static realm portrayed by Tennyson in "The Lotos-Eaters," becomes an emblem for the death-in-life which Latimer will find
in his own present and future. History, he will realize, instead of
moving toward a better future, reveals but a successive casting-
off of values. Ideals held in the past become petrified by time.
Arnold's Empedocles, another seer capable of piercing "mysteries"[14] hidden from ordinary men, cynically views a similar
past:

> We scrutinize the dates
> Of long-past human things,
> The bounds of effaced states,
> The lines of deceased kings;
> We search out dead men's words, and works of dead men's hands.[15]

Like Empedocles, Latimer will succumb to despair over the
flux which can deaden all ideals. The stony inhabitants of his vision, as "doomed to be old and undying" as Tennyson's Tithonus,
seem to him to be "the *real* inhabitants of the place." His later
experiences will only confirm his suspicion. The impotence of
the mummified inhabitants stems from the shifting, mutable re-

[14] See Arnold's manuscript outline, Yale Papers, reprinted by C. B.
Tinker and H. F. Lowry, *The Poetry of Matthew Arnold: A Commentary* (London, 1950), p. 291. Arnold's description of Empedocles fits Latimer: "He sees things as they are—the world as it is—God as he is: in their
stern simplicity. The sight is a severe and mind-tasking one: to know the
mysteries which are communicated to others by fragments, in parable."

[15] "Empedocles on Etna," I, ii, 322–326.

ality of "the busy trivial men and women, hurrying to and fro" —the reality of the time-bound world which George Eliot had first tried to vindicate in "Amos Barton." For Yeats, the stasis of saints and kings frozen in their "regal gold-inwoven tatters" was to represent a desirable, ideal refuge from the world of flux; for that self of George Eliot who is Latimer, this same stasis only represents the cruelty of that flux. Dinah Morris, who was able to pierce the "soft, liquid veil" which enveloped Hetty, complained of a "strange deadness to the Word" (AB, chap. 9, p. 146; chap. 8, p. 134). But, whereas Dinah's vision could be adjusted to her creator's hopeful belief in a temporal order moving towards the realization of "Love," Latimer's vision of the lovelessness that lies beneath mutability is confirmed when, in Prague, actuality corresponds to his dream.

Yet before he encounters the stony saints prefigured by his imagination, Latimer faces still another confrontation. He enters the city's medieval synagogue and is terrified by it:

But, as I stood under the blackened, groined arches of that old synagogue, made dimly visible by the seven thin candles in the sacred lamp, while our Jewish cicerone reached down the Book of the Law, and read to us in its ancient tongue,—I felt a shuddering impression that this strange building, with its shrunken lights, this surviving withered remnant of medieval Judaism, was of a piece with my vision. Those darkened dusty Christian saints, with their loftier arches and their longer candles, needed the consolatory scorn with which they might point to a more shrivelled death-in-life than their own. (chap. 1, p. 309.)

Like Daniel Deronda, who would witness a similar scene at Frankfort, Latimer perceives only the withered remains of a once-vibrant faith; but unlike Deronda's, his conclusions seem correct. Deronda is likewise repelled by the external shabbiness of worshipers who seem condemned to a stale repetition of memories; yet that later hero discovers that by lifting the veil of ordinary life he can find the Ideal. Latimer, on the other hand, by lifting that same veil, is denied all illusions. On leaving the Jewish quarters he faces the scene prefigured in his trance at

Geneva; he turns "cold under the mid-day sun" (chap. 1, p. 309).

Gradually, Latimer shrinks away from human contact. His insight into the meanness of others robs life of all positive meaning. His powers of insight allow him to detect the mendacity lurking in all human hearts, while his powers of foresight allow him to anticipate the awful circumstances of his own death. Like Swift, whose epitaph he cites with grim relish, this disciple of Rousseau will become paralyzed, impotent, denied by his own servants. Although George Eliot implies that Latimer's contempt for his fellow beings is excessive, she also makes it clear that it is warranted by his unusual predicament. The savage indignation which lacerates this former Rousseauvian's heart could only have been avoided through those "serious relations of life" she mentions in her letter to Sara Hennell. Latimer could have been saved through contact with one of those "rarities" mentioned by the narrator of *Adam Bede*—someone of a higher nature, like Mr. Tryan or Dinah Morris or a golden-haired child like the one who rescues Silas Marner from misanthropy and despair. Early in the story, Latimer is soothed by the "simple, waking prose" of his servant; later, however, he avoids and is avoided by those simpler human beings like Mrs. Hackit or Mrs. Poyser or Dolly Winthrop who might have given him the benefit of their native shrewdness and sympathy.

No such creatures cross Latimer's way. When Charles Meunier reappears at the end of the story, Latimer feels a flicker of hope: "his presence," he decides, "would be to me like a transient resurrection into a happier preexistence" (chap. 2, p. 331), a return to an era of trust and innocence such as Tom and Maggie experience shortly before their death. But the "resurrection" that awaits him is not one of feeling. Instead, by resuscitating the dead Mrs. Archer, Meunier contributes more to Latimer's final disillusion. The lifting of the veil of death by the man of science only verifies the horrors already unveiled by the unscientific seer. Meunier's experiment leads to the ultimate horror. In *Middle-*

march, the "dead hand" of neither Casaubon nor Featherstone can affect the living; but in "The Lifted Veil" the hand of the dead Mrs. Archer revengefully points at Latimer's wife, and accuses her of murder. Human hatred extends even beyond the grave. Panic-stricken, Latimer cries out: "Good God! Is this what it is to live again . . . to wake up with our instilled thirst upon us, with our unuttered curses rising to our lips, with our muscles ready to act out their half-committed sins?" (chap. 2, p. 339).[16] Even Meunier looks paralyzed: "life for that moment ceased to be a scientific problem for him," as it will be for that other physician in Middlemarch who must adjust his scientific view of woman.

Mrs. Archer's accusation reveals to Latimer the evil of the creature he had romanticized as a "Water-Nixie." The cleared vision of his own past ends what the vision of the dead city had begun. By admitting to himself the full depravity of his wife,

[16] It is noteworthy that what is a *question* in the 1877 version of the story was originally a *declaration* in the 1859 version, which reads, "Good God! This is what it is to live again . . ." (*Blackwood's Edinburgh Magazine*, LXXXIX [July 1859], 47).

By coincidence, the same issue of *Blackwood's* also contained Lewes' article on "The Novels of Jane Austen" and an anonymous review of H. L. Mansel's *Limits of Religious Thought*. In his otherwise very perceptive discussion of Jane Austen, Lewes alludes to her "sympathy with ordinary life," apparently for the sole purpose of slipping in "a striking passage from one of the works of Mr. George Eliot, a writer who seems to us inferior in the art of telling a story, and generally in what we have called the 'economy of art'; but equal in truthfulness, dramatic ventriloquism, and humour, and greatly superior in culture, reach of mind, and depth of emotional sensibility" (p. 104). Few readers would have suspected at the time that the writer thus puffed was appearing in the same issue. Gifted with hindsight, modern readers of the magazine can savor a further irony: George Eliot, whose description of Amos Barton's homeliness ("in no respect an ideal or exceptional character") was instanced by Lewes as evidence for "his" sympathy with ordinary life, had also created the exceptional Latimer, whose visions transcended the very "limits of the human mind" which Mansel discussed in his treatise (p. 48) and which Jane Austen had exploited in her fiction.

he is stripped of his very last illusion and brought to the "Center of Indifference." Like Adam Bede, he has willfully deluded himself by loving a creature incapable of love. But the blind Adam is rescued from his infatuation with Hetty; he is allowed to marry the soulful Dinah. The all-seeing Latimer, however, has married Bertha Grant, fully aware of her contempt for him. If Hetty is made to seem too insignificant to be Adam's wife, Bertha is of a piece with this surrealistic tale. She is "a cruel immortal, finding her spiritual feast in the agonies of a dying race" (chap. 2, p. 337). Far more openly than Hetty, she represents her creator's deep fears of the natural world's hostility to ideals, to all conscious striving towards goodness and perfection. Like the stony figures in Latimer's vision of Prague, this cruel immortal typifies imperviousness and destructiveness; she is the *"real"* inhabitant of this world, and it is her horrible reality which defeats Latimer and drains him of his last hopes. Dressed in green leaves and wearing a green emerald, this Lamia epitomizes, as poor ordinary Hetty never could, a serpentine vision of the world-as-evil. In *Adam Bede*, Hetty was ejected from her green English garden, and Adam was granted another Eve. In "The Lifted Veil," Bertha's sting poisons Latimer and forces him into exile; robbed of his one love, he becomes aimless, anticipating yet fearing the approaching death which will relieve him of his too oppressive existence.

Like *Frankenstein* or "The Ancient Mariner," George Eliot's "The Lifted Veil" belongs to that mode which Walter Pater in his essay "Coleridge" defined as "that taste for the supernatural, that longing for *le frisson*, a shudder, to which the 'romantic' school in Germany and its derivation in England and France, directly ministered."[17] George Eliot's adoption of this mode has roots which are both personal and philosophical. Latimer represents a state of mind which clearly corresponds to that nihilism

[17] Walter Pater, "Coleridge," *Appreciations*, Library Edition (London, 1910), p. 96.

which all of her fiction was designed to resist: "For continual suffering had annihilated religious faith within me: to the utterly miserable—the unloving and the unloved—there is no religion possible, no worship, but a worship of devils" (chap. 2, pp. 329–330).[18] In Latimer, torn between two outlooks, two cultures, yet belonging to neither, his creator dramatized some of her own self-divisions: Europe and England, Rousseau and Swift, poetry and science, subjectivity and objectivity, trust and doubt, were the polarities which she herself tried to master and combine. Yet, whereas in her other novels she tried to connect and balance opposing categories in order to be true to a "reality" that could equally encompass her belief in objective veracity and her faith in ideals, she deliberately dispensed with all such restrictions in this tale. Latimer is confounded by the temporal reality which offers solace to Adam Bede. Yet his creation was obviously as necessary to George Eliot's well-being as Maggie Tulliver's mutilation of her dolls. Cut off from the past, finding the present as intolerable as the future he foresees, Latimer dies, not as Frankenstein had, for merely daring to lift the veil of nature, but rather for learning afterwards that the reality he has uncovered is unbearable without "mystery" or the "delicious illusion" of love.

It may be pointless to enumerate the personal elements which went into this disturbing vision: to insist that Latimer's "yearning for brotherly recognition" corresponds to George Eliot's deep need for acceptance by her brother Isaac and to speculate why the cursed "gift" of vision which separates the suffering Latimer from England and the English should first manifest itself, after

[18] The reviewer in *Blackwood's* (William Henry Smith, the philosopher) who attacked Mansel for constricting the limits of human understanding to such an extent "as to render a system of revealed religion impossible," may well have read the tale which ended on the same page where his article began. If so, Smith would have seen that by "lifting" the epistemological restrictions which Smith had deplored in Mansel's philosophical outlook the author of the tale had only found religion to be an even greater impossibility.

an illness, in Geneva, where Marian Evans first breathed the freedom of an unencumbered intellectual life.[19] To schematize the story by saying that in it the novelist turned against both the English ties she had lost and the Continentally inspired values she had adopted, is to simplify. As we shall see, "The Lifted Veil" is much more than a personal allegory; it is, as Lewes declared, also a poignant story of a "philosophical kind," perfectly self-consistent and compatible with the rest of George Eliot's fiction. Yet it is significant, nonetheless, that she had to resort to this private fantasy tale in order to accommodate Latimer's horror of existence. By writing out his story, she perhaps hoped to avoid a recurrence of the dream he was condemned to repeat: "The more I lived apart from society . . . the more frequent and vivid became such visions as that I had had of Prague—of strange cities, of sandy plains, of gigantic ruins, of midnight skies with strange bright constellations" (chap. 2, p. 329). For once in her fiction, the parched landscape of the city that "looked so thirsty" could not be overcome by her insistence on the redemptive power of love.

PUBLIC PARABLE: THE DENIAL OF DOUBT

When George Eliot sent Blackwood her epigraph for "The Lifted Veil" fourteen years after its composition, she was neither trying to impose a new meaning on it nor to disguise whatever personal relevance this dark tale might have held for her back in 1859. The positive "idea" which she expounded in that motto, with its emphasis on the need for the "energy of human fellow-

---

[19] Cf. George Eliot's second letter to D'Albert Durade, December 6, 1859: "When I was at Geneva, I had not yet lost the attitude of antagonism which belongs to the renunciation of *any* belief—also, I was very unhappy and in a state of discord and rebellion towards my own lot. Ten years of experience have wrought great changes in that inward self." (GEL, III, 231.)

ship," was implicit in the story's negations. Although Latimer acts out a nihilism which George Eliot at her most pessimistic quite obviously shared, he also becomes the vehicle for the moralism always present in her fiction.

Like Janet Dempster, Adam Bede, and Maggie Tulliver, this idealist confronts an Everlasting No. But unlike them, he is a Diogenes who cannot rise above denial and despair. Like Arnold's Empedocles, he seeks out his own isolation. Although he even lacks the will by which his Greek counterpart could leap into the crater, he is, in his way, just as suicidal. Deliberately painted as most unattractive, his morbid personality contains the seeds for its own destruction. Thus, even though George Eliot partakes of Latimer's negative vision, she simultaneously brands it as an extreme and denies him the very means by which ordinary mortals —bound by time and space—can be saved from anarchy and destruction. In Arnold's "Empedocles," the despairing philosopher shuns his double, Pausanias the physician, who, like Walton, can "live free from terror" (II, ii, 26); in George Eliot's story, Latimer seals his doom when he proves himself incapable of trusting his friend Meunier, also a medical man. In each case, the protagonist is no more a spokesman for the author's views than those other nineteenth-century malcontents, Hawthorne's Reverend Mr. Hooper or Melville's Captain Ahab are the mouthpieces of their creators.

Like all of these figures, Latimer is the creation of an anti-Romantic romantic. For those English Romantics at the beginnings of the nineteenth century who regarded time and space as purely subjective forms of the intelligence, the phenomenal world was but a "veil" preventing man's highest fulfillment. Thus, to penetrate the illusory veil that Blake personified as "Vala" was both a glorious and a necessary task. In "The Destiny of Nations: A Vision," Coleridge extolled human freedom as being not only the full exercise of all "the powers which God for use had given," but also the power to reach out at the Deity, "Effulgent, as though clouds that veil his blaze" (ll. 14, 17). Yet even the

Romantics found it increasingly difficult to approach an Ideal which was blocked out by the actuality of the temporal world. Wordsworth was accused by both Coleridge and Blake of mistaking the veil for the higher reality behind it. When Wordsworth asserted in "The Recluse" that man's individual mind was perfectly attuned to "the external World," and, conversely, that "the external World is fitted to the mind" (ll. 65, 68), he invoked Blake's apocalyptic wrath: "You shall not bring me down to believe such fitting & fitted I know better & Please your Lordship."[20] For Blake, "This World <of Imagination> is Infinite & Eternal whereas the world of Generation or Vegetation is Finite & [*for a small moment*] Temporal."[21] But to link this finite and temporal world to the eternal, beneficent order beyond it became more and more problematic. Keats and Shelley, those potential Victorian poets, emphasized the dangers of transgressing into the unreality beyond the "veil." In "Mont Blanc" Shelley echoes the question mark which ends "The Ode to a Nightingale" : "Has some unknown omnipotence unfurled / The veil of life and death? or do I lie / In dream . . . ?" (ll. 53–54.) In his 1818 sonnet, he describes the predicament of those who, like Alastor or Frankenstein, have dared to lift "the painted veil which those who live / Call Life."

Yet even for Shelley, with whom Latimer may have been vaguely identified in George Eliot's mind,[22] the Promethean seer

---

[20] *The Poetry and Prose of William Blake*, ed. David V. Erdman, comm. Harold Bloom (Garden City, 1965), p. 656.

[21] *Ibid.*, p. 545.

[22] Latimer approvingly quotes the Latin inscription on Swift's epitaph; on visiting Shelley's tomb in April 1860, George Eliot claimed: "it was like a personal consolation to me to see that simple outward sign that he is at rest, where no hatred can ever reach him again. Poor Keats' tombstone, with that despairing bitter inscription, is almost as painful to think of as Swift's" (GEL, III, 288). Like Ladislaw in *Middlemarch*, who is openly identified with Shelley, Latimer is an outcast who can find no fulfillment in England.

was still a figure of awesome proportions, a hero who dared to uncover the sublime. For those post-Romantic novelists who feared there might be nothing beyond the veil of actuality, however, this seeker bore quite different implications. Hawthorne's Mr. Hooper, the veiled Puritan minister, and Melville's Ahab, the frenzied monomaniac, like Latimer, recognize a reality other than that which protects ordinary men. Mr. Hooper wears his black veil to signify his recognition of universal evil; Ahab hunts the White Whale in order to rend the veil of a malevolent deity. In its nihilism, Latimer's vision resembles theirs: "I saw that darkness had hidden no landscape from me, but only a blank prosaic wall" (chap. 2, p. 323). Like them, he is consumed by the same evil he attributes to others: "The quick thought came, that my selfishness was even stronger than [Alfred's]—it was only a suffering selfishness instead of an enjoying one" (chap. 2, p. 312). Thus, although the "horror" that Latimer comes to recognize is partially correct, he also contributes to its perpetuation and perishes unloved because unloving.

For Latimer lacks the qualities which allow an Ishmael to resist that fascination with horror which draws his antitype into the vortex of destruction. Instead, he becomes a captive of his vision, engulfed by the city of the dead. The landscape he has seen turns out to be an emanation of his own self. In *Romola*, the heroine's brother Dino conjures up a ghastly vision of a city with gaping graves; in *Daniel Deronda*, Gwendolen Harleth beholds, "with a change of expression that was terrifying in its terror" (chap. 6, p. 86), the dreadful picture of an uplifted dead face. These omens correspond to a "reality" which is potentially true, representative of the spiritual emptiness of a diseased Florence and a diseased England; in both cases also, this reality must be surmounted if men are to retain a will to live, to believe in values which can save them from the nihilism of sheer despair.

The diseased Latimer lacks that will; he cannot accept life amidst an actuality which he has emptied of meaning. He is "perpetually exasperated" by his brother and despises the "coarse, narrow nature" of all such men: "This man needed no pity, no love; those fine influences would have been as little felt by him as the delicate white mist is felt by the rock it caresses" (chap. 2, pp. 312–313). The egotism of Bertha only makes him more passive and condescending: "she found herself powerless with me, except to produce in me the chill shudder of repulsion— powerless, because I could be acted on by no lever within her reach. . . . I lived under influences utterly invisible to her" (chap. 2, p. 324). The thought that his wife might respond to a lever within his own reach does not occur to him; he makes no effort to overcome the alienation that has crept into his marriage. The idea that Bertha, too, might "really be pitiable to have such a husband" momentarily crosses his mind, but he dismisses it sarcastically by attributing such "regard and pity" to those lesser beings who cannot fathom her true nature. His kindness to his servants, he feels bitterly, has provoked no such regard. Their "shrinking, half-contemptuous pity" he rejects with a fully contemptuous epigram: "They judge of persons as they judge of coins, and value those who pass current at a high rate" (chap. 2, pp. 324–325). Like Swift, Latimer cannot give his love to that fallible creature called man.

On one occasion only does Latimer feel resurgence of the affection that had once bound him to Charles Meunier. After his brother's accidental death, which, unlike Bertha's evil, he was unable to predict, he senses "the presence of a new element" which for a while unites him to his father, "as we had never blent before" (chap. 2, p. 316). This new element is the same which, under different circumstances, had brought Adam Bede the "completer manhood" denied to Latimer. It is, quite simply, suffering. His father's pain arouses in Latimer "the first deep compassion I had ever felt." But his sympathy is short-lived. At the same time that he feels attracted to his father's grief, he is also repelled by the old man's "mortified sense that fate had compelled him to the unwelcome course of caring for me as an important being" (chap. 2, p. 317). Once again, Latimer's insight into the motivations of others proves to be a curse.

Latimer therefore can never move beyond the self-pity which paralyzed Adam Bede for only a brief spell. At the high point of his despair Adam had blamed an unjust God for Hetty's irreparable evil; but, by recognizing the sympathy which even a woman-hater like Bartle Massey could muster, Adam turned again into a man of action willing to embrace his creator's creed of "sorrow and duty and endurance." Latimer, however, chooses to remain in the slough of despond. He asks for sympathy, but can give none. Meunier's return leads him to consider whether, "I might possibly bring myself to tell this man the secrets of my lot. Might there not lie some remedy for *me*, too, in his science?" (chap. 2, p. 332.) But he shrinks away from an act demanding trust in man, faith in life. Sure that sympathy is an illusion, Latimer rejects the opportunity for a confession such as that which liberates Janet Dempster, in "Janet's Repentance," or which will alleviate Lydgate's bondage in *Middlemarch* to a creature so similar to Latimer's own blonde water nixie. Janet and Lydgate disparage their confessors before yielding "to the exquisite sense of leaning entirely on a generous sympathy, without any check of proud reserve" (M, chap. 76, p. 353). Latimer does not dare to trust a proven friend. His lack of faith in human nature thus contributes to his destruction: "The horror I had of again breaking in on the privacy of another soul, made me, by an irrational instinct, draw the shroud of concealment more closely around my own, as we automatically perform the gesture to be wanting in another" (chap. 2, pp. 332–333).

Thus it is that this "miserable ghost-seer," like Hawthorne's Mr. Hooper, creates a new veil as illusory as that which he has lifted. His self-imposed veil becomes a shroud which separates him from the living and denies him the possibility of salvation in life. He has had "one chance / One few years' term of gracious life,"[23] but in his fear he refuses to test his vision. George Eliot goes out of her way to make it clear that Meunier might well have given Latimer the sympathy he wishes for but is afraid to request. There is no reason to suppose that his former friend, whose "large and susceptible mind" even Latimer praises, lacks charity. He is never tried. In the early days of their friendship Latimer's powers of insight had not yet manifested themselves; when he sees Meunier again, he has lost them: "My insight into the minds of those around me was becoming dimmer and more fitful, and the ideas that crowded my double consciousness became less and less dependent on personal contact" (chap. 2, p. 329). More personal contact might have led Latimer, like that other misanthrope, Silas Marner, to detect light among darkness. But Latimer has lost the ability to trust. He universalizes the evil he finds in his wife and ceases to search "among my fellow-beings [for] the blessed possibility of mystery, and doubt, and expectation" (chap. 2, p. 322). By fearing to test the possibility of his old friend's sympathy, Latimer has denied himself the opportunity of being saved. He has lifted the "veil that shrouded Bertha's soul," but the "shroud of concealment" which he now draws around himself is the shroud that marks his extinction as a human being and consigns him to the dreadful city of his vision.[24]

Bereft of the faith of the orthodox Christian or of the Romantic believer in a higher order beyond the veil of nature, Latimer perishes because of his inability to believe in man. He is, to be sure, more a victim than a sinner. Like Adam Bede, he is beset by forces beyond his control; like Maggie or Tom Tulliver, he is the sacrificial victim of capricious circumstances, created in order to validate the author's humanist ideals. But Maggie's death

[23] James Thomson, "The City of Dreadful Night," ll. 807–808.

[24] His predicament is very much like that of the speaker in Thomson's poem: "This chance was never offered me before; / For me the infinite Past is blank and dumb. / This chance recurreth, never, nevermore; / Blank, blank for me the infinite To-come." (ll. 823–826.)

seems unsatisfactory in a novel where George Eliot again pretended to adopt the standards of probability observed in *Adam Bede* and *Scenes of Clerical Life*; in "The Lifted Veil," where improbability is the rule, we cannot question the capriciousness of the circumstances leading to Latimer's ruin: capable of foreseeing some events, he fails to foresee others; free to see depravity, he is denied an opportunity to see altruism and love. This arbitrariness is deliberate: his negative conclusions must be founded on a partial vision of reality.

Latimer's "horror of [the] certitude" he has experienced falsely leads him to abandon the pursuit of "that doubt and hope and effort which are the breath" of the souls of more ordinary men (chap. 1, p. 306; chap. 2, p. 318). Though appropriating Swift's motto of "Sweetness and Light" for his own purposes in *Culture and Anarchy*, Matthew Arnold accused the Dean of possessing too much light and too little sweetness; George Eliot's Swiftian narrator, who regards the "vagrant, frivolous ideas and emotions of some uninteresting acquaintance" as the "loud activity of an imprisoned insect," is likewise too much of a spider and too little a honeybee. He rips apart the motives of men with a cruel light: "the kindly deeds which used to make the web of their characters, were seen as if thrust asunder by a microscopic vision, that showed all the intermediate frivolities, all the struggling chaos of puerilities, meanness, vague capricious memories, and indolent makeshift thoughts, from which human words and deeds emerge like leaflets covering a fermenting heap" (chap. 1, p. 295). Too certain of the meanness of human existence, Latimer denies life its "honey of probability" (chap. 2, p. 318).

Read in that fashion, "The Lifted Veil" becomes a celebration of doubt. Through Latimer's despair George Eliot represented the same state of mind which still another eminent Victorian had tried to overcome, some years before, in his verses:

O life as futile, then, as frail!
O for thy voice to soothe and bless!

> What hope of answer, or redress?
> Behind the veil, behind the veil.

Like Tennyson, George Eliot had dramatized the plight of one of the two voices within her. Latimer, too, was a projection of that self who had once trusted "God was love indeed / And love Creation's final law," a self who could no longer find a corroboration of that love in a visible universe foreshortened in "the tract of time." Tennyson's betrayed idealist gradually works himself out of his despair; George Eliot's succumbs to the certitude of his disbelief.

Yet "The Lifted Veil" is but a demonstration *a contrario* of the same faith in "honest doubt" which Tennyson reached in *In Memoriam*: in the face of an inhospitable reality, man can only trust in doubt itself. One of the stanzas which Tennyson placed as an introduction to his poem—

> We have but faith: we cannot know
>   For knowledge is of things we see;
>   And yet we trust it comes from thee,
> A beam in darkness: let it grow.

—is quite analogous in its implications to the epigraph George Eliot sent to John Blackwood:

> Give me no light, great heaven, but such as turns
> To energy of human fellowship;
> No powers save the growing heritage
> That makes completer manhood.

Tennyson's doubter finds faith in his uncertainty; Latimer finds that the light of certainty incapacitates him from living a life which must be based on trust, a life which must be spent in that opaque veil or web whose texture George Eliot chose to analyze in her more realistic novels.

Far from being a curious anomaly, "The Lifted Veil" is as

central to a century obsessed with epistemology as it is to the pre-occupations of its author. George Eliot's epigraph could easily have been appended to either *Adam Bede* or *The Mill on the Floss*, both of which deal with the relation between knowledge and faith in the temporal world. Her Adam, like Milton's, learns to accept an existence in which man can no longer be "illumined" by God's celestial light: Maggie, who wants "some explanation of this hard, real life," is partly punished for nibbling like Eve at "this thick-rinded fruit of the tree of knowledge" (MF, Bk. IV, chap. 3, pp. 28, 29). Adam finds fulfillment in the penumbra of that veil "which those who live / Call Life"; Latimer shrinks from its imperfections: "nor was there aught / The world contains, the which he could approve"; Maggie must die in order to inspirit St. Ogg's with the higher beams of "Love."

As an important "mental phase," "The Lifted Veil" is essential to our grasp of George Eliot's development as a philosophical novelist. It demonstrates primarily the extent of her own self-division: "Are you unable to imagine this double consciousness at work within me, flowing on like two parallel streams that never mingle their waters and blend into a common hue?"[25] In recent years we have come to regard George Eliot's fiction as but the even exposition of one "Religion of Humanity," and have paid insufficient attention to her own doubts in the efficacy of her prescriptions. These doubts found expression through her experi-

---

[25] The passage bears contrasting to Coleridge's famous statement in his notebooks: "I have read of two rivers passing their streams wholly distinct —if I mistake not, the Rhone and the Adar, through the Lake of Geneva. In a far finer distinction, yet in a subtler union, such, for the contemplative mind, are the streams of knowing and being. The lake is formed by two streams in man and nature as it exists in and for man; and up this lake the philosopher sails on the junction-line of constituent streams, still pushing upward and sounding as he goes, toward the common fountain-head of both, the mysterious source whose being is knowledge, whose knowledge is being—the adorable I AM IN THAT I AM." (*Animae Poetae*, ed. Ernest Hartley Coleridge [London, 1895], pp. 261–262.)

mentations with various fictional forms. Without the unreality of a tale like "The Lifted Veil," George Eliot might never have been able to channel the "two parallel streams" which led her, in novels like *Silas Marner, Romola, Felix Holt,* and *Daniel Deronda,* to create double plots which stressed salvation as well as extinction, regeneration as well as denial. Even the partial fulfillment she granted, in the greatest of her novels, to that other Swiss-educated idealist whose "nature, like the river of which Cyrus broke the strength, spent itself in channels which had no great name," might not have come about without Latimer's relegation to the parched city crossed by a metallic river.

More specifically, George Eliot's horror tale allows us to appreciate the differences between the novels immediately before and after it. In *Adam Bede,* Dinah Morris claims that she "could sit all day long with the thought of God overflowing my soul— as the pebbles lie bathed in the Willow Brook" (chap. 8, p. 131). Yet the negativism which lies half-submerged in the idyllic atmosphere of Loamshire, surfaced again in *The Mill on the Floss.* Critics who have correctly deplored the unsatisfactory conclusion of the latter novel might do well to reappraise "The Lifted Veil." For it is no coincidence that in *The Mill,* though she returned to the rules of probability observed in *Adam Bede,* George Eliot should have used an apocalyptic flood to purge St. Ogg's of its hostility and indifference. The thirsty city seen by Latimer was destined to remain a part of her own completer vision.

6. Tragedy and the Flux:
The Mill on the Floss

Never did sun more beautifully steep
In his first splendour, valley, rock or hill;
Ne'er saw I, never felt, a calm so deep!
The river glideth at his own sweet will:
Dear God! the very houses seem asleep;
And all that mighty heart is lying still!
       —WORDSWORTH, "Composed upon Westminster Bridge"

You could not live among such people; you are stifled for want of
an outlet towards something beautiful, great, or noble; you are ir-
ritated with these dull men and women, as a kind of population out
of keeping with the earth on which they live—with this rich plain
where the greater river flows for ever onward, and links the small
pulse of the old English town with the beatings of the world's
mighty heart.

                                             —*The Mill on the Floss*

The Mill on the Floss is unquestionably the most ambitious of the
seven works of fiction belonging to George Eliot's first phase of
development. From Bulwer-Lytton in 1860 to F. R. Leavis in
our own time, critics have repeatedly faulted the novel for some
of its undeniable artistic defects; however, its reputation as one
of the great novels of the Victorian period has been even more
consistent than that of *Middlemarch*.[1] Although there is little

---

[1] For Bulwer-Lytton's criticism, see GEL, III, 314–315 note, and the
introduction to Professor Haight's Riverside Edition of *The Mill on the
Floss* (Boston, 1961), p. xv; Mr. Leavis' objections are made in *The
Great Tradition* (New York, 1954), p. 58. For a discussion of the com-
parative reputations of *The Mill* and *Middlemarch*, see James Donald

doubt that *The Mill* is far less even in its craftsmanship than either *Adam Bede* or *Silas Marner*, its very unevenness is also a mark of George Eliot's greater aspirations. For the novelist's progress from her three *Scenes* to *Adam Bede* to *The Mill* can be regarded as a Victorian equivalent of the classical Virgilian procession from "small things to great." Within three years, George Eliot had moved from her rustic "scenes" to a pastoral epic, and now she hoped to achieve an even greater scope and depth by writing a new kind of novel, a tragedy for her times in which she would try to relate the fate of individual characters to the forces of historical change.

Adam Bede's Loamshire had been semimythical and self-contained. In it a giant Saxon carpenter could loom as a patri-archal hero. In *The Mill*, however, the pastoral Eden which sustained Adam is disintegrating. The "emmet-like Dodsons and Tullivers" are dwarfed by the immense river "which flows for-ever onward," and Adam's world has shriveled into the childhood world of Tom and Maggie, who, as adults, can no longer cling as he had done to "that child-like spelling out of what nature has written, which gives its poetry to peasant life."[2] The village life of Hayslope has disappeared. Instead, the environment portrayed in the later novel belongs to that diseased modern age in which, according to Matthew Arnold, "the calm, the cheerfulness, the disinterested objectivity have disappeared."[3] This movement from

---

Barry, "The Literary Reputation of George Eliot" (unpublished disserta-tion, Northwestern University, 1955), pp. 144, 207, 217, 262–276, 288–299, 302.

[2] MF, Bk. IV, chap. 1, 5–6. The references to this novel will include citations to the seven "books" into which it is divided, since George Eliot did not number the chapters consecutively throughout, but began each book with chapter one.

[3] Preface to the 1853 edition of the *Poems* in *The Poetical Works of Matthew Arnold*, ed. C. B. Tinker and H. F. Lowry (London, 1957), p. xvii.

an age of faith to one of doubt and self-division required, in George Eliot's view, a new artistic genre, a change in form such as Virgil himself had reflected in moving from his *Georgics* to the *Aeneid*, and Milton in proceeding from *Comus* or "Lycidas" to *Paradise Lost* and *Samson Agonistes*.

As a Victorian tragedy, *The Mill* is not wholly successful, although it is certainly more so than either Arnold's classical *Merope* (1858) or Meredith's quasiromantic *Richard Feverel* (1859), the two English attempts at tragedy closest in time. George Eliot was herself aware of the partial failure of her novel when she returned immediately after its composition to the pastoral mode she had first experimented with in *Adam Bede*. She claimed that *Silas Marner* "thrust itself between me and the other book I was meditating on" (GEL, III, 360). That other book was *Romola*, the first of those ambitious works of her second phase in all of which she would likewise attempt to connect individual fate to historical determination. In *Romola* she would vainly try to portray an even more momentous collision than that depicted in *The Mill*, and she would resort to an improbable romance in order to protect Romola from the river which devours Maggie Tulliver.

OF TIME, RIVERS, AND TRAGEDY

The Mill on the Floss, then, breaks new ground. In their correspondence with Blackwood, both George Eliot and Lewes at first described the book as but "as sort of companion picture" to *Adam Bede* (GEL, III, 41, 55). But soon the novelist spoke of her new work as being of a higher order than the pastoral epic she had concluded. Before finishing even the first third, she already asserted that "the book might be in some respects superior to Adam, and yet not continue . . . to excite the same interest in the mass of readers" (GEL, III, 151). When, during the novel's composition, a professor of Greek at Edinburgh University, J. S. Blackie, asked her to continue "to give pictures of the deeper life of this age," she felt inspired to sit down at her desk "with a delicious confidence that my audience is not made up of reviewers and literary clubs" (GEL, III, 241). As we shall see, *The Mill* clearly displays the marks of her conscious striving for a greater allusiveness and scope, that *"epische Breite"* which she eventually was to feel she had achieved only in the book's first two volumes (GEL, III, 317).

Shortly after the publication of *The Mill*, George Eliot became highly indignant to find that a French reviewer had compared her to the then popular English novelist Dinah Maria Mulock: "The simple fact is that 'The Mill on the Floss' has had much more time and labour bestowed on it than 'Adam Bede.' But the most ignorant journalist in England would hardly think of calling me a rival of Miss Mulock—a writer who is read only by novel readers, pure and simple, never by people of high culture. A very excellent woman she is, I believe—but we belong to an entirely different order of writers" (GEL, III, 302). The tone of this self-vindication is revealing. Only a few years before, George Eliot would have been more than content to capture the public of "novel readers, pure and simple." Now, however, the philosophical novelist who hoped to address herself to "the deeper life of this age" wanted to be appreciated by "people of high culture," the audience of Victorian prophets such as Carlyle, Ruskin, and Matthew Arnold. Significantly, her derogation of the ordinary novel-reading public closely resembles that of Arnold, whose *Poems: Second Series* (1855) she had reviewed sympathetically and whose views on "culture" were almost identical to her own.[4]

[4] See "George Eliot, Matthew Arnold, and Tradition," in my *Religious Humanism and the Victorian Novel* (Princeton, 1965), pp. 60–71. In the "Belles-Lettres" section of the *Westminster Review*, LXIV (July 1855),

Arnold's more gradual shift from "Empedocles on Etna" (1852) to "Sohrab and Rustum" (1853) and *Merope* (1858), resembles George Eliot's from "The Lifted Veil" to *The Mill*. As George Levine points out in his perceptive essay on this novel,[5] both Arnold and she believed that the Victorian artist should inspirit his age. Arnold had asked for an art "dedicated to Joy"; George Eliot later insisted that "the art which leaves the soul in despair is laming to the soul."[6] Both therefore demanded an art which would depict action rather than inaction; both looked to Wordsworth as a precursor who had found a "cheerful faith" in the natural world.[7] Yet both contravened their aesthetic credos when they had portrayed situations "from the representation of which, though accurate, no poetical enjoyment can be derived." Arnold removed his "Empedocles" from the 1853 edition of his poems; George Eliot did not acknowledge the authorship of "The Lifted Veil" until the very end of her career. Despite the moralism imposed on the stories of Empedocles and Latimer, both productions illustrated also their creators' own despair of finding in the transient world the unity still perceived by the Romantics. Arnold and George Eliot thus faced a common dilemma: How can the artist who despairs of the crippling caused by the flux of time address himself to his own time-ridden age of

---

297–298, George Eliot singled out "Resignation" and the first two portions of "The Harp-Player on Etna" (the truncated remnants of "Empedocles"). She felt that these poems best displayed Arnold's kinship to both Wordsworth and Tennyson.

[5] "Intelligence as Deception: *The Mill on the Floss*," *PMLA*, LXXX (September 1965), 402–409.

[6] "Notes on *The Spanish Gypsy*," in J. W. Cross, *George Eliot's Life as Related in her Letters and Journals* (Edinburgh and London, 1885), III, 48.

[7] I have more fully discussed Arnold's dependence on Wordsworth in "Dover Revisited: The Wordsworthian Matrix in Matthew Arnold's Poetry," *VP*, I (January 1963), 17–26.

transition? By turning to the mode of tragedy both writers detected a way out of their predicament. Through tragedy, they hoped to elevate the conflicts which had lamed both Empedocles and Latimer. Action rather than inaction, catharsis rather than self-pity, would be the result of their endeavors.[8]

Yet the form chosen by Arnold was to differ radically from that adopted by George Eliot. In his 1853 Preface Arnold attacked those modern artists who had tried to reproduce the baffling complexities of the Zeitgeist. He had, five years earlier, written to Clough that he, for one, would not "be sucked for an hour even into the Time Stream."[9] In the Preface he again maintained that the modern artist should move away from works "conceived in the spirit of passing time." By turning instead to the limited but perennially enduring actions of the ancients, the modern writer could impress on his own poetic efforts the fixity and permanence of great art. To be sure, he would have to be selective in his choice of models. He could not write another *Antigone*, Arnold contended, for its conflicts had become dated; nor could the nineteenth-century writer simply feign a classical repose by turning his back on the turbulence of his own times. In his preface to *Merope*, Arnold agreed with George Henry Lewes who in his *Life of Goethe* had criticized *Iphigenie auf Tauris* for its avoidance of all emotional "agitation." Yet though

---

[8] In his 1853 preface, Arnold argues: "In presence of the most tragic circumstances, represented in a work of Art, the feeling of enjoyment, as is well known, may still subsist: the representation of the most utter calamity, of the liveliest anguish, is not sufficient to destroy it: the more tragic the situation, the deeper becomes the enjoyment" (p. xviii). In her "Notes on *The Spanish Gypsy*," George Eliot likewise holds that, despite its "calamitous issue," tragedy can instill the emotions of "love, pity, constituting sympathy, and generous joy with regard to the lot of our fellowmen" (Cross, III, 47).

[9] *The Letters of Matthew Arnold to Arthur Hugh Clough*, ed. H. F. Lowry (London and New York, 1932), p. 95.

Arnold agreed that the "repose" in Goethe's play was artificial, he insisted nonetheless that the Greek tragedians, too, had avoided turbulence. Their repose, however, was achieved without the sacrifice of passion: Sophocles, according to Arnold, exhibited always "the most agitating matter under the conditions of severest form."[10]

In both "Sohrab and Rustum" and in his pseudo-Sophoclean tragedy of *Merope*, Arnold tried to impose the severeness of "form" on the same matters which had agitated his Empedocles or George Eliot's Latimer. Like the novelist, he hoped to conduct his readers "to a state of feeling which is the highest aim of tragedy to produce, to *a sentiment of sublime acquiescence in the course of fate, and in the dispensations of human life.*"[11] Arnold regarded "Sohrab and Rustum" and *Merope* as mere preparations for another tragedy, which was to be his *chef d'oeuvre*. But he never was to write *Lucretius*. For, in his handling, both "Sohrab and Rustum" and *Merope* became nineteenth-century allegories like those he had asked the modern poets to discard. Despite its Miltonic echoes and epic similes, the action of "Sohrab and Rustum" merely dramatizes *externally* the internal conflicts which had led Empedocles to submit to the destructiveness he saw in all modes of life. On "the low flat strand / Of Oxus, where the summer-floods o'erflow" (13–14), the old kills the new—an exacting Hebraic father mistakenly slays his loving, idealistic son.

Arnold's "Sohrab and Rustum" opens and ends, as George Eliot's novel would, with a description of a mighty river. In both works, this river is an emblem for the stream of change, the permanence of impermanence. Like the Floss, the Oxus acts as the *deos* of the tragedy of modern existence. The same "mighty

---

[10] *Merope: A Tragedy* (London, 1858), Preface, p. xli.

[11] *Ibid.*, p. xl (Arnold's italics). George Eliot likewise regards the sentiment of "grand submission" as being the central aim of tragedy (Cross, III, 46).

tide" that in the novel's opening paragraph carries blackened ships to St. Ogg's will eventually hurl the splintered pieces of some "wooden machinery" at the last of the Tullivers. Arnold's epic machinery likewise stresses the implacability of change.[12] Young Sohrab dies by the yellow river's "brink"; old Rustum wails: "Oh, that its waves were flowing over me! / Oh, that I saw its grains of yellow silt / Roll tumbling in the current o'er my head" (ll. 768–780). But even though the father's misjudgment proves as fatal as Mr. Tulliver's, his own death wish is not fulfilled. As in *The Mill on the Floss*, the young must die for their elders' mistakes.

In *Merope*, despite its Sophoclean treatment, the situation is reversed: the new slays the old. Innovation, represented by young Aepytus, overcomes reaction, represented by the aged Polyphontes. Aepytus' allies are the Messenian city-dwellers who hate "their present"; Polyphontes' allies are the conservative Dorian lords. In *The Mill on the Floss*, Tom Tulliver adapts himself to the city ways of St. Ogg's. Like Aepytus, he wants to revenge his father; like Aepytus, he has lived in Arcadia and yet must embrace the ways of the future. George Eliot's novel ends with the catastrophe of the flood; Arnold's play culminates in an "all-flooding ocean of blood" (l. 1246). Significantly, the inertness of his tragedy is relieved only at two points: when Merope almost repeats Rustum's mistake by killing her own son, and when that son, the disguised Aepytus, describes with extraordinary vividness the purely imaginary circumstances of his death. Those circumstances are noteworthy in themselves; for Aepytus graphically relates his own supposed drowning in the tumultuous torrent of a

---

[12] In *The Poetry of Matthew Arnold: A Commentary* (London, 1950), C. B. Tinker and H. F. Lowry maintain that the Oxus acts as a reminder of "another order than the temporal and transitory one in which the immediate action moves" (p. 81). I cannot agree with this view. The river *is* the temporal order; "the immediate action," is but a ripple in its larger flow.

"rumbling subterranean stream." Merope, wooed by both extremes—Polyphontes and Aepytus—stands by as paralyzed as Empedocles had been. If Maggie must yield to the moving river, Merope can at least avoid all internal commotion by being as impassive a spectator as the poet who was to look at the ebb and flow of human misery from a perch on the cliffs of Dover. Around her, Ionian disruption and Dorian order collide in one further cycle of that systolic expansion and contraction which is history.

If George Eliot wanted "people of high culture" to understand the full import of her tragic novel, Arnold hoped that ordinary "John Bull" might also recognize his play as more than an incursion into classical antiquity.[13] The newly elected Oxford professor of poetry wrote a long explanatory preface to the play in which he broadly hinted that the "events on which the action turns belong to a period of transition" like his own era. He also tried to stage his tragedy in order to make it accessible to more than the reading public. As drama, however, the play was as unsuccessful as Dr. Johnson's *Irene*. Though not perhaps the "utter failure" that Lionel Trilling declares it to be,[14] *Merope* founders because, as Mr. Trilling puts it, Arnold refused "to see that the subjectivism in romantic poetry had its roots in historical reality, that it could not be dismissed by turning away to its seeming opposite, 'classical' objectivity" (p. 143).

George Eliot never lost sight of this "historical reality." In her 1856 essay on "The Antigone and Its Moral," she framed what seems to be a careful answer to Arnold's objections to that tragedy. To her, far from being invalid for her contemporaries, the play depicts a universal historical struggle: "Wherever the strength of a man's intellect, or moral sense, or affection brings him into opposition with the rules society has sanctioned, *there* is renewed the conflict between Antigone and Creon."[15] Yet this

[13] *Ibid.*, p. 279.
[14] *Matthew Arnold* (New York, 1955), p. 142.

universality, George Eliot felt, could not be attained simply by borrowing the classical Greek forms. To her, as to Arnold, man's temporal life was essentially gloomy: death merely confirmed each man's defeat by the flux which governed all existence. She therefore spoke of some of her ordinary *Scenes of Clerical Life* as being, loosely, tragedies. Even many of those superb comic touches always present in her novels are mere mechanisms to help divert her natural inclination towards a tragic sense of life.[16] Like Arnold, George Eliot sought a more elevated form to express her tragic sense; yet she recognized far more clearly than Arnold the need to devise new ways of embodying the conflicts that they both wanted to portray.

In 1854 George Eliot read and supported the views of one of her German friends, the classicist and philosopher Otto Friedrich Gruppe, whose treatise on Greek tragedy she declared to be "one of the best books, if not the very best we have on Greek Drama."[17] In that work, *Ariadne: Die Tragische Kunst der Griechen* (1834), the Hegelian Gruppe bitterly declaimed

[15] "The Antigone and Its Moral," *Leader*, VII (29 March 1856), 306; reprinted in *Essays of George Eliot*, ed. Thomas Pinney (London, 1963), p. 265.

[16] In "Menander and the Greek Comedy," a review of Guillaume Guizot's study of Menander, George Eliot claimed that the highest comedy was really "tragedy in the disguise of mirth" (*Leader*, VI [16 June 1855], 579). It is true, as Mr. Darrell Mansell, Jr., asserts, that George Eliot regarded all her fiction as "a kind of tragedy" ("A Note on Hegel and George Eliot," *Victorian News-Letter*, 27 [Spring 1965], pp. 12–15). But his discussion of all her novels as identical representations of "tragic conflicts" is not only highly reductive, but also, as Mrs. E. Anne Kilcullen points out in a letter (*VNL*, Spring 1966), is based on some serious misreadings. Even as fine a formalistic critic as Mrs. Barbara Hardy tends to underestimate the variation in the form of George Eliot's novels, regarding them all as identical "unheroic tragedies."

[17] "The Future of German Philosophy," *Leader*, VI (28 July 1855), 723–724; in *Essays*, p. 149. The article was a review of Gruppe's later work, *Gegenwart und Zukunft der Philosophie in Deutschland* (1855).

against all those moderns who (like Goethe in *Iphigenie*) had merely tried to emulate classical tragedy. Greek tragedy, he argued, had sprung from a gradual historical process. Had German writers only understood that process, he believed, they might have turned to a comparable rich fund of myth provided by their own native folklore or "*Volkspoesie*." Gruppe, who might have been mollified by the later use of the Germanic sagas by Wagner and others, lamented that the Nibelungen cycle could no longer evolve into tragedy: "Those myths have waned away, disappeared from our racial consciousness: what can a learned inquiry do at this point? Even if we could convince our modern tragedians that it is impossible for them to emulate the Greeks in general and Sophocles in particular . . . how could this insight help us any more? It is too late."[18]

Gruppe's thesis—important because of its connections to George Eliot rather than for its originality or validity—is inimical to a neoclassical approach like Arnold's. Greek tragedy, Gruppe asserts again and again, cannot be reproduced; but the modern tragedian may tap similar sources of poetic belief. For Arnold, *Hamlet* marks the beginning of modern self-division; for Gruppe, Shakespeare's plays point the way for those moderns who must admit the reality of history: "He stands, as did

---

George Eliot had met the philosopher during her 1854 sojourn in Germany: "He has written books on everything—on the Greek drama—a great book on the Cosmic Systems of the Greeks—an epic, numberless lyric poems, etc.—he has a philosophical work and a history of literature in the press" (GEL, II, 192). She probably had Gruppe in mind when she had Ladislaw remark that Casaubon's German contemporaries would laugh at his results, and she remembered him as late as 1878, two years after his death, when she found the Crown Prince of Germany to be just as amiable "as if he had been a Professor Gruppe" (GEL, VII, 29).

[18] *Ariadne: Die Tragische Kunst der Griechen in ihrer Entwicklung und ihrem Zusammenhang mit der Volkspoesie* (Berlin, 1834), pp. 655–656 (my translation).

Sophocles, at the end of a developmental period of folk-literature" (p. 656). The modern artist, he implies, might likewise enlist the poetic belief of predecessors living in a simpler, yet immediate past. Gruppe's work or the ideas which it reflects probably came to the attention of the Swiss Gottfried Keller, who is usually credited with being the father of the German realistic novel.[19] It is easy to see why Gruppe's views should also have appealed to the English novelist who wanted to see life steadily and see it whole. In her 1856 essay on Riehl, for instance, George Eliot asked that both German and English novelists turn to the poetry still extant in their rural communities. In her own *Scenes of Clerical Life*, she took for her starting point that "naturalistic" stage which, in Gruppe's view, had also set in after the fragmentation of the ancient Greek religion. In that historical stage, the German contended, the pictorial art of the Greeks had depicted "scenes" which were not unlike those painted by the

---

[19] George Henry Lewes' article, "Realism in Art: Modern German Fiction," *Westminster Review*, LXX (October 1858), 488–518, contains a four-page discussion of Keller's *Die Leute von Seldwyla*. The review was written in Germany in 1858; George Eliot claimed that her "only contribution to it was reading the novels aloud after dinner" (GEL, II, 486). Using this as his point of departure, Allan Casson devotes two pages to presumed parallels between one of the novellas Lewes discusses, *Romeo und Julia auf dem Dorfe*, and *The Mill* (*MLN*, LXXV [January 1960], 20–22). Although I have no quarrel with his findings, I believe the links between Keller and George Eliot to be far more significant than such a study might suggest. Like George Eliot, Keller was born in 1819; like her, he was influenced by Strauss and Feuerbach (whose lectures he attended) and later turned from journalism to fiction. He, too, tried to validate his agnostic philosophy by going back to an agrarian past he had personally known; he, too, experimented with novellas and with the more capacious *Bildungsroman*. The aggregate stories in *Die Leute von Seldwyla* (1856–1874) resemble the larger series which George Eliot had originally planned in her own *Scenes of Clerical Life*. *Der Grüne Heinrich* (1854–1855; 1879–1880) is a tragic novel of education like *The Mill on the Floss*. I hope to develop some of these links in the future.

"Dutch genre-painters"; even sculptors, he maintained, had turned to the portrayal of an "old woman" (p. 769). George Eliot's remarks in *Adam Bede* about "the many Dutch paintings which lofty-minded people despise" immediately come to mind: "I turn from cloud-borne angels . . . to an old woman bending over her flower pot." In the *Scenes*, she had tried to dramatize the "tragedy" of old age through Mr. Gilfil's story and to create a catharsis through Mr. Tryan's death. Yet by the time of *Adam Bede*, where "Nature" herself becomes a "great tragic dramatist," she had begun to chafe at the limitations imposed by her realistic art. *The Mill*, she hoped, would be a modern analogue of those great tragedies by Sophocles, Aeschylus, and Euripides which Gruppe had described as being historically unique.

Gruppe had pointed out that Sophocles had availed himself of the organic art evolved for him by epic poets such as Homer. Similarly, in *Adam Bede*, as we saw, George Eliot took for her subject the myth of man's fall which had been developed for her by Milton. What is more, her reliance on the poetry of William Wordsworth in all the novels of her first phase also illustrates her essential agreement with Gruppe's ideas. For she regarded Wordsworth as writing a *Volkspoesie* such as the German had called for in his own country; though devoid of her predecessor's romantic faith, she could knit her own experience to the world of fable he had bequeathed her, and thereby, as Gruppe had put it, stand on the "shoulders" of an earlier age of belief. In her review of Arnold's poems, George Eliot had praised him for the "expression of exquisite sensibility united with deep thought, in which he reminds us of Wordsworth."[20] In the early portions of *The Mill*, whose heroine bears the same name as Arnold's romantic Marguerite, Wordsworth's influence can be felt on almost every page. (In *Silas Marner*, the novelist would not only recur to Wordsworth with new zest, but would also turn to the

---

[20] "Belles-Lettres," *Westminster Review*, LXIV (July 1855), 298.

Volkspoesie of that other Warwickshire provincial who had conquered London's literary world in a much earlier era.)

The Mill on the Floss has often been described as a "Wordsworthian" novel. But the description should be qualified, for the romantic subjectivism of Maggie, which lies at the core of the book, is viewed rather skeptically by a Victorian who cautiously eyes her Romantic counterpart. In the novel's superb opening, the narrator who directs our eyes from the wide Floss to the tributary Ripple forces us to behold the small girl who has been watching the moving mill wheel. Her eyes, the narrator's eyes, and our eyes converge, hypnotized by the "unresting wheel." Time seems to stop. And then the narrator breaks the repose. He severs past from present, illusion from reality, and reveals himself as a dreamer dreaming about an irretrievable past of one winter afternoon "many years ago."

Yet, just as Arnold's *Merope* vainly tries to reproduce the Sophoclean repose, so does George Eliot's Wordsworthian novel vainly enlist the Romantic's power of memory. Arnold elegized the "eternal note of sadness" which Sophocles had long ago heard by the Aegean; George Eliot lamented the lost childhood from which Wordsworth had drawn the sustenance of faith. In "Tintern Abbey," by the "banks / Of this fair river," a brother oppressed by mutability and change had looked into the "wild eyes" of his romantic sister. Summoning his confidence, he placed his faith in the changeful ways of Nature:

> Oh! yet a little while
> May I behold in thee what I was once,
> My dear, dear Sister! and this prayer I make,
> Knowing that Nature never did betray
> The heart that loved her; 'tis her privilege,
> Through all the years of this our life, to lead
> From joy to joy: for she can so inform
> The mind that is within us, so impress
> With quietness and beauty, and so feed
> With lofty thoughts, that neither evil tongues,

> Rash judgments, nor the sneers of selfish men,
> Nor greetings where no kindness is, nor all
> The dreary intercourse of daily life,
> Shall e'er prevail against us, or disturb
> Our cheerful faith, that all which we behold
> Is full of blessings.

("Lines Composed a Few Miles Above Tintern Abbey," ll. 119–134)

Wordsworth's apotheosis bears comparing to a scene near the end of George Eliot's novel. Here, too, a brother looks into his sister's wild romantic eyes; here, too, memory will revive the latent emotions of childhood. Yet we are on a different sort of river, where evil tongues, rash judgments, and the sneers of selfish men cannot be disregarded. The "dreary intercourse of daily life" is about to triumph. As Tom looks into Maggie's eyes, he can hardly wax as loquacious as the rapturous William:

They sat mutely gazing at each other: Maggie with eyes of intense life looking out from a weary, beaten face—Tom pale with a certain awe and humiliation. Thought was busy though the lips were silent: and though he could ask no question, he guessed a story of almost miraculous divinely-protected effort. But at last a mist gathered over the blue-gray eyes, and the lips found a word they could utter: the old childish— "Magsie!" (Bk. VII, chap. 5, p. 399.)

Here, too, there is catharsis, a purification; but significantly enough Tom's recognition of the strength of his bonds to Maggie comes *before* the novel's final action. The wooden fragments are about to destroy the last of the house of Tulliver. The novelist's words are therefore pregnant with bitter irony: Maggie's "intense life" will soon be extinguished by the capricious river which devours her and her brother; the "divinely-protected effort" which Tom assumes is but an empty illusion. Like Arnold's Empedocles or George Eliot's own Latimer, Tom and Maggie can discover the unity they desire only through the repose of death.

In *The Mill on the Floss* George Eliot did not completely succeed in converting the laming paralysis of despair into the stirring motions of a tragic action. Like Matthew Arnold, she concluded that the only catharsis a Victorian tragedy could offer was an acceptance of the ineluctable flux. The saddened narrator who surveys the graves of Tom and Maggie finds some comfort in seeing that the churchyard which had been uprooted by the river has recovered "all its grassy order and decent quiet" (Conclusion, p. 402). But there is no promise of a purified future as in a traditional tragedy. As in Arnold's play, the catastrophe seems capricious. The chorus in *Merope* imputes the slaughter of Polyphontes and his court to the inevitable "will of the Gods." But Merope herself cannot account for the strife she has witnessed; she can at best hope for the prospects of "moderation." Her wish does not differ considerably from the moral which George Eliot extracted from *Antigone*: man's hope for ideal permanence should be tempered by resignation—"our protests for the right should be seasoned with moderation and reverence."[21]

After *Merope*, Arnold rejected the role of poet. He abandoned his plan to write the tragedy *Lucretius* and turned to the critical essay. The "spirit of passing time" could be mastered only in those occasional elegiac poems where he would exploit his melancholic vision of perennial change. In the essays the quarrel between Sohrab and Rustum, or Aepytus' Messenians and Polyphontes' lords, was to become the quarrel between Philistines and Barbarians, Hellenism and Hebraism, science and religion. In *Merope*, the heroine stands at the sidelines and witnesses the collision of ignorant armies; in the essays, the learned poet who had demanded the "repose" of a great action becomes the ironic advocate of the inaction of "Culture." The "confluent streams" which once watered the Messenian plains could now be avoided.

George Eliot would not abandon the collisions she had tried to portray in her novel. If, after *Merope*, Arnold would desist from

---

[21] "The Antigone and Its Moral," *Essays*, p. 265.

writing poetry, she would even more unsuccessfully try her hand at a poetic tragedy in *The Spanish Gypsy* (1868). Eventually, she was to profit from her experimentation. In *The Mill*, where life at the Ripple becomes subsumed by life on the Floss, the extraordinary Maggie is devoured by the angry river. In *Middlemarch*, however, the extraordinary Dorothea Brooke can find the "moderation" denied to Maggie. For, by the time she came to write her greatest novel, George Eliot had come to adapt her tragic vision to her acceptance of the rhythm of ordinary life:

That element of tragedy which lies in the very fact of frequency, has not yet wrought itself into the coarse emotions of mankind; and perhaps our frames could hardly bear much of it. If we had a keen vision and feeling of ordinary life, it would be like hearing the grass grow and the squirrel's heart beat, and we should die of the roar which lies on the other side of silence. (M, chap. 20, pp. 297–298.)

Latimer and Empedocles, Maggie and Sohrab, die of that "roar"; Arnold became content to listen to its grating sound by proclaiming that Sophocles, too, had heard it long ago by the Aegean. Yet Dorothea Brooke, the modern Antigone, was destined to resist her creator's tragic sense of life. She would be allowed to merge with the maelstrom of human existence.

Binding Small Things to Great

Just as she did in "Mr. Gilfil's Love-Story" and in the seventeenth chapter of *Adam Bede*, George Eliot interrupts her narrative in the first chapter of Book IV of *The Mill on the Floss*. In order to define the atmosphere of her novel, she metaphorically juxtaposes two different orders of "reality" by contrasting the imposing castles along the Rhine with the ruined villages along the Rhone. Life "on the banks of the Floss," she declares, belongs to the "oppressive" existence typified by the deserted villages. The Rhine castles fill the beholder with "a sense of poetry," for they are the surviving monuments of a "grand" era, an age

of faith, "nay, of living, religious art and religious enthusiasm."
By comparison, existence on the Floss seems paltry. Like the life
by the Rhone, it epitomizes the ravages of change: "these dead-
tinted, hollow-eyed, angular skeletons of villages on the Rhone
oppress me with the feeling that human life—very much of it—
is a narrow, ugly, grovelling existence, which even calamity does
not elevate, but rather tends to exhibit in all its bare vulgarity of
conception" (Bk. IV, chap. 1, p. 4).

In "Mr. Gilfil's Love-Story" or in *Adam Bede*, such remarks
would immediately have been answered with an ironic rebuttal.
In "The Lifted Veil," they would have been attributed to the
jaundiced Latimer. Here, however, the remarks are neither as-
cribed to some reader desirous of romance nor to a disappointed
idealist, but they are made by the narrator himself. For the novelist asserts that this oppressiveness is essential to her subject:

I share with you this sense of oppressive narrowness; but it is necessary
that we should feel it, if we care to understand how it acted on the lives
of Tom and Maggie—how it has acted on young natures in many generations, that in the onward tendency of human things have risen above
the mental level of the generation before them, to which they have been
nevertheless tied by the strongest fibres of their hearts. The suffering,
whether of martyr or victim, which belongs to every historical advance
of mankind, is represented in this way in every town, and by hundreds
of obscure hearths; and we need not shrink from this comparison of
small things with great; for does not science tell us that its highest striving is after the ascertainment of a unity which shall bind the smallest
things with the greatest? In natural science, I have understood, there is
nothing petty to the mind that has a large vision of relations, and to
which every single object suggests a vast sum of human conditions. It
is surely the same with the observation of human life. (MF, IV, chap.
1, p. 6.)

In *Adam Bede*, such a defense would have been unnecessary.
For Hayslope, like those grand castles on the Rhine, had belonged
to an age of faith, to an era which Matthew Arnold (after the
fashion of the St. Simonians and German historicists) was to label

a period of "concentration." Loamshire's organization had been centripetal: characters from different stations of life converged at the communal gatherings held in Hayslope Church, at Arthur's birthday feast, and at the Poysers' harvest supper. Just as the visitor from the outside world finds himself transfixed by Dinah's preaching, so is Dinah herself drawn from the periphery of Stonyshire to the story's center, which is marked by Adam's commanding figure. Neither Arthur nor Hetty can break away from the moral judgment which radiates from the core of this agrarian community. Even time, as Dorothy Van Ghent points out, is measured by the eight-day clock implanted in Mrs. Poyser's room at the Hall Farm.[22]

The Mill on the Floss, however, returns to the era of conflict and change already portrayed in "Amos Barton" and "Janet's Repentance." This is an era of "expansion." If *Adam Bede* shows the fulfillment possible in the temporal world, *The Mill* dramatizes "the suffering, whether of martyr or victim, which belongs to every historical advance of mankind." Accordingly, while *Adam Bede* opens by focusing on its larger-than-life protagonist amidst his narrow workshop, the later novel begins by calling our attention to the "broadening Floss" which dwarfs both Tullivers and Dodsons. For George Eliot, as for Arnold, the river becomes a metaphor for the sweeping progress of history, which she attempted to depict in all the productions of her second phase from *Romola* to *Daniel Deronda*. Its motion is centrifugal: the "unresting wheel" which so entrances the imaginative narrator and the equally imaginative Maggie can no longer be controlled by the proud miller and his descendants. The mill wheel which spins out of control symbolizes the capriciousness of forces which pitch man up, only to plunge him down again.[23]

[22] "On Adam Bede," *The English Novel: Form and Function* (New York, 1953), p. 177.

[23] Cf. Mr. Kenn's allusion to John Keble's *The Christian Year* in Book IV, chap. 9, p. 265: "The souls by nature pitched too high, / By suffering plunged too low."

Thus it is that in *The Mill on the Floss* the novelist herself must try to control forces still checked in the quiescent world of *Adam Bede*. Despite the exorbitant punishment meted out to Hetty Sorrel in that novel, the survival of the fittest still corresponded to the survival of the best. In *Adam Bede*, as in Elizabethan tragedy, the wheel of fortune presumably was turned by a just Providence capable of punishing men for their vaulting ambitions. If Hetty aspired too high, so did Adam mount "hup'ards apace" (chap. 22, p. 267). But Adam's fall was cushioned; his pride turned into resignation. If, as he admitted, "there's no slipping up-hill again, and no standing still" (chap. 4, p. 46), it was nonetheless possible for him to fall in step with the gentle motions of Hayslope life. In *The Mill on the Floss*, however, history or temporal "Nature" is far more turbulent a force. In this period of intense change, there can be no such justice as reigned in the earlier novel. Neither Maggie's expiation for her impulsive flight nor Tom's final softening towards his sister can prevent their uprooting and death. The time has come for a new turn of the wheel. Industrial St. Ogg's displaces the pre-industrial existence of the Tullivers: "Mr. Deane had been advancing in the world as rapidly as Mr. Tulliver had been going down in it" (Bk. III, chap. 3, p. 323). A new cycle has begun. Tom and Maggie will be its martyrs or victims.

In *Adam Bede*, the organism of Hayslope, momentarily disrupted by Arthur and Hetty, regroups and contracts to its former shape around Adam, Dinah, and the Poysers; in *The Mill*, however, the expanding waters of the river do not contract until they have done their damage. In the "changing world" portrayed in *The Mill*, there can be no thorough repair. Like *Paradise Lost*, the novel enlists the flood as an agent for its catharsis. In Milton's great epic, the poet not only forces Adam to see his beloved Eden washed away by a "sea without shore," but also compels the horror-stricken Adam to witness the end of his offspring, "all in view destroy'd at once" (XI, 755). By making us see this terrifying scene through Adam's eyes, Milton can also move us to pity the grieving father of mankind: "thee another Flood, / Of tears and sorrow a Flood thee also drown'd, / And sunk thee as thy Sons" (XI, 756–758). We are at the turning point of the poem. Our overflowing emotions are skillfully channeled by the poet: awe and pity now generate a countermovement of new hopes. The vision of the rainbow which follows the deluge gives us and Adam our first glimpse of a destiny "far happier" than that which he had dared to foresee. In George Eliot's novel, however, the retreating waters of the flood only reveal the impress of change: "if there is a new growth, the trees are not the same as the old, and the hills underneath their green vesture bear the marks of the past rending" (Conclusion, p. 401). Our emotions are elegiac; we must linger on the past, for that past has not been channeled into the assurances of a better future. Our pity and fear remain unrelieved. Though Maggie's death is intended to be an inspiriting sacrifice which will teach the reader to acquiesce in the inevitability of change, it remains a senseless sacrifice nonetheless.

Dr. Johnson was undoubtedly wrong in his feeling that the ending of *King Lear* could not be reread without excessive agitation; John Forster's similar statement about *The Mill on the Floss* may be more excusable.[24] Cordelia's death is a painful yet necessary event which arises logically from the previous action; the catharsis of Lear and of Kent, Albany, and Edgar is our catharsis as well. In *The Mill*, Maggie's death, like the deaths of so many other martyrs in Victorian literature (one thinks of Arnold's Sohrab as well as of Meredith's Richard Feverel, Pater's Marius, and Hardy's Jude), is a cosmic irony which can at most be related only symbolically to the action. The small procession of mourners which visits the graves of Tom and Maggie cannot produce in us the purifying emotions which we do derive from Lear's grief and from the awe of his survivors. For Mag-

[24] Forster, Dickens' biographer, told Blackwood that after reading the novel he could not turn to it again (GEL, III, 306).

gie's fate only confirms her earlier suspicions about the universe in which her creator has placed her: "Memory and imagination urged upon her a sense of privation too keen to let her taste what was offered in the transient present: her future, she thought, was likely to be worse than her past." (Bk. VI, chap. 2, p. 167.)

Tom and Maggie are a pair whose opposing temperaments ought to have brought a much-needed synthesis. Like Adam Bede, Tom is practical, self-reliant, intolerant of the failings of others; though a far more complex character than the ethereal Dinah Morris, Maggie, too, is a feminine dreamer whose dreams complement the pragmatism of a male realist. But Adam and Dinah are joined, while Tom and the sister who loves him with a passion bordering on the incestuous can remain together only in death. Despite Adam's lack of charity toward his fallible father, he was acclaimed for his Carlylean dedication to his work; yet Tom, who labors so obsessively to restore his father's good name and fallen fortune, is presented as a far less attractive character than Adam. Each man possesses the same eye for what is practicable; each man learns to adjust himself to change. But what passes as a virtue in the rural sphere of *Adam Bede* is treated almost as a defect in *The Mill*. For the "transient present" of St. Ogg's, to which Tom so ably adapts himself, has become nearly as intolerable for the author as it has for Maggie. In Hayslope, man seems free, "working for himself, with choice / Of time, and place, and object."[25] Adam can face his present unflinchingly because it is so firmly anchored in the traditions of the past. In the fluctuating world of *The Mill*, where traditions have been uprooted, the present becomes as unbearable as it had been in "The Lifted Veil." As in that story, the past itself can acquire its fullest meaning only through retrospection at the very threshold of death.

If *The Mill on the Floss* is indeed a "companion picture" to

[25] Wordsworth, *The Prelude*, VIII. 152–153.

Adam Bede, it is so only in that George Eliot moved her usual values to a far more precarious testing ground. In the rural atmosphere of Loamshire, those values could be spelled out by Mrs. Poyser's sharp tongue; as John Paterson has convincingly shown,[26] the authorial voice in that novel is deliberately simple and restrained. In *The Mill*, however, we have the voice of that Victorian sage who was to speak with far greater assurance in *Middlemarch*.[27] Multiple allusions to Greek, Shakespearian, and Romantic tragedy, to natural science, history, and legend are made by a bookish commentator who even possesses "several manuscript versions" of the history of St. Ogg, the city's patron saint. This narrator differs considerably from the limited observers who had pretended to know Adam Bede and Amos Barton personally. Unlike the earlier works, *The Mill* never disguises the fact that its author is a sage eager to influence her own age. The same writer who in "Amos Barton" professed to be neither "erudite or eloquent," now openly is personified as a figure who wants us to share his capacity to connect and interrelate: "there is nothing petty to the mind that has a large vision of relations."[28]

In "Amos Barton," George Eliot's attempts to invest the curate's story with the sublimeness of tragedy were almost as incongruous as Wordsworth's verses on Harry Gill or Coleridge's earnest apostrophe to a young ass. In *The Mill*, however, the setting and mode of the entire novel allow her to make even

[26] *Adam Bede*, ed. John Paterson (Riverside Edition, Boston, 1968), pp. xviii–xix.

[27] In *The Victorian Sage* (London, 1953), John Holloway could have analyzed George Eliot's rhetoric far more fruitfully if he had examined the emergence of the *persona* of the prophet-sage in her fiction. By including in one chapter everything from her characterization to her ethics and by ranging from "Amos Barton" to the *Impressions of Theophrastus Such*, Mr. Holloway treats George Eliot far less successfully than he does Carlyle and Arnold.

[28] Cf. *Middlemarch*, chap. 7, p. 49: "it is a narrow mind which cannot look at a subject from various points of view."

the most inconsequential impulses of a passionate child seem part
of "an action that is important, complete, and of a certain magnitude."[29] When little Maggie pushes her cousin Lucy into the
muddy pond, the narrator remarks: "There were passions at war
in Maggie at that moment to have made a tragedy, if tragedies
were made by passion only; but the essential τι Μέγεθος which
was present in the passion was wanting to the action: the utmost
Maggie could do, with a fierce thrust of her small brown arm,
was to push poor little pink-and-white Lucy into the cow-trodden
mud" (Bk. I, chap. 10, p. 154). Taken by itself, such unheroic
action certainly lacks Μέγεθος—magnitude: a resourceful little
brat has pushed another child into the mud. Maggie's motivation
is perfectly plausible; she is jealous of Tom's preference for her
blonde cousin. To mess up Lucy's immaculate frock is the most
logical retaliation available to this three-feet-tall avenger. But
George Eliot's handling endows the episode with subtle ironic
overtones which greatly outweigh its ostensible importance.

For the description which leads up to this miniscule "action"
contains transcendent meanings. Though Maggie is only a tiny
delinquent, she is potentially the future malcontent who cannot
bring herself to accept the restrictions more readily embraced by
her unquestioning brother. The allusions to the "small demons"
taking possession of this little Faustian's soul, and the likening
of Maggie to a "small Medusa with her snakes cropped," only
heighten our sense of the acute differences which separate this
child from her more ordinary brother and cousin. Whereas Tom
scientifically tickles a fat toad in order to elicit its responses, Maggie is capable of giving it a name and of inventing a history built
around it. The squatting toad, the allusions to demons and ser-
pents, the "temptation" which causes Tom and Lucy to walk to
the forbidden end of the garden, Maggie's revolt against Tom's
male superiority, her sudden outburst of passion, the tree she leans

[29] Aristotle, *Poetics*, VI. 2.

against so impenitently, the "justice" which will soon punish both boy and girl, invest this scene with mock-heroic dimensions. The "passions at war in Maggie" are clearly analogous to those which led another female in another garden to commit an action which was of the proper magnitude. The link is ironic, of course, but we are not allowed to escape it: " 'O Tom, *dare* you?' said Lucy. 'Aunt said we mustn't go out of the garden.' " God in this child-world is any adult, even one as severely limited in authority and understanding as Mrs. Tulliver's favorite sister.

But the little girl's "passions" *will* make a tragedy. The narrator's remark helps to remind us that there is nothing petty to the mind that has a large vision of relations. For in her Lilliputian action Maggie displays the same rashness that will be so ruinous to her as an adult. Her passions will lead her to hurt Lucy far more cruelly later, when she elopes with her cousin's fiancé. Then, as now, she will be displaced, at odds with the reality that is accepted by her more normal brother and cousin. The Tom who dares to trespass into the far end of the garden tells Lucy that, if discovered, he will run home. But he stands his ground as firmly as he will do later, after the loss of the home of Dorlcote Mill. It is Maggie who flees. She runs away from home to an illusory life among the gypsies, just as she will escape, years later, when her alienation from Tom draws her to the illusory life promised by Stephen Guest. But whereas now the punishment which awaits her barely corresponds to her action, her later punishment is meted out by forces which show no mercy. Now, "justice" is represented by her indulgent father; later, she is martyred by the river which devours her *after* she has fully paid for a nonexistent "crime." The difference is clear. In the child's world, where act corresponds to will, she can be held responsible; in the transient, adult world of St. Ogg's however, she herself will be pushed into the water, and killed by capricious forces beyond her control. After the muddy Lucy presents herself in her aunt's parlor, Mrs. Tulliver is overcome by fear. She wishes the river to stay away "far enough" from her children. Although her fear seems ridiculous at the time, it is justified. For when these children become adults, the angry river will come to claim them as its victims. If the child is father of the man, the fate of that adult differs considerably in this novel from that so confidently projected by William Wordsworth.

The narrator tells us that we must rely on him to find for us "that unity which shall bind the smallest things with the greatest."[30] Yet that unity is difficult to find in the fragmented world where old and new collide, brother and sister become alienated, and the Ripple gives way to the Floss. In her acknowledged search for such a unity, George Eliot removes the mask which led the readers of her earlier fiction to identify her with someone like Joseph Liggins, the presumed author of the *Scenes* and *Adam Bede*. Liggins' defenders had regarded him, like Stephen Duck the Thresher Poet or Anne Yearsley the Milkwoman of Bristol, as a "natural" like those discussed by Robert Southey in *Lives of Uneducated Poets* (1835). The opening paragraphs of *The Mill* allow no such misconception. Not only do they foreshadow the novel's scope and theme, but they also serve to acquaint us with its narrator.

In *Adam Bede*, the vatic "I" who so awkwardly compares himself to an Egyptian sorcerer disappears as soon as he has ushered us into the confines of Master Burge's workshop; in *The Mill*, the "I" who skillfully displays the vast panoramic scene before us, refuses to leave until he has fully asserted his authority as our guide and medium. As in *Adam Bede*, we are once again asked to see and hear; but this time our sight and hearing

---

[30] In "Great Things and Small: The Virgilian Progression," *CL*, XVII (Winter 1965), 1–23, John S. Coolidge points out that Milton uses the phrase "to compare great things to small" three times in the course of *Paradise Lost* (II, 921–922; VI, 310–311; X, 306). George Eliot could also have found the phrase in writers from Herodotus to Wordsworth.

are wholly dependent on the ever-present narrator. It is he who foreshortens the picture and relates the small girl to the enormous river; and he who shocks us back into our own present. Clearly this imaginative observer is no Stephen Duck or Joseph Liggins. He is a poet recollecting in tranquillity what he has once felt in agitation. He is the creator described by Wordsworth as a "man who, being possessed of more than usual organic sensibility, has also thought long and deeply. For our continued influxes of feeling are modified and directed by our thoughts, which are indeed the representatives of all our past feelings."[31] Yet Wordsworth's ideal poet could fuse thought and feeling, merge past and present, and find the unity which might lift man out of his temporal bondage. Though also possessed of unusual organic sensibility, George Eliot's narrator must rely on contrast and juxtaposition in order to yoke what can no longer be united.

In the opening chapters of the novel, the narrator plays with the relative levels of awareness of the various characters. The Hetty-like Mrs. Tulliver is conscious only of what is most immediate and tangible: the Holland sheets are safely stored away, and that is all that matters to her. Her world does not extend beyond the linen cabinet: "An' if you was to die to-morrow, Mr. Tulliver, they're mangled beautiful, an' all ready, an' smell o' lavender as it 'ud be a pleasure to lay 'em out; an' they lie at the left-hand corner o' the big oak linen-chest at the back." (Bk. I, chap. 2, p. 10.) Wider distances alarm Mrs. Tulliver. The belated realization that Tom might be a full fifteen miles away taxes her powers of understanding: "is it so far off as I couldn't wash him and mend him?" (Bk. I, chap. 3, p. 22.) Temporal distances are equally awesome to her. Incapable of thinking about any remoter future, she threatens Maggie that her sisters might not love the girl "when they come *next*

[31] Wordsworth, "Observations Prefixed to *Lyrical Ballads*," in *Criticism: The Foundations of Modern Literary Judgment*, ed. Schorer, Miles, McKenzie (New York, 1958), p. 32.

week." The miller is far more imaginative. It is he who demands a better "eddication" for his son in order to prepare Tom for the future: "why, if I made him a miller an' farmer, he'd be expectin' to take the mill an' the land, an' a-hinting at me as it was time for me to lay by an' think o' my latter end." (Bk. I, chap. 3, p. 19.) But though Mr. Tulliver may not want any competition from his son, he does want Tom to compete for him against the incomprehensible new order represented by Lawyer Wakem, Old Harry himself. Unlike his wife, the superstitious miller is at least capable of being puzzled by what he does not understand. While she resembles a dull goldfish who retains the illusion "that it can swim in a straight line beyond the encircling glass," he is smart enough to sense his confinement: "Everything winds about so—the more straightforrard you are, the more you're puzzled." (Bk. I, chap. 8, p. 113; chap. 3, p. 25.)

When sufficiently aroused, Mr. Tulliver is capable of coining aphorisms in which the words "stand for summat else." His literalistic wife, on the other hand, accepts at face value even his remark about not hiring a waggoner with a mole on his cheek. Yet the miller himself is deluded by externals. For all his suspicion that "one mustn't judge by th' outside," Mr. Tulliver consults a man who, on the surface, may look "Lawyer Wakem i' the face as hard as one cat looks another," but who otherwise is no match for the foxy lawyer. Mr. Riley proves to be a false counselor. He gives the wrong advice, not out of malice or calculation, but because "even he was more under the influence of small promptings than of far-sighted designs" (Bk. I, chap. 3, p. 33). Though he ranges beyond the sphere of the miller, he, too, is severely limited: he recommends Tom's new teacher because "Stelling was an Oxford man, and the Oxford men were always—no, no, it was the Cambridge men who were always good mathematicians." But he delivers his advice nonetheless, for a man must have an opinion. If Mr. Tulliver understands more than his wife and if Mr. Riley knows more than the miller, none

of the three characters is fit to cope with the new world of Lawyer Wakem and Mr. Deane.

Mr. Riley even compares poorly with the little girl whose own
"eddication" has already exceeded Tom's. When Mr. Riley tells
Maggie that she will need seven-league boots to get to Tom, she
brands his condescending remarks as "nonsense." The child is
also quick to sense the egotism in her father's desire to prevent
Tom from becoming a miller or a farmer: "Tom, it appeared,
was supposed capable of turning his father out of doors, and of
making the future in some way tragic by his wickedness" (Bk.
I, chap. 3, p. 19). To Maggie, such dire prospects are not to be
borne, for they do not correspond to the future she imagines.
Her sensitivity has been stimulated by her reading. After Mr.
Riley fails to be amused by her unorthodox interpretation of
Defoe's *History of the Devil*, she tries to impress Luke, the
head miller, with her superior knowledge about pipe-smoking
Dutchmen and exotic animals. Yet Luke's disconcerting reply
("Nay, nay, I aren't goin' to bother mysen about Dutchmen.
There's fools enoo—an' rogues enoo—wi'out lookin' in books
for 'em") is followed by his even more disconcerting announcement that Tom's rabbits have died of starvation. The girl who
knows all about elephants and kangaroos in faraway countries has
lost sight of the animals she was to care for at her own father's
mill. Knowledge, as Luke puts it grimly, can bring "folks to the
gallows."

The differing levels of awareness of these characters reveal
the range of their knowledge as well as their attitudes about
knowledge. There is a hierarchical arrangement from Mrs.
Tulliver and her Holland sheets up to the child who will as an
adult try to escape to Holland with Stephen Guest. Mr. Tulliver
flaunts his superiority over his wife, and yet he avails himself of
Mr. Riley's poor advice; Mr. Riley, in turn, reveals his limitations when he is made to look ridiculous by a nine-year-old who
has read the *History of the Devil*, *Pug's Tour of Europe*, and

Animated Nature. Each character is paired with the preceding one. Yet Luke, the Wordsworthian rustic who goes by experience, does not, as Mrs. Poyser did, represent the author's final point of view about knowledge. His limitations are, after all, not unlike Mrs. Tulliver's; and his distrust of the printed word is similar to his master's. The lop-eared rabbits have died, he assures Maggie, not only because she (or Harry the helper) has failed to look after them, but also because "Things out o' natur niver thrive: God A'mighty doesn't like 'em" (Bk. I, chap. 4, p. 42). Unbeknown to Luke, his words have an ominous ring. Mr. Tulliver has already complained that he finds the world to be different from the way "as God made it"; he has already admitted that, in his marriage to a Dodson, "the crossing o' breeds" in his own children has run counter to his expectations. Maggie, the result of that breeding, has already been described as a *lusus naturae* like the lop-eared rabbits—a "small mistake of nature," are the words with which the narrator first describes her. Yet Luke's implicit warning is not consciously made, as Mrs. Poyser's remarks to Dinah would have been. Whereas in *Adam Bede* Luke's homespun wisdom might have acted as a corrective to Maggie's search for higher knowledge, it cannot act as a bulwark against the world which so puzzles his master. Luke, too, will be dragged along by the same currents of change.

Thus, in order that we may understand the insufficiency of each character's response to the reality which will defeat him, each of these opening scenes has to be manipulated for us by an ironic commentator whose own superior intelligence constantly makes itself felt. It is the narrator who damns Mrs. Tulliver by slyly likening her to those Madonnas whose "somewhat stupid expression" might have grown even more stunned and stupefied by their later experiences; again, with tongue in cheek, this narrator compares the impetuous miller to Hotspur, refers to Mr. Tulliver's "rampant Manichaeism," and probes into "all the pleasant little dim ideas" which lead Mr. Riley to dispense such poor advice. This speaker is a psychologist as well as a student of that shifting "Nature" he so consistently alludes to. If the puzzled Mr. Tulliver only imperfectly perceives that one must not judge by the outside, the narrator who knows that an ugly duckling will turn into a beautiful young woman can assert that, "Nature has the deep cunning which hides itself under the appearance of openness, so that simple people think they can see through her quite well, and all the while she is secretly preparing a refutation of their confident prophecies" (Bk. I, chap. 5, p. 45).

Only the narrator can project Tom and Maggie's story into the future and emphasize truths as yet ungrasped by any one character: "Life did change for Tom and Maggie; and yet they were not wrong in believing that the thoughts and loves of these first years would always make part of their lives." (Bk. I, chap. 5, p. 58.) But "the thoughts and loves" of childhood comedy will be insufficient to withstand the tragedy of adult life. The associations made by the narrator point to inevitable disparity and conflict. The opening chapters exploit this disparity with consummate skill. The mismatch between Mr. Tulliver and his hen-like wife is as brilliant an introduction to all the novel's conflicts as is the mismatch between the proud Mr. Bennet and his spouse in *Pride and Prejudice*. In Jane Austen's world, however, such conflicts could be resolved within the mode of comedy; through Darcy's and Elizabeth's enlarged understandings, pride and prejudice can gradually merge; incompleteness can give way to fruition. In *The Mill on the Floss*, the incompleteness persists. Instead of a comic narrowing of the gap which separates Mr. and Mrs. Tulliver, there is the widening of tragedy. The same differences which set apart the miller and his wife will cut Maggie off from Tom and divorce her from the past. In an unstable world where fragmentation is inherent, there can be no fruition.

Collision or antithesis, then, is the foundation on which the entire novel is built. The use of this tactic has its theoretical basis.

George Eliot accepted the Hegelian view of tragedy as the clash between two irreconcilables. Yet whereas Hegel's view of history had still allowed for the existence of an all-pervasive essence or divinity, she sees history itself as only a ceaseless strife between extremes. In a larger sense, both Mr. Tulliver's and Maggie's tragedies are therefore part of the inevitable clash between the two different realities represented by St. Ogg's and Dorlcote Mill. Both father and daughter find their subjective wishes at odds with outward fact. Their struggles are therefore quite similar to the conflict which had paralyzed Latimer. The "painful collisions" between "the outward and the inward" which both Mr. Tulliver and Maggie experience can be resolved only through their deaths (Bk. III, chap. 5, p. 369).[32]

In *Adam Bede*, Adam and Dinah submit to the present. Adam learns not to make faulty projections into the future; Dinah learns that the past is meaningful only in its most direct bearing on her own present. In *The Mill*, Mr. Tulliver's education resembles Adam's; Maggie's, that of Dinah. Yet the catastrophes which cut short the aspirations of both father and daughter only demonstrate how much more difficult it is to connect past and future to the unpoetic present of St. Ogg's-on-the-Floss than to the life in Loamshire. The relation between past, present, and future exploited thematically in all of George Eliot's earlier works becomes in *The Mill on the Floss* an integral part of the novel's very structure.

The Bewildering Future: The Tragedy of Edward Tulliver

The Mill on the Floss is divided into seven books, which can be separated into two movements: in the first, Mr. Tulliver, like Amos Barton, vainly tries to shore his present against the im-

[32] This struggle becomes externalized in the fifth chapter of Book V, which was originally entitled "Collisions."

pending future; in the second, where that future becomes the present of his children, Tom and Maggie vainly try to recover their childhood at Dorlcote Mill. The first movement concludes with Mr. Tulliver's death at the end of Book V; the second culminates with the drowning of Tom and Maggie. Like *Antony and Cleopatra*, the novel thus contains two related tragedies, which I shall examine individually only for the sake of making critical distinctions. In Shakespeare's play, Cleopatra's sacrifice is meant to exalt Antony's bungling death; in her tragic novel, George Eliot likewise intends Maggie's sacrifice to lend a wider meaning to the little world ignobly lost through Mr. Tulliver's recklessness. The miller's gradual ruin and self-destruction are deftly handled by a novelist sure of her control. The rash miller is in his way as convincing a tragic figure as the impetuous Antony. But George Eliot could not handle Maggie's fate with the same assurance. For reasons which I shall examine in the last section of this chapter, George Eliot failed to convert Maggie's immolation into an action as world-stirring as that of Shakespeare's Cleopatra.[33]

Mr. Tulliver's story introduces all the basic collisions of the novel: the antithesis between the worlds of the Mill by the Ripple and of St. Ogg's-on-the-Floss, the contrast between Dodsons and Tullivers, the resulting oppositions between parents and children, brother and sister, and Maggie's consequent self-division. Yet the unit which ends with the miller's deathbed recognition that the "world's been too many" for him, possesses the tragic requisites which the remainder of the novel lacks. Like Oedipus, to whom he is compared by the narrator, Mr. Tulliver has become entangled in "the skein of life" through his own blind pride. Unlike

[33] These and future references to *Antony and Cleopatra* (like those to *King Lear*) are introduced for contrast only; still, the association may have a factual basis, as well: the only quotation from *Antony and Cleopatra* in all of George Eliot's letters occurs while she was writing *The Mill* (cf. GEL, III, 53).

the symbolic flood which executes Tom and Maggie, the catastrophe which marks his downfall is the direct result of the interaction of character and destiny, will and fate. Mr. Tulliver falls
victim to his own faulty choices. He first selects a spouse for her
presumed submissiveness and stupidity; then, betrayed by the unexpected biological "crossing o' breeds," he prefers his Tulliver
daughter over his Dodson son. To prepare for Tom's future, he
chooses a "gentleman's" education which is as unprofitable as that
of Amos Barton or Dickens' Pip; he adopts the advice of Mr.
Riley instead of enlisting the better judgment of Mr. Deane, his
brother-in-law, whom he regards as "the 'knowingest' man of his
acquaintance," but whom he does not consult on family matters
because of vanity and pride. Able to avoid a costly litigation, the
imprudent miller opts a lawsuit instead and thus finally places
himself in the power of Chancery, that Victorian embodiment of
ancient "Fortuna." Incapable of adapting to the changes taking
place around him, he escapes, as Maggie will, into rebellion, fantasy, and, eventually, death. Unlike his daughter, however, he is
far more the victim of his own hubris than of capricious chance.

Mr. Deane is the miller's exact counterpart. A self-made city
man, he knows the ways of the world. The foolish Mr. Tulliver
congratulates himself for having chosen a classicist as Tom's
teacher. Always impulsive, he soon convinces himself that the
boy's tutor is a "clergyman whose knowledge was so applicable
to the everyday affairs of this life. Except Counsellor Wylde,
whom he had heard at the last session, Mr. Tulliver thought the
Rev. Mr. Stelling was the shrewdest fellow he had ever met with
—not unlike Wylde, in fact: he had the same way of sticking his
thumbs in the armholes of his waistcoat" (Bk. II, chap. 1, p.
211). The utilitarian Mr. Deane, on the other hand, soon brands
Tom's education as utterly useless. Even after the youth pathetically promises to unlearn his Latin and ancient history, Mr.
Deane presses on contemptuously: "Your Latin and rigmarole
may soon dry off you, but you'll be but a bare stick after that.

Besides, it's whitened your hands and taken the rough work out of you. And what do you know? Why, you know nothing about book-keeping, to begin with, and not so much of reckoning as a common shopman. You'll have to begin at the low round of the ladder, let me tell you, if you mean to get on in life. It's no use forgetting the education your father's been paying for, if you don't give yourself a new un." (Bk. III, chap. 5, pp. 361–362.) Ironically, the very man whose advice Mr. Tulliver shunned, now teaches his Dodson son how to repair the father's mistakes.

Mr. Deane typifies the new ways of St. Ogg's. Like Lawyer Wakem, he plays Octavius to Mr. Tulliver's Antony. The miller who gallops incessantly around his threatened land is impulsive and sentimental; his unlanded brother-in-law exerts himself only by "taking snuff vigorously, as he always did when wishing to maintain a neutral position" (Bk. I, chap. 7, p. 105). Like Wakem, Mr. Deane remains evasive and noncommittal. Whereas Mr. Tulliver identifies his archenemy with "old Harry" himself, Mr. Deane cautiously respects Lawyer Wakem as a powerful business rival. Mr. Tulliver vows that he will not allow "anybody get hold of his whip-hand" (Bk. I, chap. 5, p. 53), but when he loses control of his lands, it is his brother-in-law who asks the stricken miller to accept Wakem's demeaning offer to let him manage the property he formerly owned. Mr. Deane could easily have outbid the lawyer in order to salvage Mr. Tulliver's pride, but he does not "carry on business on sentimental grounds" (Bk. III, chap. 7, p. 383). In his unromantic world a man can succeed only by waiting patiently, as he has done, "before he got the whip in his hand" (Bk. VI, chap. 5, p. 200). If the descendant of the fiery Ralph Tulliver rides against the times, his prudent counterpart moves with the tide. Once regarded as the worst match made by the Dodson sisters, Mr. Deane has gradually risen to eminence in the Guests' "great mill-owning, ship-owning business." Progress is his motto as much as it is that of Dickens' Podsnap or Gradgrind: "I don't find fault with the change, as some people do. Trade, sir, opens a man's eyes; and if population is to get thicker upon the ground, as it's doing, the world must use its wits at inventions of some sort or other." (Bk. VI, chap. 5, p. 201.)

While Mr. Tulliver loses control of his mill wheel by entering useless litigations over his decreasing "water-power," the self-controlled Mr. Deane steadily gains in influence by harnessing new sources of power: "It's this steam, you see, that has made the difference: it drives on every wheel double pace, and the wheel of fortune along with 'em, as our Mr. Stephen Guest said." (Bk. VI, chap. 5, p. 201.) If Mr. Tulliver is the enfeebled survivor of Carlyle's "Heroical Age," Mr. Deane belongs to the new mechanical era "which, with its whole undivided might, forwards, teaches, and practices the great art of adapting means to ends."[34] Deane's sphere of action seems every bit as removed from Dorlcote Mill as Caesar's Rome is from Cleopatra's Egypt. At the mill, the relation between Luke and his master still resembles that of a vassal and his feudal lord; Luke's loyalty is not unlike the devotion of a Kent or Enobarbus. For the world soon to be lost by the miller is archaic enough to harbor what Hegel had called "romantic fidelity."[35] In it the ideal of service remains as untouched as the urge for revenge which dominates the "pagan" Mr. Tulliver and his son. Like old Adam in *As You Like It*, Luke wants to give his earnings to his master, for he feels, "after

[34] "Signs of the Times," *Critical and Miscellaneous Essays*, I, *The Complete Works of Thomas Carlyle* (New York, 1901), p. 465.

[35] Cf. Hegel's discussion of dramatic motivation in *Aesthetik*. Citing the swineherd's loyalty to Ulysses and Kent's loyalty to Lear, he comments: "This borders as close as possible on that which we would make clear as romantic fidelity. Fidelity at this stage is not the loyalty of slaves and churls . . . [but] the liege-service of chivalry, in which each vassal preserves his own free self-dependence as an essential element in the attitude of subordination to one of higher rank, whether lord, king, or emperor. This type of fidelity . . . forms the fundamental bond of union in a common [i.e., communal] society" (*Hegel on Tragedy*, ed. Anne and Henry Paolucci [New York, 1962], p. 204).

the manner of contented hard-working men whose lives have been spent in servitude, that sense of natural fitness in rank which made his master's downfall a tragedy to him" (Bk. III, chap. 8, p. 405).

In St. Ogg's no such "natural fitness" exists. Luke and his master are equals despite the difference in rank; but Mr. Deane and Lawyer Wakem head a society in which mastery can be established only by competition and strife. Mr. Deane will not try to outbid Lawyer Wakem; he cannot afford to be ruled by sentiments such as Luke's. Tom, on the other hand, immediately on accepting the responsibilities of his father's position, decides to pay Luke, "if in no other way, out of his own and Maggie's money." In *As You Like It*, freed by old Adam's money, Orlando and his father's servant jointly escape into the Forest of Arden. In George Eliot's novel, there is no sanctuary. Luke's refusal to accept the payment due him cannot free either him or his young master. Tom must go to St. Ogg's to restore his father's good name. The irony is bitter. Simply by walking across the "stone bridge" that leads into the city he enters a different world. Before crossing that bridge, Tom still looked at reality with his father's eyes: "he saw the distant future before him, as he might have seen a tempting stretch of smooth sandy beach beyond a belt of flinty shingles; he was on the grassy bank then, and thought the shingles might soon be passed." But he returns as Mr. Deane's disciple: "now his feet were on the sharp stones; the belt of shingles had widened, and the stretch of sand had dwindled into narrowness" (Bk. III, chap. 5, p. 366). His vision has been adjusted. To fight Lawyer Wakem he has submitted to Wakem's oppressive world.

Like Lawyer Dempster before him, Wakem is identified with the devil himself. Although the association is made by the superstitious Mr. Tulliver, there is a tinge of truth to it. For even more than Dempster's Milby, St. Ogg's is a modern equivalent of the "city of destruction" from which Bunyan's Christian had

escaped.[36] In Milby, Mr. Tryan had been able to rescue Janet
Dempster from damnation and despair; in St. Ogg's, no such
Evangelist can rescue the modern pilgrim. Even the kindhearted
Dr. Kenn must yield to the pressure of his parishioners and evict
Maggie from his house. The historical past of St. Ogg's only
confirms the nature of its present. Like the Rome described in
Middlemarch, the city is merely an aggregate of historical strata,
each of which has stifled and suppressed the one beneath it. In
"The Lifted Veil," Latimer had seen one such layer in his vision
of Prague. Here, the narrator mercilessly uncovers all the calci-
fied deposits of the past. The intermittent floods have only separated one age of strife from another. The present warehouses
of Guest & Co. rest on the site of struggle far bloodier than
those of industrial competition. Only less than two centuries ago,
the town had witnessed "worse troubles even than the floods—
troubles of the civil wars, when it was a continual fighting-place,
where first Puritans thanked God for the blood of the Loyalists,
and then Loyalists thanked God for the blood of the Puritans"
(Bk. I, chap. 12, p. 181). Digging deeper, the narrator unearths
further collisions: the era of the church displaced the invasion of
the Norman conquerors; the Danish raiders overcame the Saxon
settlers; the Vikings ended the predominance of the Roman le-
gions. Even in the days of St. Ogg, the son of Beorl, hardhearted
and indifferent men repulsed the sufferer he ferried across the
river. In the city's present historical phase, where religion has
given way to politics, only one superannuated inhabitant still rec-

---

[36] There are several allusions to *Pilgrim's Progress* in *The Mill*. Maggie is haunted by "images of Apollyon" on visiting the gypsy camp; after
the loss of the family's property, she particularly misses "our dear old Pilgrim's Progress"; when she and Tom enter "The Valley of Humiliation"
(the title of Book IV) they are, of course, entering Apollyon's domain.
As a child, Maggie identifies the Floss with "the river over which there
is no bridge." The analogy is ironic: Christiana will ford that river;
Maggie will drown in it.

ollects having heard that same John Wesley whose words Dinah Morris had carried into Loamshire's green pastoral land.

If Mr. Tulliver's latter-day agrarian existence is threatened by the industrial present of St. Ogg's, his defeat is not as inevitable as it would be in a dialectic Marxist view. For George Eliot carefully contrasts the miller's failures with the success of the Dodsons. Both families are equally archaic in their "pagan" clannishness and social orientation. Yet while Mr. Tulliver and his only sister, Mrs. Moss, find their strength depleted, the Dodsons manage to conserve their power. Once regarded as the "buck of Basset," Mr. Moss, Gritty Tulliver's husband, has become a dehumanized "machine-horse"; his farm yields diminishing returns. The husbands of the Dodson sisters, however, have all added to their wives' dowries. Like Dickens' Wemmick, both the landed Mr. Pullet and the unlanded Mr. Glegg understand the value of "portable property." If Mr. Tulliver's aggressiveness is ineffectual, their defensive tactics prove to be invincible. The Gleggs have even moved into the enemy citadel, St. Ogg's itself. Financially secure as a moneylender, Mr. Glegg can, like Wemmick, that other amiable Harpagon, easily transfer the country into the town. Contentedly, he follows his farming instincts by cultivating his back yard. His house affords two vistas, "two points of view." It faces the busy world of St. Ogg's and the road which leads out of the city into Tofton, the suburb where both Mr. Deane and Lawyer Wakem have built handsome houses (building materials dislodged from Tofton's wharves will kill Tom and Maggie). The back windows reveal a more idyllic scene, "the pleasant garden and orchard which stretched to the river" (Bk. I, chap. 12, p. 185). In that makeshift Eden, Mr. Glegg can relax by doing "the work of two ordinary gardeners." While his brother-in-law Mr. Deane exploits the river, Mr. Glegg enjoys its shores and remains unaffected by its motions.

Tragedy cannot touch Mr. Glegg. He picked the eldest Miss Dodson as a "handsome embodiment of female prudence and thrift." His choice of a partner is made after his own image: "being himself of a money-getting, money-keeping turn, [he] had calculated on much conjugal harmony" (Bk. I, chap. 12, p. 186). As always in George Eliot's fiction, his "calkilations" are not wholly correct. But though Mrs. Glegg is somewhat of a shrew, she does not really impede her husband's well-being. Mr. Tulliver, on the other hand, must very definitely pay for having picked a wife so unlike himself. He chose Elizabeth Dodson, he smugly informs Mr. Riley, because "she was a bit weak, like; for I wasn't agoin' to be told the rights o' things by my own fireside" (Bk. I, chap. 3, p. 24). Like Lydgate in *Middlemarch*, Mr. Tulliver should not have dabbled in natural selection. For not only does his choice result in the unforeseen Mendelian "crossing" which gives Maggie her father's characteristics and endows Tom with those of the Dodsons, but it also contributes directly to his own downfall.

As an "amiable hen" who usually defers to her husband, children, and sisters, Mrs. Tulliver resembles Mrs. Bennet rather than Antony's Cleopatra. Nonetheless, her husband's tragic fate is tied to the rudder of his chosen queen. Passive as she is, Mrs. Tulliver's few actions always have an effect opposite from that which she intends. Although she knows that her splenetic husband will be incensed by any opinion contrary to his own, she dutifully invites all her sisters and their husbands to discuss Tom's education—even though the miller has already made a decision. The meeting sets in motion the sequence of events which will lead to the loss of Dorlcote Mill. Angered by Mrs. Glegg's criticism, Mr. Tulliver vows to pay back the five hundred pounds she had loaned him. His wife's attempts to mediate only rankle his pride. Even though he also is in debt to Mr. Furley, the miller insists on returning the money to his sister-in-law at once. But by refusing to be indebted to Mrs. Glegg or Mrs. Pullet, this Chanticleer closes his eyes and only places himself a step closer to the fox. Against his will or better judgment, Mr. Tulliver becomes bonded to one of Lawyer Wakem's clients: " 'It must be no client of Wakem's,' he said to himself; and yet at the end of a fortnight it turned out to the contrary; not because Mr. Tulliver's will was feeble, but because external fact was stronger. Wakem's client was the only convenient person to be found. Mr. Tulliver had a destiny as well as Œdipus, and in this case he might plead, like Œdipus, that his deed was inflicted on him rather than committed by him." (Bk. I, chap. 13, p. 202.)

But Mr. Tulliver's mate contributes still further to his self-inflicted "destiny." After the miller loses a lawsuit in which he has foolishly supposed that he can best Lawyer Wakem on the lawyer's own terrain, his henlike wife takes up her husband's cause by making a foray into the enemy camp. But her undiplomatic efforts to dissuade Wakem from bidding for her husband's land only put a new thought into the shrewd lawyer's mind. Before her visit, he had no intention of bidding against Mr. Deane. Now, however, he decides on the very course of action she had set out to prevent. Although George Eliot probes into the lawyer's motives, she also suggests that he is only an agent for the fate brought on by the miller's own rashness. If Octavius is too cold-blooded to hate his hot-tempered rival, Wakem is no more guilty of wrath "than an ingenious machine, which performs its work with much regularity, is guilty towards the rash man who, venturing too near it, is caught up by some fly-wheel or other, and suddenly converted into unexpected mince-meat" (Bk. III, chap. 7, p. 388). After flogging one of Octavius' messengers, Antony whips himself into a frenzy and wins a land battle against the enemy who had defeated him by water. Mistaking a minor skirmish for a major triumph, Antony is soon driven to suicide. Mr. Tulliver also wins a minor engagement when he repays his creditors through the efforts of his son. Yet foolishly flushed by his success, he dies of apoplexy after flogging Wakem with his whip. The lawyer escapes with a sprained arm. Like Antony, the romantic Mr. Tulliver has even bungled his exit from life.

In an essay entitled "Tragedy and the Common Man," Arthur Miller once argued that the terror and fear of tragedy could still be evoked in a modern everyman's exposure to the pressures of social change. Defending *Death of a Salesman*, the playwright contended: "I believe that the common man is as apt a subject for tragedy in its highest sense as kings were."[37] To the reader of *The Mill on the Floss*, the statement carries a somewhat familiar ring:

"Mr. Tulliver, you perceive, though nothing more than a superior miller and maltster, was as proud and obstinate as if he had been a very lofty personage, in whom such dispositions might be a source of that conspicuous, far-echoing tragedy, which sweeps the stage in regal robes, and makes the dullest chronicler sublime. The pride and obstinacy of millers, and other insignificant people, whom you pass unnoticingly on the road every day, have their tragedy too." (Bk. III, chap. 1, p. 308.)

But George Eliot's superior miller is a much more tragic figure than Miller's Loman; there is more poetry in the loss of an ancestral mill than in an aging salesman's loss of his former "territory." Like Willy Loman, Mr. Tulliver, incapable of adjusting himself to the ways of the future, escapes into a dreamworld and ponders what might have been. But Willy's end is pathetic, whereas there is a magnificence in Mr. Tulliver's impenitent death. The miller who demands a "retributive justice" barely recognizes that he also must pay for his mistakes. Yet his nemesis does inspire us with the true terror of tragedy. The impersonal order which pushes him aside seems more fearsome than Willy's displacement by a boss who plays with a tape recorder. Willy smashes his car so that his wife and children can collect his insurance money; his death is a deliberate act by which he intends to repair the damage he has done. Mr. Tulliver's injuries to his family, however, cannot be repaired. His fall is more momentous. The indifference with which Mr. Deane and Mr. Glegg regard their brother-in-law's lost "water-power" is far closer, artistically, to the indifference which Goneril and Regan display

[37] *New York Times*, 27 February 1947, Sec. II, p. 1.

toward Lear's regal attributes than it is to Howard's refusal to augment Willy Loman's Social Security payments. In the eyes of St. Ogg's, Mr. Tulliver is incompetent. In his archaic world, however, Maggie's fond and foolish father remains a "lofty personage." Accordingly, his fall is far more princely than that of the "hardworking, unappreciated prince" who is the father of the neurotic Biff.

Before dying, King Lear recognizes the goodness of the daughter he has so unjustly spurned; before his death, Mr. Tulliver must acknowledge his debt to the son he had tried to keep away from his own mill. He hopes that Tom will take care of the little "wench" who is the true bearer of his Tulliver blood. Yet, like Lear's kingdom or the "patrimonial fields" of Wordsworth's Michael, Dorlcote Mill is an heirloom that will go to no direct successors. Held by the Tullivers for "a hundred years and over," it will not be repossessed by the miller's descendants. Wordsworth's guiltless Michael loses lands that once were free like himself when his son Luke goes to the "dissolute city" and gives himself to "evil courses." Though they too must go to that city, neither Tom nor Maggie really fails their father. Yet they lack his freedom. Michael asks his son to reclaim the land which otherwise would not endure another master. Mr. Tulliver, on the other hand, dimly senses that the mill is lost forever. He tells his servant: "There's a story as when the mill changes hands, the river's angry—I've heard my father say it many a time." (Bk. III, chap. 9, p. 414.) His prophecy proves true. The angry river will claim his Dodson son and Tulliver daughter. Freedom of will gives way to accident and capricious forces. A different order of reality has taken over.

THE DISINURED PAST:
THE SACRIFICE OF MAGGIE TULLIVER

The opening books of *The Mill on the Floss* contain some of George Eliot's finest writing. Comedy and tragedy are combined through the "negative capability" which Keats recognized in Shakespeare. Ironic, tough-minded, the novelist is capable of moving our deeper emotions without ever lapsing into sentimentality. The story of a superior miller and maltster contains analogues to the stories of Lear or Antony for the mind willing to connect the smaller to the greater. Yet though we sense Mr. Tulliver's greatness, we are never allowed to forget his limitations. High and low, heroic and mock-heroic, are held in perfect equipoise through the Victorian device of "inverse sublimity."[38] It is therefore all the more shocking to watch this equipoise break down completely in the last volume of the novel (Books VI and VII). After Mr. Tulliver's death, Maggie displaces Tom on George Eliot's stage. The tiny girl of the earlier portions of the novel is now aggrandized into a "fallen princess" who is denied her regal robes by her unheroic inferiors. Conversely, the St. Ogg's which was so terrifying to the puzzled miller becomes shrunken, exposed in its full pettiness. From Shakespeare and Wordsworth we have moved to Pope: in the opening of Book VI, Stephen Guest stands poised with a pair of scissors, ready to shear off one of Lucy's straying curls. Teacups, ratafias, a piano, have replaced the poetic Dorlcote Mill. The narrator's voice has lost its sureness, shifting uneasily between satire and sentimentalism with the same uncertainty that George Eliot had exhibited in "Amos Barton."

The narrator describes Stephen's dandified attire as "the graceful and odoriferous result of the largest oil-mill and the most extensive wharf in St. Ogg's" (Bk. VI, chap. 1, p. 149). He suggests sarcastically that there is only an "apparent triviality in the action of the scissors," hinting thereby that the actions of this young man (whose appearance in the book is so sudden and un-

---

[38] I have borrowed this term from Max Keith Sutton, who uses it to designate the more ludicrous analogies between small and great, and the nonhuman and human in writers like Dickens, Thomas Hood, and W. S. Gilbert (" 'Inverse Sublimity' in Victorian Humor," *VS*, X [December 1966], 177–192).

expected) are every bit as trivial as the activities of the society to which he owes his wealth. But the attempt to typify in Stephen the society headed by his father and by Mr. Deane, his prospective father-in-law, seems heavy-handed. The satire misfires rather badly, for it has the effect of reducing the scope of the very forces that had led to Mr. Tulliver's downfall. The clear-cut, all-too-explicit picture of the "small world" that stifles Maggie with its puerilities, can hardly disturb us as deeply as the more general picture of the impersonal flywheel which had vanquished her father. The disparity between the small and the great is no longer handled ironically. In the previous portions of the book the actions of Mr. Tulliver and of little Maggie, though insignificant, were prompted by the Μέγεθος of true passion. But later not even so imposing an agent as a biblical flood can impress tragedy on the world of "The Rape of the Lock." The machinery of Pope's mock-epic jars with that used in earnest by such nineteenth-century imitators of Milton as John Abraham Heraud in his twelve-book epic *The Judgement of the Flood* (1834). The small and the great have become arbitrarily reversed, as well as sundered.

Even before the opening of the novel's third volume, there is a marked shift in treatment and style. If Maggie the child and Mr. Tulliver were viewed by a narrator able to maintain an aesthetic distance, the young woman's story is writ "large" whenever she makes her appearance. Whereas the commonplace miller became an Œdipus only by a stretch of our imaginations, George Eliot now tries to assist us whenever possible by likening the miller's daughter to a "tall Hamadryad" whose "queenly head" is juxtaposed to a hastily introduced backdrop of "grand Scotch firs." The ideological skeleton of the novel, so superbly enfleshed in the first half of the narrative, shows increasingly through a veneer of skin. Only by implication was Mr. Tulliver a prince falling from high to low; Maggie, however, is actually described as a regal figure without the kneeling subjects she so richly deserves. The child who wanted to be crowned as queen of the gypsies, who invented a world in which Lucy was queen, "though the queen was Maggie herself in Lucy's form" (Bk. I, chap. 7, p. 90), now must escape with Lucy's Prince Charming before discovering that he too is hopelessly unworthy of her. And we are not allowed to forget the "jet crown" upon this exquisite creature's head.

Though Maggie is presumably guilty of the Tulliver pride, she is made to seem far less culpable than her willful father. Mr. Tulliver's exchanges with his wife, her relatives, or Mr. Riley always revealed his own deficiencies. The adult Maggie's exchanges with Philip or Stephen Guest seem by comparison to be hollow recitations. When Philip tells her that he has "nothing but the past to live upon," and plaintively asks her whether "the future will never join on to the past again," Maggie answers in similar abstractions: "I desire no future that will break the ties of the past" (Bk. VI, chap. 10, p. 278). To Stephen's entreaties that she accept the future he offers her, Maggie replies: "You feel, as I do, that the real tie lies in the feelings and expectations we have raised in other minds. Else all pledges might be broken, when there was no outward penalty. There would be no such thing as faithfulness." (Bk. VI, chap. 11, p. 287.) When, drifting down the river, she suddenly awakes to Duty and Memory, she proclaims: "If the past is not to bind us, where can duty lie? We should have no law but the inclination of the moment." (Bk. VI, chap. 14, p. 329.) Such speeches belong to a thesis-novel. They ought to come from a ventriloquist's puppet and not by the rounded human being whose growth we have observed. George Eliot has dropped all indirection. She glosses Maggie's willingness to be led by Stephen in the boat with a laconic statement, "Memory was excluded," as if an explicit stage direction could substitute for what the reader ought to feel through his own experience. Yet Maggie must be readied to play out her role as victim or martyr.

Though pitiful, Mr. Tulliver was not spared the ironic treatment accorded to his rivals in St. Ogg's; the adult Maggie, however, is untouched by the sarcasm with which the author ridicules the pretensions of a society far more sterile than Milby. Pretending to adopt the voice of "not the world, but the world's wife" (Bk. VII, chap. 2, p. 350), the narrator becomes a satirist who blames society for barring its doors to an innocent victim. Maligned and defamed as Mr. Tryan had been, the "large-souled" Maggie becomes too precious for this world—even for the aunt who now surprises us by welcoming the young outcast. Life at the Ripple cannot be recovered. Rowing towards the Mill, Maggie notices a "rushing muddy current that must be the strangely altered Ripple" (Bk. VII, chap. 5, p. 396). Paradise has been washed away and soiled by the irresistible flux. Maggie must surrender. Only death can rescue the girl who demanded a higher life: in "dreadful clearness" she and Tom behold the "hurrying, threatening masses" which will engulf them in the river's current.

The concluding portions of *The Mill on the Floss* not only lack, in Professor Haight's words, "the same degree of realism" found in the earlier parts,[39] but they also betray a severe loss of artistic control. Although George Eliot spent but nine weeks on the last two books of her novel, it is highly doubtful that more time and care might have made Maggie's tragedy seem more appropriate.[40] Several reasons have been advanced for the unsatisfactory resolution of the novel.[41] Of all the explanations, that

[39] Introduction, Riverside Edition, p. xix.

[40] Barbara Hardy contends that this "cursoriness" may even be a virtue, since it makes Maggie's attraction to Stephen seem all the more rapid, violent, and superficial (*The Novels of George Eliot: A Study In Form* [London, 1959], p. 56). The observation, however plausible, does not quite account for those changes in perspective and tone which go far beyond Maggie's brief entanglement with her new lover.

[41] Mr. Haight assumes that only the very ending of the novel is unsatisfactory, and he generously attributes the dissatisfaction to "George Eliot's lack of familiarity with boats and rivers" (Introduction, p. xix). F. R. Leavis advances a psychological hypothesis: it is George Eliot's

offered by George Levine comes closest to the heart of the matter. To him, the conclusion indicates the novelist's need to "escape from the implications of her most deeply felt insights."[42] Pulling back from the nihilism inherent in "modern sensibility," George Eliot was able to dignify the amoral and accidental existence she distrusted only by treating Maggie's death as an extraordinary martyrdom. Mr. Levine's argument seems generally cogent, even though he almost seems to blame George Eliot for not being William Faulkner. What is more, since he advances his thesis for all of George Eliot's fiction, it is his burden to show whether his conclusions apply equally to her other works. Indeed, his statement does not adequately explain why the author who had succeeded so admirably with Mr. Tulliver's tragedy should have failed in depicting Maggie's plight.[43]

"self-pity" and "self-idealization" through the adult Maggie which, in his view, determine the way in which the novelist beholds her character (*The Great Tradition* [New York, 1954], p. 58). Though shrewd, this thesis seems insufficiently developed. It does not explain how George Eliot could maintain an ironic distance with the little child whose shortcomings anticipate the "immaturity" which Mr. Leavis attributes to the adult Maggie. Indeed, the precocious little Maggie, whose eyes are so "full of unsatisfied intelligence, and unsatisfied, beseeching affection," is as much a projection of Marian Evans as the young woman who cannot turn her back on St. Ogg's provincial life.

[42] "Intelligence as Deception," p. 402.

[43] Though his artistic judgment is correct, Mr. Levine occasionally employs the wrong tools: he assumes, for example, that the waters of the Floss have regenerative qualities by referring to the symbology in *Adam Bede*; but *The Mill* is not *Adam Bede*. It is a very different "mental phase," and portrays a different historical era, belongs to a different genre, and therefore also relies on correlatives other than the Feuerbachian symbols which George Eliot gradually discarded after *Adam Bede*. The river is far less the baptismal symbol of Feuerbach (or of Milton) than it is a symbol of destruction, like the "River of Suicides" of James Thomson's "The City of Dreadful Night." It is closer to the metallic river in "The Lifted Veil" than to the water imagery in *Adam Bede*.

George Eliot's variation can be accounted for only if we carefully examine some of the difficulties she faced in relating Tom's and Maggie's stories to that of their father. That these difficulties had their origins in Marian Evans's need to define her own identity through her precarious relationship with both her father and brother, though undeniably true, need not concern us in this study of the novelist's more conscious intentions. (I leave it up to critics more versed in Freud to interpret the significance of the two dreams Maggie has before her "real waking" on Stephen's boat.) Both Tom and Maggie, we are told by the narrator, have evolved "above the mental level of the generation before them." In Tom, the Dodson strain has been magnified; in Maggie, the "richer blood" of the Tullivers is dominant (Bk. IV, chap. 2, p. 9). Though Tom has inherited his mother's literalism, his tenacity is even greater than that of the strongest of her sisters. Though Maggie possesses her father's faculty for perceiving that words can stand for "summat else," her greater imagination demands a more grandiose outlet for her unsatisfied intelligence and affection. Tom embraces the reality of St. Ogg's; Maggie yields to the fantasy life that was her father's destruction.

If Mr. Tulliver refused Mr. Deane's advice, Tom not only works for his uncle but also lets himself be guided by the practical Bob Jakin. Bob's strength, like Mr. Deane's, lies in his adaptability. Even as Tom's boyhood companion, he had boasted of his instinct for survival: " '*I* don't care about a flood comin',' said Bob; 'I don't mind the water, no more nor the land. I'd swim— *I* would.' " Like some of the organisms mentioned by the narrator, the amphibian Bob belongs to a species hardy enough to adapt himself to a change in environment. Aware that there is no future for him as a bargeman or rat-catcher, he chooses what to him is a less appealing profession. Bob prospers as a packman; Tom rises in his uncle's firm. Both turn their backs on a "paradisiac picture," determined to get on in the world. Yet Tom's fierce determination lacks Bob's warmth and humor. He has no time for such amenities as a wife and family. Tom's words shock even his uncle: "I want to have plenty of work. There's nothing else I care about much." (Bk. VI, chap. 5, p. 206.) Transplanted to St. Ogg's, Adam Bede's doctrine of work seems grim and materialistic. In his monomaniac desire to recover Mr. Tulliver's mill Tom inherits only the miller's intolerance: "his inward criticism of his father's faults did not prevent him from adopting his father's prejudice" (Bk. VI, chap. 12, p. 299). In his desire to vindicate the past, he betrays all that was best in it by yielding uncritically to his present.

Maggie, on the other hand, cannot at all adapt herself to this changed present. As a child she fancied a world where people never got larger than the children of her own age. This fantasy sets her apart from Tom and links her to her father. The miller's incapacity to grow, his paranoid hostility toward the incomprehensible world that impinges on him, prefigures the predicament of his daughter. His maladjustment, however, is treated with an almost clinical objectivity. The novelist makes it clear that, like Mr. Toobad in Peacock's *Nightmare Abbey*, Mr. Tulliver blames his own irresponsibility on the machinations of the devil. But whereas she exposes the simplicity of the miller's evasions of reality, George Eliot cannot bring herself to do the same when she depicts his daughter's plight. Instead, significantly enough, the narrator now appropriates the miller's hostility against the world at large. If Mr. Tulliver foolishly blames "old Harry" for his own inability to find fulfillment, our intelligent narrator is forced to blame a different fiction—"the world's wife." In the second chapter of the last book, "St. Ogg's Passes Judgment," the narrator pauses to satirize this imaginary figure for maligning poor Maggie. The world's wife, he tells us, has its own favorite abstraction, called "society." Yet the narrator does not hesitate to vent his own spleen on this same abstraction. As Mr. Levine suggests, intelligence can often lead to self-deception; so, obviously, can emotion.

In "The Lifted Veil," the disabled Latimer helplessly awaited the moment of his death; in *The Mill on the Floss*, Mr. Tulliver watches the auctioning of all his belongings after he has been immobilized by a stroke, and Maggie and Tom stand paralyzed in their boat as they see "death rushing on them." All four characters are equally defenseless. Yet it is Maggie, rather than her masculine brother or father, who most resembles the passive and prostrate Latimer. Like the protagonist of George Eliot's horror tale, Maggie is choiceless, the victim of her creator's apprehension over the blind chance which may determine identity and fate. To an even greater extent than Latimer (who might have been saved by Meunier), Maggie is powerless to alter her fate. While George Eliot makes Mr. Tulliver seem blameworthy for his imprudence, she comes close to pretending that Maggie's destiny is absolutely sealed because predetermined by "the irreversible laws within and without her" (Bk. IV, chap. 3, pp. 31–32).

The outside forces affecting Maggie are withstood by her brother by virtue of his Dodson tenacity; the inner forces weakening her come from the characteristics she has inherited from her father. Like Mr. Tulliver, the girl possesses a "soul untrained for inevitable struggles"; like the miller, she is deeply neurotic, incapable of accepting what Freud would call the "reality principle." Maggie therefore not only succumbs to the social changes which destroy her father, but she is also victimized by a trick of heredity, by the "crossing of breeds" by the miller who had perversely chosen a wife so unlike himself. Had Maggie, and not Tom, been a man, she might have profited from Mr. Stelling's education, gone on to the university, and become a "gentleman" like Pendennis or even a gentleman-novelist like Thackeray himself. Had she, instead of Tom, retained her mother's characteristics, or, better still, have remained at the "mental level" of Mrs. Tulliver, she might have become an ordinary governess in a world without Byronic Rochesters or Gothic manor houses, contentedly mangling her master's sheets instead of having the world mangle her psyche. But, by a hereditary caprice, Mr. Tulliver's favorite child is a throwback to the heroic Ralph Tulliver, and hence is all the more unfitted to cope with the world than her father. She may well wish to remain insignificant, to lead the untroubled life of a child, "easy and simple, as it might have been in Paradise" (Bk. VI, chap. 11, p. 288); but in George Eliot's deterministic view of existence, such regression is not only unhealthy but also impossible. In a simpler era when Tom could have been an Adam Bede, unseduced by the ways of St. Ogg's, Maggie might have become a Dinah embracing the "reality principle." But in her stage the chasm has become too wide. The re-entry into a less troubled stage of life can come only through the return to those "daisied fields" which Tom and Maggie are allowed to revisit in the flash of time which elapses before their drowning. Though treated as a greater character than her father, Maggie seems infinitely punier because she is so irrevocably determined by his genes. Character may not be destiny, as the narrator warns us, but neither are chromosomes. As Ibsen was to discover later in the century, tragedy and heredity are difficult to mix.

Like the witch in the book she shows to Mr. Riley, Maggie is condemned, regardless of her choice. Whichever way she turns lies hell. The moral which this shrewd little girl derives from her book applies to her later self:

O, I'll tell you what that means. It's a dreadful picture, isn't it? But I can't help looking at it. That old woman in the water's a witch—they've put her in to find out whether she's a witch or no, and if she swims she's a witch, and if she's drowned—and killed, you know—she's innocent, and not a witch, but only a poor silly old woman. But what good would it do her then, you know, when she was drowned? (Bk. I, chap. 3, p. 21.)

Her question is all the more poignant in light of the answer framed by the child herself: "Only, I suppose, she'd go to heaven, and God would make it up to her." As an adult, Maggie is denied even that consolation. Her fate must be idealized in order to become bearable for her creator. For only a god-like novelist can "make it up" to choiceless victims in a Godless world.

"Choose!," thunders the six-foot Tom on finding Maggie with Philip. Yet when, pages later, she does make her single choice and dutifully returns to Tom and to St. Ogg's, she does regret it. Though innocent, she must drown. As Professor Haight points out in his preface to the novel, George Eliot's contemporaries thought Maggie's escape with Stephen was terribly "wicked"; John Ruskin (whose own sexual life was hardly exemplary) accused Maggie and Stephen of "forgetting themselves in a boat"; even the more lenient Bulwer-Lytton felt that the very "indulgence" of her temptation had violated Maggie's large Ideality. The modern reader can hardly help being amused by such reactions. Sensing Maggie's kinship to Lawrence's heroines,[44] he might easily overreact in the opposite direction and wish that Maggie had indeed "forgotten herself" with some handsome gamekeeper instead of panting like a "wounded wargoddess" after being kissed by the insipid Stephen (Bk. VI, chap. 10, p. 275). But such an enlightened view would be as far off the mark as that of Ruskin and Bulwer-Lytton. Like Philip Wakem, Stephen is merely a convenient device. Philip, whose femininity is repeatedly emphasized, acts as a spokesman for the novelist who likewise finds herself powerless to deflect Maggie from a predetermined course. Though impotent, Philip at least can chide Maggie for her nunlike mortifications ("stupefaction is not resignation"); a sufferer himself, the deformed artist

[44] See the account, not always reliable, given by "E.T." (Lawrence's friend Jessie Chambers): "Lawrence adored *The Mill on the Floss*, but always declared that George Eliot had 'gone and spoilt it halfway through.' He could not forgive the marriage [sic] of the vital Maggie Tulliver to the cripple Philip. . . . Maggie Tulliver was his favorite heroine. He used to say that the smooth branches of the beech trees (which he especially admired) reminded him of Maggie Tulliver's arms" (*D.H. Lawrence: A Personal Record* [London, 1935], pp. 97–98).

foresees the far more bitter mortifications she will have to undergo. The pseudo-Byronic Mr. Guest, however, is primarily a listener, almost as passive as Coleridge's wedding guest. He escorts Maggie down to the boat, retreats, and reappears only as the escort of the saddened, but wiser Lucy who visits her dark cousin's grave. Maggie might have escaped alone on that river (as Romola will do in a very similar situation), but such an action would not have permitted the narrator to satirize the society which excuses Stephen but blames his female companion.

According to Professor Haight, one of George Eliot's earliest biographers G. W. Cooke claimed that it was not physical passion but a spiritual craving growing out of Maggie's yearning for a fuller life that led her to follow her abductor.[45] There is at least a partial truth in this statement. Maggie's attraction to Stephen is definitely sexual (the description of her surrender is very similar to that of Hetty's submission to Arthur Donnithorne). If the feminine Philip proves to be an inadequate substitute for Tom, the broad-chested Stephen is quite as manly as Maggie's brother. Yet she follows him because she confuses sexual impulse with rational choice. Mistakenly, Maggie believes that Stephen can lead her into a better world. The child who was so completely hypnotized by the churning mill wheel had felt a "dim delicious awe as at the presence of an uncontrollable force" (Bk. I, chap. 4, p. 39). The adult Maggie also wants to believe that "the tide was doing it all—that she might glide along with the swift, silent stream, and not struggle any more" (Bk. VI, chap. 13, p. 313). But the forgetfulness of this Lethe is imaginary. In her childhood, fantasies of a "little world apart from her outside everyday life" were always broken by Tom. Now, daylight reveals that Stephen is not the knight she had imagined him to be. Tennyson's Lady of Shalott dies when she drifts into contact with the stark reality of Lancelot's ordinary world; George Eliot's dreamy

---

[45] Riverside Edition, p. xiv.

heroine dies soon after she discovers that Stephen belongs to the same prosaic world she had tried to flee. Pain is inescapable. Philip's words come true: "there is no such escape possible except by perverting or mutilating one's nature" (Bk. VI, chap. 7, p. 229). Stephen's own appeal to Natural Law is specious: "There is nothing in the past that can annul our right to each other," he professes (Bk. VI, chap. 14, p. 331). His statement applies only to his own past, not to Maggie's. Bitterly, she discovers that she is bound by that past, even if it has been lost by her father, altered by her brother, and made irrecoverable by her own growth to adulthood.

But if Maggie bows to the past, the past lacks the authority it had possessed in *Adam Bede*. To be sure, as Thomas Pinney contends, the novel's conclusion is intended to "affirm the supreme value of the early affection of Maggie and Tom for each other."[46] But George Eliot's efforts to endow Maggie's past with a higher meaning led the novelist to inconsistencies not noted by Mr. Pinney. When Maggie and Tom become adolescents, George Eliot speaks of their having passed "the golden gates of their childhood" into a "thorny wilderness" (Bk. II, chap. 7, p. 301). This remark, like the later suggestion that Maggie's affection for Philip is "tranquil" and "tender" only because it has its roots "deep down in her childhood," seems most artificially superimposed. For Tom and Maggie's childhood had hardly been "golden"; Maggie's affection for Philip could have been just as tranquil had she met the deformed young artist only as an adult at the Charity Bazaar. Even in the novel's concluding remarks, there is a definite tinge of self-deception. George Eliot allows brother and sister to relive the "days when they had clasped their little hands in love, and roamed the daisied fields together." Yet there were few instances when Maggie the child was allowed to hold her brother's hand. The little girl asked by Tom to choose

[46] "The Authority of the Past in George Eliot's Novels," *NCF*, XXI (September 1966), 137.

between two halves of a muffin found then, as later, that any choice would make her unhappy. By resorting to the Wordsworthian myth of childhood, George Eliot apparently forgot that her heroine's agonies had begun as an infant. Maggie's first memory, after all, is that of the brother who ceases to torment her only upon his death.

For Dr. Johnson memory was not the joyful experience it was to be for Wordsworth. In one of his *Idlers*, he suggested quite realistically that the act of recollection must always be painful, since it forces us to remember the vanity of all our broken illusions. Thus, he suggested, men logically resist memory; for without its "afflictive" power the "mind might perform its functions without incumbrance, and the past might no longer encroach upon the present."[47] The Victorians also longed for "an art of forgetfulness."[48] Though they made a habit of repudiating the forgetfulness of lotos-eating, they, like the Doctor, fully recognized the painfulness of viewing the gaps between past and present. But the Victorian artist also derived a bittersweet satisfaction in conjuring up the lost simplicities of times past. The days when Maggie and Tom had roamed the daisied fields together may have been fictitious, as is the more openly metaphoric picture of another pair of infants toddling towards Avila in the prelude to *Middlemarch*; but it was necessary to invent that nonexistent past, to take refuge—ever so briefly—in its untroubled ways. (Had George Eliot ever written a novel about St. Theresa herself, the author would, most likely, have scaled the Spanishwoman's present against still another simpler, more innocent past).[49]

[47] *Idler*, No. 72.

[48] *Idler*, No. 44.

[49] Cf. the description of Arthur and Hetty's meeting, for instance: "Poor things! It was a pity they were not in that golden age of childhood when they would have stood face to face, eyeing each other with timid liking, then given each other a little butterfly kiss, and toddled off to

The fiction of childhood tranquility could at least lend meaning to Maggie's death and allow George Eliot to stir those "springs of goodness" which she had tried to touch in the death of Amelia Barton. But while she is alive, as child or adult, the complex Maggie cannot link herself to any past. Dinah could adapt the living words of John Wesley to her present; but the "Voice from the Past" which Maggie unearths in the writings of Thomas a Kempis does not speak to her own times. The author of *The Imitation of Christ* cannot really quench modern man's thirst: "She had not perceived—how could she until she had lived longer?—the inmost truth of the old monk's outpourings, that renunciation remains sorrow, though a sorrow borne willingly." (Bk. IV, chap. 3, p. 35.)[50] Like Savonarola in *Romola*, this monk can at best offer a concealed kernel of truth; it is Maggie's own experience, like Romola's, which must be her teacher, even if that experience leads her to death.

---

play together" (chap. 12, p. 193). This wishfulness carries a further dimension: had the two been young children, their sexual attraction would have been harmless, without issue. Maturity, in whatever form, is hard to bear.

[50] George Eliot may well have been aware of Ernest Renan's influential essay on "L'Auteur de l'Imitation de Jésus Christ," in his *Etudes d'Histoire Religieuse* (1857). In his essay Renan views the author of the *Imitation* (whom he assumes to be the Benedictine Jean Gersen rather than Thomas a Kempis) much as Arnold regards the Carthusians in "Stanzas from the Grande Chartreuse." As the "last voice of monachism," the book is too simple, too reactionary and uncurious ("to increase knowledge is to increase trouble") ; yet Renan holds that its incompleteness lends the work the charm of an irrecoverable simplicity: "I would not wish to exaggerate the importance of this kind of spiritual gentility, without which we can very well be useful, and even honest men. But it is certain that in losing the institution of the monastic life, the human mind has lost a great school of originality" (*Studies of Religious History* [London, 1893], pp. 231, 234, 236). George Eliot's attitude seems closer to Renan's than to Feuerbach's far harsher view of "monachism"—a view censured by Renan in another essay, "M. Feuerbach and the New Hegelian School."

Maggie must eventually bear her own crown of thorns in order to imitate Christ. But, like Hetty Sorrel, she will bear her sorrow unwillingly. Her fate seems as unjust, though for very different reasons. Hetty, like Arthur, had denied the past; Maggie, on honoring the ties of the past, finds it anachronistic, bypassed by the changes inherent in all growth, evolution, and "historical advancement." The guilty Hetty did not deserve her fate because of her ignorance; the intelligent Maggie does not deserve it because of her innocence. Maggie defends Philip by saying, "He couldn't choose his father" (Bk. II, chap. 5, p. 277). Neither could she. She is born and dies as the victim of chance. Despite the adequacy of the flood as a *deus ex machina*, despite the careful foreshadowings of the flood from the very beginning of the novel, the device, like the appearance of Stephen Guest, seems extraneous and accidental. Professor Haight detects what may well be a consciously implanted parallel to *King Lear*: "Maggie's prayer, 'O God, if my life is to be long,' is answered by the waters rising about her with something of that ironic effect of the storm that follows Lear's appeal to the gods."[51] Yet Lear, it must be remembered, is not killed by the storm, whereas Maggie is sacrificed to the river.

In a tragedy like *King Lear*, the forces of circumstance are as prominent as in a "realistic" novel like *The Mill on the Floss*. The unexpected reversal of the French army, Edmund's deception, the protracted distraction of Albany and Edgar at the very moment that Cordelia is hanged contribute to the final tragedy. But it is Lear's initial act of willfulness, committed at the height of his powers, which has precipitated the ensuing concatenation of events. Maggie's one act of willfulness, itself blamed on the hypnotic influence of her seducer and on her Tulliver blood, is unrelated to the cataclysmic circumstances of her death. Had Lear not banished Cordelia, the carnage of his house would have been avoided; but had Maggie not fled with Stephen, she

[51] Riverside Edition, p. xix.

could still have drowned like the "helpless cattle" washed away by the Floss. Notwithstanding George Eliot's identification of the overflowing river with those deterministic "laws" within and without the girl's psyche, the drowning is not tragic. For all her queenly attributes, despite the carefully implanted parallels to figures like the drowning Ophelia, despite Maggie's own firsthand knowledge about "Shakespeare and everything," she remains a figure of pathos, the prey of circumstances that are capricious and accidental. There is no causal connection between her flight and the destiny assigned to her.

Indeed, had the flood occurred at the time of Maggie's and Stephen's escape, had it then prompted her belated return to the mill and led to her reunion in death with Tom, a logical connection between her willfulness and her denial of "irreversible laws" might have been established. But George Eliot wanted Maggie to drag her bloodied feet along the streets of St. Ogg's before her final canonization. The break, though it allowed the author to pour her sarcasm on the "world's wife," unfortunately robbed Maggie's death of the desired elevation by making her all the more a victim of chance like Latimer. Tom's military drill-master complains that General Wolfe did not die heroically enough: "He did nothing but die of his wound: that's a poor haction, I consider. Any other man 'ud have died o' the wounds I've had." (Bk. II, chap. 4, p. 267.) The George Eliot who wept while writing about Maggie's death clearly did not consider her heroine's martyrdom to be a "poor haction." She wanted Maggie's final sojourn in St. Ogg's to be a true "Imitation of Christ." Even as a passive victim, Maggie Tulliver is infinitely more attractive than Walter Pater's indolent Marius, another unwilling imitator of Christ. Nonetheless, there is a similarity between Pater's lifeless pagan-turned-Christian and the intensely alive daughter of a "pagan" miller. Both of these figures are the victims of chance and change; both die of the wounds which their creators resisted and survived.

7. Reconciliation Through Fable: *Silas Marner*

My days are swifter than a weaver's shuttle and are spent without hope.

. . . . .

If I have made gold my hope, or have said to the fine gold, Thou art my confidence . . . this also were an iniquity . . . The stranger did not lodge on the street, but I opened my doors.

. . . . .

In a dream, in a vision of the night, when sleep falleth upon men . . . then he manifests himself.

—JOB, 7, 31, 33

When Marner's sensibility returned, he continued the action which had been arrested, and closed the door, unaware of the chasm in his conscience, unaware of any intermediate change, except that the light had grown dim, and that he was chilled and faint. He thought that he had been too long standing at the door and looking out. Turning towards the hearth, where the two logs had fallen apart and set forth only a red uncertain glimmer, he seated himself on his fireside chair, and was stooping to push his logs together, when, to his blurred vision, it seemed as if there were gold on the floor in front of his hearth. . . . Was it a dream? He rose to his feet again, pushed his logs together, and throwing on some dried leaves and sticks, raised a flame; but the flame did not disperse the vision—it only lit up more distinctly the little round form of the child.

—Silas Marner

The reader who vaguely remembers *Silas Marner* as a distasteful, saccharine high-school text may be every bit as startled upon rereading this fine novel as by taking a second look at that other children's classic, *Gulliver's Travels*. To Henry James, *Silas*

Marner seemed a masterpiece because of its superb craftsmanship: "it has more of that simple, rounded, consummate aspect,
that absence of loose ends and gaping issues which marks a classical work."[1] On somewhat different grounds, *The Westminster
Review* also declared the new work by its former editor to be
superior to all of her previous fiction: "the stream of thought
runs clearer, the structure of the story is more compact, while
the philosophical insight is deeper and more penetrating than in
any of her former productions."[2] Both of these estimates, artistic
and philosophic, seem correct: in *Silas Marner* George Eliot not
only eliminated all the "loose ends" which had so seriously marred
the artistry of *The Mill*, but also overcame some of the difficulties she had encountered as a thinker. Through the medium of a
"legendary tale," she reconciled the incongruities which had aris-
en, to greater or lesser degrees, in all of her former fictional attempts to find the ideal in the "real."

If *The Mill on the Floss* was intended to be a companion
piece to *Adam Bede*, the composition of this new pastoral novel
was to be wholly unplanned. Immediately upon the appearance
of *The Mill*, George Eliot and Lewes had set out for Italy,
where "rather an ambitious project" soon suggested itself to
her (GEL, III, 300). Florentine history, rich and momentous,
would—she hoped—allow her to continue her progression from
"small to great." Yet she stayed inactive after her return to

[1] "The Novels of George Eliot," *Atlantic Monthly*, XVIII (October
1866), 482.

[2] "Belles Lettres," *Westminster Review*, LXXVI (July 1861), 280.
Relying for obvious reasons on water imagery, the *Westminster* reviewer had said of *The Mill on the Floss* in an earlier article: "it affects us
like the spring in which it appeared with a weary longing and suspense
that is too forcibly contrasted with the rapid movement of the conclusion
of the story; the slow, placid, and somewhat turbid stream too suddenly
changes to a rushing waterfall; the canal ends in a cascade: this destroys
the harmonious impression that every work of art ought to leave upon our
minds". (LXXIV [July 1860], 26.)

England, finishing only the minor comic story of "The Idiot Brother" (later entitled "Brother Jacob")[3] before moving into London itself. Once she was established in the city, the "loss of the country" made her almost as despondent as Maggie Tulliver had been (GEL, III, 360). On January 1, 1861, the novelist thanked Blackwood for the profits she had reaped during the previous year and complained at the same time: "I suppose that I shall never love London, or believe that I am as well in the streets as in the fields" (GEL, III, 369).

But perhaps the streets of London helped her, as those of Munich had once done, to focus her imagination on the fields of a pastoral past. For just as George Eliot was readying herself for *Romola*, she announced that "another English story" had crossed her mind (GEL, III, 339). Amply aware by now that her stories about town life were apt to be gloomier than those set in the country, John Blackwood asked with undisguised curiosity: "Is the English Story to be Town or Country?" (GEL, III, 341.) He did not receive a reply until she was well on her way: "I am writing a story which came *across* my other plans by a sudden inspiration. . . . It is a story of old-fashioned village life, which has unfolded itself from the merest millet-seed of thought." (GEL, III, 371.) Just a month after this announcement George Eliot presented Blackwood with the first two-thirds of her manuscript. Completed in another month, *Silas Marner* was published on April 2, 1861. As if in self-amazement, its author again commented that the novel had been "quite a sudden inspiration that came across me in the midst of altogether different meditations" (GEL, III, 392).

Whatever the reasons for its suddenness, the sources of this "inspiration" are not difficult to trace. For there is little doubt that the story of Silas' regeneration was a "millet-seed" which

[3] The story was not published until 1864 in the July issue of the *Cornhill*; George Eliot sent it to the magazine's editor as a gift, to compensate him for the relative failure of *Romola*.

had resisted the grinding stones of Dorlcote Mill. Even the far-
cical story of David Faux and his idiot brother had in a way
stemmed from "the loose ends and gaping issues" left by the
tragedy of the Tullivers. The nemesis of "Brother Jacob," unlike that of *The Mill on the Floss*, is mild. In her tragic novel,
George Eliot used the myth of a happy childhood to lend meaning to the past lost by Tom and Maggie; in her comic short story,
she uses the figure of an infantile man to confront his brother
with the past the latter had hoped to erase. In both cases, old ties
assert their hold on those who would escape them. Maggie clasps
Tom in the brief instant of death; Jacob clings to David Faux
and prevents him from denying their kinship. But despite the
milder conclusion, "Brother Jacob" is rather cheerless and austere
as a comedy; it lacks those rich touches of humor evident in the
opening portions of *The Mill*. Instead, the story of David Faux's
unsuccessful efforts to rise in the dreary society of Grimworth
rather resembles, in tone and emphasis, those latter chapters of
the novel in which George Eliot had lashed out at the social pre-
tentions of St. Ogg's.

David Faux is perhaps the most unpleasant character in George
Eliot's fiction. Swollen with "an impatient sense that he ought to
become something very remarkable," this young man is dissatisfied with his station in life: "he scorned the idea that he could
accept an average" (BJ, chap. 1, p. 347). But his discontent is
unwarranted. Unlike the Tulliver children who were likewise
forced to "put up with a narrowed lot," he is hopelessly mediocre.
Tom and Maggie had, after all, evolved above the mental level
of a "superior" miller. This grumbling farmer's son is inferior
to all the members of his family, even the half-wit who will
come to haunt him. The extraordinary Maggie submits to her
fate and returns to St. Ogg's. The less-than-remarkable David,
whose imagination, like hers, "circled round and round the utmost limits of his geographical knowledge" (chap. 1, p. 348),
tries to break away from his parents and brothers. He steals his

mother's savings and escapes to Jamaica; but when he fails to make his fortune, he returns to England under an assumed name and with a face yellowed by malaria. Like Tom Tulliver, he now tries to rise in the provincial business world. But Tom went to St. Ogg's to restore his family's good name and to recover the ancestral mill across the river. The man who uses the false name of "Edward Freely" chooses the town of Grimworth because in its mediocrity it provides the least resistance to his social ambitions. David attracts the townspeople by lying about his parentage, but he exposes his identity when he learns that his benevolent father has forgiven him and left him a small legacy.[4] The disclosure of his whereabouts proves to be ruinous. His past now descends upon him in the shape of the heavy "Zacob," armed with his pitchfork, but eager to embrace his brother. Branded as a parvenu in the eyes of Grimworth, Mr. "Freely" finds himself fettered by the ties he had tried to deny. Like Bulstrode in *Middlemarch*, he is ejected by the town's society. Jacob, snorting amiably like a "heavy animal," becomes George Eliot's means of punishing this social upstart.

Though obviously related to the story of Maggie and her brother, this simple tale was hardly destined to resolve the deeper, more disturbing questions raised by the fate of that other pair. The "hard reality" that had defeated the Tullivers still needed to be amended. Increasingly sensitive about any criticism of *The Mill on the Floss*, George Eliot nonetheless was herself bothered by "the absence of things that might have been there. In fact, the third volume has the material of a novel compressed into it" (GEL, III, 285). (One of her finest Victorian critics, R. H.

---

[4] In *The Mill on the Floss*, Tom must provide for his parents, even though they are to blame for the loss of what should have been his; in "Brother Jacob," the parents, who have been robbed by David, still provide for him because they blame themselves for having brought "this ill-conditioned son into the world when he was in that entirely helpless state which excluded the smallest choice on his part" (chap. 3, p. 392).

Hutton, made the same point more bluntly: the "masterly" fragments contained in the novel's first two volumes, he maintained, had unfortunately been followed by "a second-rate one-volume novel.")[5] It is not surprising therefore that after *The Mill* the novelist should have tried to set "the remedial influences of pure, natural human relations" in a stronger light (GEL, III, 382). St. Ogg's had to be exorcised before she could look at Florence.

From Flood to Rainbow

In the letter which accompanied the manuscript of *Silas Marner*, George Eliot added a highly interesting observation: "somehow, experience and finished faculty rarely go together. Dearly beloved Scott had the greatest combination of experience and faculty—yet even he never made the most of his treasures, at least in his *mode* of presentation." (GEL, III, 378.) The remark can be read as an unintentional self-assessment. For even if the experience and finished faculty that went into her new novel are identical to those which had shaped *Adam Bede* or *The Mill*, it is the "mode of presentation" which is so surprisingly different. In searching for a form suited to her latest inspiration, George Eliot had toyed even with the notion of writing a metrical romance like Wordsworth's "Michael" (a poem from which she drew the novel's epigraph): "I have felt all through as if the story would have lent itself best to metrical rather than prose fiction, especially in all that relates to the psychology of Silas." (GEL, III, 382.) Yet the form she adopted was perfectly attuned to her aims.[6]

[5] "George Eliot," *Literary Criticism* (Philadelphia, n.d.), p. 267. Hutton might have added, however, that this "second-rate one-volume novel" gave rise to the first-rate one-volume novel *Silas Marner*.

[6] Nonetheless, those parts of the novel dealing with Silas' reawakened feelings can almost be scanned as poetry; William Wordsworth might have appreciated the following passage from chapter 14:

Few critics of *Silas Marner* have noted the actual extent to which this legendary tale is a reaction to, as well as a continuation of, *The Mill on the Floss*. At first glance, the resemblances between these two works would seem scanty indeed. *The Mill* is a sprawling *Bildungsroman* built around the aspirations of an unusual young woman; *Silas*, however, is a terse fable in which the psychology of its titular hero is definitely less interesting than that of Godfrey Cass, the young squire whose mental habits closely correspond to those of Arthur Donnithorne, Adam Bede's coarser foil.[7] Maggie Tulliver, whose charm and superior intelligence were already established as a child, dominated the stories of her father and brother. None of the figures in *Silas Marner* possesses a comparable degree of complexity. Though Eppie, like Maggie, does not "want any change," *her* wish seems to be granted. On attaining maturity, the girl rejects the advantages belatedly offered by the more sophisticated man who has at last revealed that he is her father. Instead, she chooses to remain with the weaver who has, through her, regained his own childlike awe. For Silas the foundling becomes "an object compacted of changes and hopes that forced his thoughts onward, and carried them away from their old eager pacing towards the same blank limit—carried them away to new things that would come with the coming years" (SM, chap. 14, p. 192).

Maggie, too knowledgeable and imaginative, becomes disconnected from her father's past; Silas, simple and uncomprehend-

---

> And when the sunshine grew strong and lasting,
> So that the buttercups were thick on the meadows,
> Silas might be seen in the sunny mid-day,
> Or in the late afternoon when the shadows
> Were lengthening under the hedgerows,
> Strolling out with uncovered head to carry
> Eppie beyond the Stone-pits where the flowers grew.

[7] Henry James goes a step further: "Godfrey Cass, with his lifelong secret, is by right the hero of 'Silas Marner.'" ("The Novels of George Eliot," p. 485).

ing, looks confidently at the future provided by his adopted daughter. Yet even at the very end of his experience, Silas remains far more puzzled and mystified than Mr. Tulliver had ever been. Feeble, slow-thinking, almost closer to the idiot Jacob Faux than to the enthusiast who devours *The Imitation of Christ*, the weaver nonetheless acts, just as Maggie had done, as the vehicle for a "philosophic" parable about existence in a changeful world. Like the Job he resembles, Silas remains a type: his early piety, his unexpected afflictions, the injustice he rails against, the nature of his eventual reconciliation, are handled without the loss of distance which marred the conclusion of *The Mill on the Floss*. By openly sharing Maggie's unsatisfied yearnings in her earlier novel, George Eliot dispensed with the protective mask of a detached observer. The narrator of *Silas Marner*, however, coldly observes that he finds it difficult "to enter that simple untaught state of mind" which belongs to the weaver's limited powers of comprehension (chap. 1, p. 18). Maggie's internal conflicts were nursed by Philip, the sensitive artist as a young cripple; Silas' troubles are viewed with dispassion and healthy distrust by the unsentimental gathering in the Rainbow Tavern. The Raveloers' reserve is understandable. For their strange visitor does seem truly repulsive. An automaton as mechanical as his shuttle, he cannot see any future beyond that furnished by his increasing mound of coins: "He seemed to weave, like the spider, from pure impulse, without reflection" (chap. 2, p. 23).[8] His

[8] Like that other spiderlike misanthrope in "The Lifted Veil," Silas becomes too certain of despair: "He hated the thought of the past; there was nothing that called out his love and fellowship toward the strangers he had come amongst; and the future was all dark, for there was no Unseen Love that cared for him." (chap. 2, p. 23.) If Latimer feels a tinge of affection on witnessing his father's plight, Silas likewise yields to a "rush of pity" on seeing the dropsical Sally Oates' pain. But as in the earlier tale, pity soon gives way to repulsion and makes "isolation more complete." Yet the differences are also noteworthy. Latimer sees too much light; he senses the egotism in his father's misery. Silas, however, is still unenlightened; the rustics who now rush to be cured by him will later cure his own disease.

monomania resembles that of David Faux; it is not prompted, as Tom Tulliver's had been, by any consideration outside his own self. Though he hurt Maggie, Tom had at least tried to repair the wounds suffered by their father; Silas merely swathes himself in self-pity.

On closer inspection, however, these differences only reveal the kinship between the novels. Like Maggie's, Silas' alienation stems from circumstances beyond his control. He, too, is paralyzed, and his initial paralysis is likewise identified with a city. If Maggie is seduced by the spells of an imagination as uncontrollable as Latimer's visionary fits, the simple Silas is subject to actual cataleptic seizures. Maggie, "entirely passive," awakes from her "drowsy" stupor on Stephen's boat to find that her yesterday cannot be revoked; Silas awakes from his coma to find that he has become the victim of William Dane, the schemer who has framed his trusting friend as a thief. His "loving nature" is even more cruelly thwarted than that of Maggie or Latimer. Lacking their intelligence, far more guiltless than they had been, he rails with even greater justification against a world robbed of order and justice. His trustful belief that God will immediately vindicate his innocence before the Brethren of Lantern Yard is even more painfully denied than Maggie's desire to be vindicated in the eyes of her own brother. Maggie is not wholly exempt from blame; Silas is. The injustice he suffers therefore seems to him all the more unaccountable. Like Shakespeare's Pericles—another passive Job eventually redeemed through the miraculous gift of a daughter—Silas is Fortune's fool.

The weaver's fate, then, is even more capricious than Maggie's. But whereas she must passively suffer from the errors of others, Silas just as passively benefits from the mistakes of Godfrey Cass. In fact, his story opens exactly where Maggie's had ended. Both characters are denied choice; both are defamed; both seek to escape from the changeful city which is the seat of all their misfortunes. "Unhinged," as Maggie had been, from his "old faith and love," this simpler pilgrim seeks, as she had done, that "Lethean influence of exile, in which the past becomes dreamy because its symbols have all vanished, and the present too is dreamy because it is linked with no memories" (chap. 2, p. 20).

Maggie's exile becomes a curse; Silas', a blessing. To him, as to her, there seems at first to be little "unity between his past and present life" (chap. 2, p. 25). In *The Mill*, George Eliot had labored assiduously to impress an artificial unity on her heroine's disenfranchised existence. To extricate Maggie from an impossible dilemma, she had resorted to those fictive memories which brother and sister recollect, not in tranquility, but in the agitation before death. Silas, on the other hand, calmly forms an entirely new set of memories based on his eventful life in Raveloe. By means of a new "mode of presentation," we are transported with him into that same mythical world of "daisied fields" which brother and sister glimpsed only in the act of dying. In Raveloe, a realm even more legendary than Adam Bede's Hayslope, the corpse-like weaver veritably will become "a dead man come to life again" (chap. 1, p. 8). He may not resemble the vital Maggie; yet through his resurrection, she too is given a new life.

Silas' regeneration through feeling occurs in a pastoral world which is not only hazier by far than the Shepperton which had revived Amos Barton, another grotesque intruder, but even more stylized than the Hayslope which had buoyed up Adam Bede. Like Adam Bede, this doubter, who likewise inveighs against a "God of lies, that bears witness against the innocent" (chap. 1, p. 17), comes to find meaning and purpose in the man-centered village life. Still, his reintegration is handled very differently than Adam's. For Silas' discovery of a new faith grows directly from Maggie Tulliver's objectless quest. His story represents far more than a mere revisitation of the semi-idyllic past depicted in *Adam Bede*. The change in setting goes beyond the differences between eras of "expansion" and "concentration" which had also separated "Amos Barton" from "Mr. Gilfil's Love-Story" or "Janet's Repentance" from *Adam Bede*. If the heroic Adam who accepts Hayslope life was merely restored to his former self, the Silas who accepts and is accepted by Raveloe becomes a new man as an exile from the same reality which had consumed Maggie. Maggie could find no values except in the fiction of a serene childhood; Silas, however, is redeemed by a small child on being "transported to a new land" (chap. 2, p. 20).

According to the able theological scholar, K. Gottwald, the Book of Job is "neither epic, drama, lyric, or didactic literature; and yet partakes of something of each."[9] The same statement applies to George Eliot's legendary tale. Although Shakespeare, Milton, and Wordsworth are as much blended into this fable as into the earlier novels, this mode does not call attention to the correlatives of drama, epic, and poetry. We are in a realm which generates its own poetry, the *Ur*-world of Gruppe's "*Volkspoesie*." The medium is that of a timeless legend whose wholeness stems from the perfect fusion of the expected and the unexpected, from the metamorphosis of all its constituent parts. We have no need for a sophisticated narrator to instruct the reader how to connect the lesser to the greater.

To achieve its blending, the book eschews the sharpness of photographic realism. Instead of a narrator who forces us to behold the objects in Jonathan Burge's workshop exactly as it appeared on that fateful eighteenth of June in 1799, we are thrust into what seems almost a mythological domain:

In the days when the spinning-wheel hummed busily in the farmhouses —and even great ladies, clothed in silk and thread-lace, had their toy spinning-wheels of polished oak—there might be seen in districts far away among the lanes, or deep in the bosom of the hills, certain pallid

[9] *A Light to the Nations* (New York, 1954), pp. 472–473.

undersized men, who, by the side of the brawny country-folk, looked like the remnants of a disinherited race. The shepherd's dog barked fiercely when one of these alien-looking men appeared on the upland, dark against the early winter sunset; for what dog likes a figure bent under a heavy bag? —and these pale men rarely stirred abroad without that mysterious burden. (chap. 1, p. 3.)

The passage gives us no specific time. The figure we see, pallid yet dark, is unidentified, presented only in generic terms. Darkness and light, the imagery which will dominate this slender fable as much as Job[10] or *Paradise Lost*, add to the sense of mystery. We must find our own way in the penumbra. The point of view adopted in this passage is neither that of an all-seeing "Egyptian sorcerer" nor that of a visionary narrator who restrains himself by holding onto the reality of his armchair. To the shepherd's dog, and to the shepherd himself, the burden that bends the shoulders of this apparition may well seem mysterious. Soon, of course, we shall be set at rest. The alien-looking stranger who mystifies the barking dog is none but the harmless linen-weaver. But we shall never be able to relax our guard completely. Like the villagers, we shall gradually accept Silas and overcome our distrust; conversely, we shall, like Silas, become acquainted with the ways of Raveloe and participate in the rhythm of its life. But this initial sense of unfamiliarity will persist; the aura of mystery will never quite abate. For we shall want to unravel those semivisible threads with which Silas' destiny becomes interwoven with that of Godfrey's Raveloe. We are to be teased by a novelist who, while engaging our attention with richly colored details, will constantly invite us to deduce further inferences from her careful arrangement of symbol and fact.

[10] Cf. Job, 29: "Moreover Job continued his parable, and said, Oh that I were as in months past, as in the days when God preserved me; / When his candle shined upon my head, and when by his light I walked through darkness, / As I was in the days of my youth, when the secret of God was upon my tabernacle."

It matters little for us to discover, when we do, that the events of this novel belong to "the early years of this century," that the "war times" during which they take place must correspond to the same decade which saw Arthur Donnithorne return from the Napoleonic wars. In *Adam Bede* the exactness of all dates was imperative; the novel's chronology even permitted us to savor such ironies as Arthur's puzzlement over "The Ancient Mariner." In *Silas Marner*, however, the factual and the symbolic qualify each other: the haunted pilgrim we have seen turns out to be a grotesque weaver who suffers from cataleptic fits, and yet, ordinary as he is, he nonetheless will undergo a unique experience. The man called "Old Master Marner" belongs and does not belong to that disinherited race of wanderers who roam through the *Lyrical Ballads*. Ironically enough, his Christian name stems from that of the pagan deity Sylvanus, the protector of landed "husbandmen and their crops."[11] His surname, on the other hand, suggests his kinship to Coleridge's Ancient Mariner.[12] Earth and water, fixity and motion, tradition and change, at odds in *The Mill on the Floss*, coalesce again with this wanderer's return to the lands denied to Tom and Maggie. The world of Raveloe (itself a cryptic anagram) will reveal unexpected truths, hidden from the Raveloers themselves. Although we are asked to see beyond the characters, we also surrender to the logic of their world in a way that we could not submit to George Eliot's uneasy invocation of a biblical deluge or to her conversion of the naturalistic Hetty into a

[11] Charlotte Yonge, *History of Christian Names* (London, 1884), p. 179: "His name had become a Roman name just before the Christian era, and belonged to the companion of St. Paul, who is called Sylvanus in the Epistles, and, by the contraction, Silas in the Acts. This contracted form, Silas, has been revived in England as a Scripture name."

[12] See Charles Wareing Bardsley, *English Surnames: Their Sources and Significations* (London, 1884), p. 408: " 'Henry le Mariner's name still lives among us, sometimes being found in the abbreviated form of 'Marner.' "

fallen Eve. We can suspend our belief without necessarily yielding to either the superstition of Mr. Macey or to the disbelief of Mr. Dowlas, the skeptic.

Like a ballad, *Silas Marner* soon develops a rhythm of its own by alternating between the expected and the unexpected, the complete and the incomplete. After our attention is thrice called to the gold-tipped whip which Dunstan Cass holds in his hand, we are certain that the whip will have some ulterior significance, though the exact relevance of this detail may escape us at the moment. After Silas has exclaimed for the third time, "God will clear me," we sense, even though he does not, that he will not be cleared by Lantern Yard; yet at the same time we strongly suspect that some unforeseen clarity will eventually emerge from his confusion. We are carried along by the story's rhythm, by a symmetry developing before our eyes. Silas' beloved earthen pot breaks into three pieces; his earthly life will likewise be broken into three fragments by William Dane, Dunstan, and Eppie. Godfrey's life, on the other hand, seems to be affected by only two external events—the sudden disappearance of his brother Dunstan and the equally sudden death of Molly, his unacknowledged wife. Thinking himself rid of these two tormentors, the young man looks confidently to an unbroken future. Yet fate has merely delayed a third intervention, which comes when Godfrey reaches the same age Silas was at the time he found Eppie. At the novel's end, we have a sense of completion. Our expectations have been fulfilled. If Maggie's drowning in *The Mill on the Floss* seemed arbitrary and unpredictable despite all the careful foreshadowings of that event, the symmetry which binds Silas' and Godfrey's destinies generates an irresistible logic. If we ultimately cannot account for that logic, we nonetheless feel, as Blake did in "The Tyger," a certain awe and reverence for the inescapable symmetry on which it depends.

When Silas and the grown Eppie timidly venture back into the outer world, they find that the changeful city has swallowed up Lantern Yard. But the loss of this past becomes insignificant to the old man who had expected some light to be cast on his curious fortune. Knowing by now that "things *will* change," Silas trustfully accepts a change which has been for the better. If the change in Maggie's environment was crippling to her psyche, Silas' move and adaptation to a simpler world have restored his inner sanity. The injustice he formerly suffered in "the city of destruction" (chap. 14, p. 201) no longer matters to him. In *The Mill on the Floss*, the narrator derives what little comfort he can from the fact that the graves of brother and sister have recovered their "decent quiet"; in *Silas Marner*, there is no need for such elegiac attempts at conciliation. The graves of Silas' Brethren have disappeared, but death has yielded to a new life:

"The old place is all swep' away," Silas said to Dolly Winthrop on the night of his return—"the little graveyard and everything. The old home's gone; I've no home but this now. I shall never know whether they got at the truth o' the robbery, nor whether Mr. Paston could ha' given me any light about the drawing o' the lots. It's dark to me, Mrs. Winthrop, that is; I doubt it'll be dark to the last." (chap. 21, p. 269.)

Demanding more light, the Faustian Maggie had died in the swirling darkness of the waters which spanned two irreconcilable worlds; Silas, however, gladly trots back to his checkered Eden. He has found a new paradise through the foundling he named after his dead mother and sister. Ruined by Mr. Tulliver's mistakes, ruled by his family's hectic blood, Maggie appropriately bore the name of her father's short-lived mother, Margaret Beaton. The beaten, stooped linen-weaver who gives his adopted daughter a "Bible name" does not even fathom its full significance: "thou shalt no more be termed Forsaken; neither shall thy land anymore be termed Desolate; but thou shalt be called Hephzibah."[13] Through Eppie he has been led away

---

[13] Isaiah, 62, 4.

from "threatening destruction" into a "calm and bright land" (chap. 14, p. 201).

Maggie perishes in the flood; Silas' first promise of salvation comes when he ventures among the humanity gathered in a tavern called "The Rainbow." The villagers who stare at the weaver are no more idealized than the townspeople attracted by the multicolored display in David Faux's confectionery shop, where a rainbow seems to have "descended into the market-place" (chap. 2, p. 368). But unlike the materialistic inhabitants of Grimworth, the Raveloers can be moved by a stranger's plight. They become the means for Silas' regeneration. As in *Paradise Lost* or in Shakespeare's *Pericles* and *The Tempest,* the covenant for such a redemption is signified by the rainbow which followed the tempestuous flood. Milton's Adam first re-vives at the sight of the three-colored bow "Betok'ning peace from God, and Cov'nant new" (XI, 867). Prospero's recon-ciliation to a world of darkness likewise begins when, in the masque, Iris, the "many-colour'd messenger," spans earth and heaven with her "wat'ry arch" (*The Tempest,* IV, i, 76, 71). But if the renewed confidence of Adam and Prospero still de-pends on a supernatural power, Silas' regained faith is made possible by "the remedial influences of pure, natural human relations." The power behind these human relations remains dark and inscrutable. Silas wracks his brain to understand the dispensation which seems to repay him for his former misfor-tunes. His puzzlement is shared by the superstitious rustics who had even regarded him (much as Mr. Tulliver viewed Lawyer Wakem) as a "queer-looksed thing as Old Harry's had the making of" (chap. 10, p. 96). Yet their awe and his awe must be ours as well. Though their perplexity seems as simplistic as their feeble attempts at explanation, the narrator refuses to ad-vance any theories of his own.

Were George Eliot to have written the sentimental tale that *Silas Marner* is still thought to be, she would not have felt compelled to connect the weaver's story to that of Godfrey Cass. Instead, Silas' regeneration by the golden-haired child could have been simply a wishful fantasy designed to help the author purge herself of the fears that had surfaced in "The Lifted Veil" and *The Mill on the Floss.* By merely adopting the superstitious attitude of Silas and the Raveloers, the novelist could safely have regressed into a simpler, untroubled world in which men could remain children. In this wishful realm—a realm as beneficent and wholesome as the one in "The Lifted Veil" had been terrifying and repellent—the accidents which led to Silas' regeneration could have gone wholly unexplained; the weaver's fate might simply have appeared as the opposite of the sadder destinies of Latimer and Maggie. Yet George Eliot does not escape into Maggie's arrested fantasy world. She deliberately links Silas' strange story to Godfrey's and makes Godfrey's fate as fully understandable as that sequence of events which had brought the nemesis of David Faux. And by so doing she emphasizes the very questions her previous fiction had tried to disguise. In *Silas Marner* the novelist squarely confronts the disparities which resulted from her previous treatment of moral justice in a world of fortuitous change.

Division as Unity: Godfrey and Silas

In the fiction before *Silas Marner*, George Eliot met considerable difficulties in trying to extract moral sanctions from a world ruled by random change. As I have tried to show in this study, her novels inevitably try to master the conflicts arising from two different ways of beholding reality. George Eliot demanded of her characters that they accept a natural order devoid of the providential dispensation she had once believed in. As we saw, accident had dominated in *Scenes of Clerical Life*: even in the most positive of those stories, Janet Dempster could believe in a moral order only through the accident which freed her from her husband's tyranny. In *Adam Bede*, George Eliot had been far more successful in staking out a domain in which morality might exercise its own logic; still, Dinah's trustful belief in a "Divine Love" was qualified by her creator's deep reservations about the capriciousness of the material world. And, in what certainly are the novelist's gloomiest projections, both Latimer and Maggie Tulliver succumbed to combinations of fortuitous circumstances.

In "The Lifted Veil" and *The Mill on the Floss*, George Eliot had tried to disguise her personal fear of a hazardous reality. She resorted to the irrationality of the fantasy tale in order to account for Latimer's inability to trust in a better future; in the more realistic mode of her tragic novel, she tried to advance a series of logical explanations for Maggie's passivity as a victim: Mr. Tulliver's and Tom's mistakes in judgment, the "richness" of the Tulliver blood, the dangers inherent in too rapid a variation, the obduracy and insensitivity of St. Ogg's, were among the many reasons adduced for the girl's collapse. Still, Maggie's destiny seemed as arbitrary as Latimer's. Neither the unusual circumstances which prevented Latimer from seeing goodness nor the apotheosis of the flood could lead the reader from nihilism to the recognition of a beneficent order akin to the divine dispensation George Eliot had rejected. Unlike her father's, Maggie's fate seems only capricious and unjust.

Silas Marner relies on the oppositions depicted in *The Mill*. Two modes of life, agrarian and urban, once again typify two different realities—the one ruled by freedom of choice, the other governed by impersonal and irresistible forces. But whereas in *The Mill* George Eliot pretended that Maggie's downfall was precipitated by the same interaction of imprudence and "external fact" which caused her father's tragedy, in *Silas Marner* she openly distinguishes between the chance which affects Silas Marner and the processes which bring on Godfrey's nemesis. Although the novel relies on the familiar contrast of city and country ("what could be more unlike the Lantern Yard world than the world in Raveloe?"), chance and free will coexist in the same environment. If accident influences Silas' life in the city, it equally affects his life in Raveloe. And Raveloe is far more stable than the world of Dorlcote Mill: "the fall of prices had not yet come to carry the race of small squires and yeomen down that road to ruin for which extravagant habits and bad husbandry were plentifully anointing their wheels" (chap. 3, p. 32). In his threatened agrarian world, Mr. Tulliver's extravagance and bad husbandry contributed to his downfall. In the more stable order of Raveloe, Godfrey Cass is wholly responsible for all of his actions. His secret marriage to a barmaid, which exposes him to his brother's blackmailing, is as foolish as Mr. Tulliver's marrying the weakest of the Dodson sisters. But Godfrey's freedom of choice is even greater than that of the imprudent miller who was ground by the wheels of St. Ogg's.

The freedom and accident which are irrevocably at odds in *The Mill* ultimately become indistinguishable from each other in *Silas Marner*. As David R. Carroll has pointed out, the novel presents two alternate explanations of reality: "In the frenetic atmosphere of Lantern Yard, Silas sought to explain life in terms of the miraculous; in the materialistic, indulgent atmosphere of Raveloe, Godfrey, as his surname suggests, seeks to explain life in terms of Chance (*casus*).[14] Yet *Silas Marner* depicts a curious transference. As in *Middlemarch*, where Lydgate the scientist and Dorothea the religious enthusiast will find their original explanations of life to be incomplete, here too the beliefs of Godfrey and Silas qualify each other. Godfrey, the onetime worshiper of luck, will come to acknowledge the mandates of a power he identifies with an exacting God; Silas, the

[14] "Silas Marner: Reversing the Oracles of Religion," *Literary Monographs* (Madison, Milwaukee, and London, 1967), p. 175. For a different connotation of Godfrey's surname see note 17, below.

plaything of chance, finds that he is unable, "by means of anything he heard or saw, to identify the Raveloe religion with his old faith" (chap. 14, p. 191). And yet, though their initial explanations do not account for the strange connection between their fates, both Godfrey and Silas are brought to acknowledge the justice of whatever dispensation has tied them inextricably together. The "mystery" previously denied to Dinah, Latimer, or Maggie, is allowed to survive in this legendary tale.

Godfrey Cass is ironically named. His Christian name suggests that he is free, at peace with God.[15] Yet, like the David Faux who chose the name of "Mr. Freely," this young man will be punished by the past he tries to deny. Even at the beginning of the novel, he already tugs at the chains his own imprudence has forged. For Godfrey has foolishly misspent his freedom by marrying Molly. Revolted by his own folly ("an ugly story of low passion, delusion, and the waking of delusion"), afraid that his brother Dunstan will reveal his secret to Squire Cass and the whole of Raveloe, the well-meaning Godfrey yields to a life of hazard. Seeing no way out of his sensual enslavement, he indulges in the same "excitement of sporting, drinking, card-playing" which led Chaucer's young rioters to their spiritual deaths and which, in *Middlemarch*, will lead Tertius Lydgate to opium and the gaming table. Though Godfrey hates Dunstan, another worshiper of Dame Luck, his brother becomes an extension of his worse self. Godfrey regards Nancy Lammeter, whose steadying influence he desires, as his better angel and the opium-eating Molly Farren, as the cause and emblem for his own paralysis and "natural irresolution." The immobilized Godfrey hopes that fortune will somehow break the manacles he has forged for himself and allow him to live

[15] Godfrey (Geoffroi, Gofredo, Gottfried) is a combination of *got* (the deity) and *fri* (peace or freedom). The name thus signifies "divine peace"; it can connote the freedom granted by God, as well as (in this case) the desire to be free of God, or "god-free."

an unencumbered life with Nancy. In the manner of Arthur Donnithorne, he expects "some unforeseen turn of fortune, some favourable chance which would save him from unpleasant consequences—perhaps even justify his insincerity" (chap. 9, p. 112). His expectations, like Arthur's, are destined to be shattered. In one of those ominous authorial asides so rare in this novel, the narrator warns that "Favourable Chance is the god of all men who follow their own devices instead of obeying a law they believe in" (chap. 9, p. 112).

Yet Silas Marner, who believed in precisely such a moral law, at first seems to fare even worse than Godfrey. If Godfrey's acknowledged guilt does not allow him to regard himself as "simply a victim," Silas is clearly victimized in both Lantern Yard and Raveloe. Chance, which already had allowed William Dane to frame Silas for a crime he did not commit, again presents itself in Raveloe. The unsuspecting weaver is but a hundred yards away during Dunstan's entry into his open cottage. He has left the door ajar because, bereft of his belief in Providence, he has come to rely on simple common sense: "What thief would find his way to the Stone-pits on such a night as this? and why should he come on this particular night, when he had never come through all the fifteen years before?" (chap. 5, p. 62.) But this logic proves to be faulty. When Silas arrives at his cottage, Dunstan, the "lucky fellow" who has lighted on an unguarded treasure, has already retreated into the darkness.

Thus, while Silas, the former believer in an exacting divine law finds his luck waning, Godfrey discovers that his prayers seem to have been answered by his own goddess, "Favourable Chance." First, Dunstan, who had professed himself to be "always lucky," ever able to land on his feet, unaccountably disappears; then, Molly, the denied wife, dies before she can confront Godfrey with his child. The past seems miraculously annulled. Relieved, the young man now regards himself as free at last; Nancy Lammeter can be wooed and won. Yet the same

event which Godfrey falsely interprets as a fortunate intervention in his behalf, comes to Silas' rescue: the child whose
paternity Godfrey hides from Raveloe in order to retain his
freedom frees Silas from his disappointment over an amoral
world devoid of law and justice and earns this outsider a place
among the Raveloers. Although Godfrey must eventually recognize that there is no such thing as "Favourable Chance," some
arbitrary power has nonetheless favored Silas Marner.

The book's parallels at first seem simple—simple enough to
force them on school children: Attracted by the light of Silas'
cottage, Dunstan steals the miser's painfully accumulated past;
attracted by the same light, little Eppie brings a more refulgent
future. Dunstan meets death in darkness; Eppie is preserved in
the room lit by the "red uncertain glimmer" of the dying hearth.
As Silas pushes the two logs together so the fire reveals the
form of the child, his life, broken in two, begins to be mended
once again. Yet the pattern appears more complicated as soon
as we become aware of the relation between the changes which
Dunstan and Eppie induce in Silas and Godfrey. For Silas, the
loss of the coins had meant the extinction of feeling; when
Eppie comes, however, life comes out of death, fire out of ashes
—like the "squire's child" found by the shepherd in *The
Winter's Tale*, the foundling's value will exceed that of "fairy
gold."[16] Against his own will, the benumbed weaver who wanted
to shun all human fellowship is drawn to the villagers. An ungainly misanthrope is transformed into the placid Master
Marner, who will obediently smoke the daily pipe urged on him
by "the sages of Raveloe." Godfrey, on the other hand, had
wanted "the tender permanent affection" of Nancy, as well as

---

[16] In Act III, scene 3, the clownish shepherd finds Perdita while his
son discovers the dying Antigonus: "thou mettest with things dying, I
with this new-born." I am originally indebted to Mr. Lee Sterrenburg
for this insight; more recently, the parallel has also been pointed out by
David R. Carroll in his essay.

the esteem of the villagers. The young squire who fathered the child had inwardly wished the disappearance of his brother and the death of his first wife. His wish is granted. The child itself seems conveniently removed. Presumably, like Silas, Godfrey can now be reinstated into the society which has frowned on his excesses. But while Silas' open consternation and helplessness endear him to Dolly Winthrop and the townspeople who gather at "The Rainbow," Godfrey can regain their esteem only by keeping his secret. Silas, by accidentally opening his door, has found the world opening to him; Godfrey, by deliberately shutting within himself the secret of his paternity, locks out even the being dearest to him, Nancy. Once again, freedom will elude him.

Godfrey has inherited his father's "large red house"; though he does not make official use of the title, he is the new Squire Cass.[17] The self-contained world he had envisioned has become a reality. After the disappearance of Dunstan and the death of Molly, Godfrey eagerly looks forward to a closed room "with all happiness centered on his own hearth, while Nancy would smile on him as he played with the children" (chap. 15, p. 203). But, after sixteen years of waiting for a legitimate child, when he finally "opens his home" to Eppie and confesses to her and Silas the secret he has encased for so long, it is too late. He assures his daughter that he can give her a greater freedom than the weaver can. Yet his "natural claim" upon her proves to be as empty as Stephen Guest's invocation of that "natural law" which "surmounts every other." The unnatural barriers he has erected now deprive him of the child who had entered through Silas Marner's unintentionally opened door. The man who once tried to lock out his daughter from the room reserved for his

---

[17] The Middle English word "cass" (box, chest, container) is derived from the Latin *capsa* (cf. *casa*, the Spanish word for house), which stems from *capere* (to hold, to contain).

and Nancy's children, now goes "straight to the door, unable to say more" (chap. 19, p. 260).

Before the theft of his gold, Silas had also tried to shut out others: "at night he closed his shutters, and made fast his doors, and drew forth his gold" (chap. 2, p. 30). His treasure had "fenced him in from the wide, cheerless unknown"; his money's disappearance, however, left him exposed: "But now the fence was broken down—the support was snatched away" (chap. 10, pp. 116–117). Indifferent, he no longer cares "to close his shutters or lock his door" (chap. 10, p. 132). His faith in goodness, divine or human, has been "blocked up." But with Eppie a new life opens for the former miser. His cottage will eventually be enlarged "at the expense of Mr. Cass" in order to accommodate Aaron and Eppie and their future children. Appropriately enough, the frontage is left semi-open: "The garden was fenced with stones on two sides, but in front there was an open fence, through which the flowers shone with answering gladness" (Conclusion, p. 273). Silas can look at the prospects of a widening future; his glance no longer rests on a "blank." Godfrey, on the other hand, sadder and wiser, absents himself from the wedding of his daughter, while his barren wife Nancy remains ensconced in the Red House. Like his brother Dunstan, Godfrey has taken "one fence too many"; he suffers from the very secret he must now forever hide from Raveloe.[18]

[18] The significance of obstacles and fences, doors and windows—opened and closed—has been discussed by several critics of *Wuthering Heights*, notably Dorothy Van Ghent. George Eliot's own metaphoric treatment of confinement and freedom, here and in "Mr. Gilfil's Love-Story," the two most romance-like of her "realistic" stories, may well be derived from Emily Brontë's novel. According to Lewes' diary, she read *Wuthering Heights* in June 1858, although she may have come across the novel once before, in the late 1840's. In Brontë's novel, Lockwood, as appropriately named as young Squire Cass, must also beat a hasty retreat in the face of domestic felicity; he escapes just as Cathy and Hareton enter the open front door of the Heights. The window Lockwood opens

Immediately on finding the squirming child, Silas begins to regain his "old impressions of awe at the presentiment of some Power presiding over his life" (chap. 12, p. 171). On finding the skeleton of Dunstan when he drains the water off his land, Godfrey, too, senses that he has been judged by some outside power. Though he fears public opinion, he now confides his secret to his wife in one of those confessional scenes so dear to George Eliot's "religion of humanity": "Everything comes to light, Nancy, sooner or later. When God Almighty wills it, our secrets are found out. I've lived with a secret on my mind, but I'll keep it from you no longer." (chap. 18, p. 243.) Chance, favorable or unfavorable, has in the eyes of Silas, Godfrey, and Nancy been replaced by the workings of a just power.

Silas' "sense of mystery" over Eppie's appearance seems almost as infantile as the baby's own absorption with "the primary mystery of her toes." Twice he repeats: "The money's gone I don't know where, and this is come from I don't know where" (chap. 14, p. 186). His consternation is rather amusing. As Eppie grows older and wiser, she acquires new interests. The infantile Silas, however, remains as perplexed as before, even after he learns where his money had gone and after he discovers Eppie's origin. He is still befuddled, still awed by his good fortune. Just as he had refused to accept a "medical explanation" for his cataleptic seizures, he now rejects any purely rational explanation for his fate. Irrationally, he fears that with the restoration of his coins Eppie may disappear or "be changed into gold again." For he has fallen back on the earlier belief in magical signs and omens on which the religion of Lantern Yard

---

in Cathy's room and the window left ajar on Heathcliff's death contribute to an aura of mystery quite similar to that which George Eliot wants to produce in the key scene of her novel. Dolly Winthrop insists: "The door was open, and it walked in over the snow, like as if it had been a little starved robin. Didn't you say the door was open? (chap. 14, p. 186.)

had depended. Convinced that God has personally looked after his interests, Silas rebukes Godfrey with unexpected fierceness, "God gave her to me because you turned your back upon her, and He looks upon her as mine" (chap. 19, p. 254). The weaver refuses to be cut "i' two" again. But George Eliot makes it clear that Silas' belief in a protecting deity is precarious. His faith depends on the child that is so precious to him. He admits that if he were to lose Eppie, he might again also "lose the feeling that God was good to me."

Godfrey's and Nancy's own conclusions about the powers that have affected their lives are somewhat less simpleminded. But although Godfrey's recognition of his dereliction of duty is couched in religious terms, it does not differ greatly from that forced on Amos Barton or Arthur Donnithorne. His allusion to a "God Almighty" merely represents an acknowledgement of the impossibility of his ever amending the mistakes of the past. As in Silas' case, his belief is based on events that have happened in the material world, events which could have happened without the aid of any supernatural power. George Eliot declared Godfrey's nemesis to be "very mild" (GEL, III, 388), and milder it is certainly than the circumstances which force Amos Barton away from Milly's grave in Shepperton or the circumstances which push Arthur away from Hayslope into the Napoleonic wars.[19] But even though Godfrey is allowed to remain in Raveloe and to retain his wife, his nemesis is appropriately severe: left without an acknowledged heir, he, like Arthur Donnithorne, stands to lose his patrimony.

Yet it is Nancy, rather than Godfrey or Silas, who best asserts the justice of the novel's retribution. Like the chorus in a Greek drama, she is not necessarily all-seeing. In her superstition, Nancy shares the limitations of both Silas Marner and Dolly

[19] Cf. chap. 3, p. 41: "[Godfrey] could imagine no future for himself on the other side of confession but that of 'listing for a soldier'—the most desperate step, short of suicide, in the eyes of respectable families."

Winthrop: "She would have given up making a purchase at a particular place if, on three successive times, rain, or some other cause of Heaven's sending, had formed an obstacle; and she would have anticipated a broken limb or other heavy misfortune to any one who persisted in spite of such indications" (chap. 17, p. 235). In a story where obstacles come in threes, where rain[20] and snow have affected the main events of the plot, such beliefs cannot be laughed away. In the simpler world of belief that George Eliot has created, Nancy can stand as a partial spokesman for her author's far more complex moral vision. Nancy refuses to accept any explanation of a life that is not arranged by some higher dispensation. Determined, resolute, the girl who had once refused to sit by the card tables, cannot accept a belief in chance.[21] After the death of her and Godfrey's infant, she rejects his suggestion that they adopt Eppie. Although she does not yet know that the child was fathered by her husband, she is convinced that the adoption "would never turn out well, and would be a curse to those who had wilfully and rebelliously sought what it was clear that, for *some high reason*, they were better without" (chap. 17, p. 234; italics added).

[20] In chapter three, Dunstan tells Godfrey: "I'm always lucky in my weather. It might rain if you wanted to go yourself" (p. 43); in chapter four, as he approaches Silas' cottage, "the lane was becoming unpleasantly slippery, for the mist was passing into rain" (p. 56). Loaded with the bags of gold, clutching Godfrey's golden whip, Dunstan closes the door behind him to "shut in the stream of light." The concealment leads to his death: "The rain and darkness had got thicker, and he was glad of it." In that darkness, he meets the fate of Chaucer's gold-obsessed rioters. Holding on to his heavy treasure, he slips on the wet ground and falls into the Stone-Pit where he belongs.

[21] In chapter eleven, when Godfrey tries to lead Nancy into the "adjoining parlor, where the card-tables were set," she objects: " 'O no, thank you,' said Nancy, coldly, as soon as she perceived where he was going, 'not in there' " (p. 161). Although she later accedes, her resistance is as significant as her sister's humorous rejection of chance: " 'My pork-pies don't turn out well by chance' " (p. 151).

Although George Eliot does not share the crude superstitions which shape Nancy's intuition, she definitely wants the reader of *Silas Marner* to believe in any "high reason" that can validate what is morally right. Nancy's refusal prepares us for Godfrey's retribution. And that retribution must, in this novel, depend on some such power as that which Nancy calls "the will of Providence."[22]

It might seem singular that Nancy—with her religious theory pieced together out of narrow social traditions, fragments of church doctrine imperfectly understood, and girlish reasonings on her small experience —should have arrived by herself at a way of thinking so nearly akin to that of many devout people whose beliefs are held in the shape of a system quite remote from her knowledge: singular, if we did not know that human beliefs, like all other natural growths, elude the barriers of system. (chap. 17, pp. 235–236.)

Nancy's "small experience" contains the essence of all belief in moral right. Here, even more than in the early portions of *The Mill on the Floss*, the lesser holds the seeds for the growth of larger universals. Although the explanations advanced by Silas, Godfrey, or Nancy belong to a narrower world view rejected by the novelist, their credulity is necessary to the "human beliefs" which her tale tries to generate. Like the Book of Job, *Silas Marner* asks: "But where shall wisdom be found? and where is the place of understanding?" Like Job, Silas learns that this understanding cannot be extracted from the material world: "It cannot be gotten for gold, neither shall silver be weighed for the prize thereof."[23] Yet neither is there a God speaking

---

[22] In his otherwise excellent introduction to the Rinehart edition of the novel, Jerome Thale argues that Nancy's view is either "at variance with or irrelevant to the human facts" (p. xvii). I would argue that, to the contrary, Nancy's supernatural explanation is essential as a perfect point of connection between the fairy tale of Silas and the "realistic" story of Godfrey. The device allows George Eliot to be true to two separate orders of "human facts."

[23] Job, 27.

through the whirlwind. If in Job the simple man called Elihu prepares the doubter for God's veiled answers, in this novel the complex woman who called herself "Eliot" for once refuses to unveil the contradictory ways of existence: " 'Ah,' said Dolly, with soothing gravity, 'it's like the night and the morning, and the sleeping and the waking, and the rain and the harvest—one goes and the other comes, and we know nothing how nor where.' " (chap. 14, p. 186.)

The scriptural tone and rhythm of this statement are intentional. Like Nancy, whose deepest thoughts are always stimulated by the copy of "Mant's Bible before her," the wheelwright's wife clings to what is elementary. To her surprise, Dolly discovers that, notwithstanding the theological differences between the Brethren of Lantern Yard and the indulgent religion preached by the Reverend Mr. Crackenthorp, her Bible and Silas' Bible are the same:

"And yourn's the same Bible, you're sure o' that, Master Marner—the Bible as you brought wi' you from that country—it's the same as what they've got at church, and what Eppie's a-learning to read in?"

"Yes," said Silas, "every bit the same; and there's drawing o' lots in the Bible, mind you," he added in a lower tone. (chap. 16, p. 214.)

The Evangelical who had once clung to her Bible and the agnostic who translated Strauss and Feuerbach could never again become "every bit the same." From "Amos Barton" to *The Mill on the Floss*, George Eliot oscillated between alternate explanations of reality. The fable of Silas Marner allowed her to balance these opposites. The conflicting impulses underlying her previous fiction finally found a common resting point.

THE CULMINATION OF A PHASE

In one of her essays for the *Leader*, George Eliot had argued that lying between the deductive bibliolatry of the extremely orthodox and the inductive historical mode of the extremely heterodox, there was a middle ground occupied by those biblical scholars who believed in the "accommodation" theory: "As the Deity, it is said, in speaking to human beings, must use human language, and consequently anthropomorphic expressions, such as 'eye of God,' the 'arm of God,' the 'laughter and jealousy of God,' which we have no difficulty in understanding figuratively, so he must adapt the form of His revelations to the degree of culture, which belongs to men at the period in which His revelations are made."[24] Her essay was written in 1856, in the same year in which she turned to the novel in order to reshape the figurative truths of the Bible. In *Silas Marner*, she profited from all her previous efforts to find a form for her revelations. By adapting herself to a simpler "degree of culture," by mediating between irreconcilable explanations, she was able to create a reality that could shelter reason and faith, the actual and the ideal.

Silas Marner succeeds in establishing, from beginning to end, that invisible rhythm which George Eliot had first suggested but then shied away from, in *Adam Bede*. The rider observing Dinah Morris' preaching on the village Green had briefly suspended his disbelief. In the green world of Raveloe, the simple Silas' final sense of wonder becomes ours as well. Like the weaver, we are satisfied by the protracted wonder which rises from a mixture of light and darkness, the transparent and the unintelligible. Godfrey's plausible loss is interwoven with Silas' strange gain. Mystery, rejected by Dinah, lost by Latimer, denied to Maggie, survives next to the clarity of reason. Like Mr. Snell, the evasive landlord of the Rainbow Tavern, George Eliot manages to suggest that there can be two irreconcilable, yet equally valid ways of beholding reality.

As David R. Carroll convincingly demonstrates, the discussion in the Rainbow Tavern which occupies the entire sixth chapter of the novel is integral to its meaning.[25] A triumph of

24 "Introduction to Genesis," *Leader*, VII (12 January 1856), 41.
25 "*Silas Marner*: Reversing the Oracles of Religion," pp. 190–194.

George Eliot's comic powers, drawn in a wide spectrum of rich colors, this scene refracts the same oppositions between the known and the unknown, the expected and the unexpected, on which the entire novel is built. From an abortive argument over the concealed reasons for slaughtering a cow, the debate slowly moves into what amounts to a philosophical dispute between two alternate modes of belief. The contest is not unlike that enacted in the barnyard of Chaucer's "Nun's Priest's Tale." The disputants are as ridiculous as the knowledgeable Chanticleer and the superstitious Pertelote. Pitted against each other are the aggressive farrier Mr. Dowlas (whose Scottish name suggests his skepticism in matters spiritual) and the oracular Mr. Macey, the parish clerk who believes in ghosts. When Mr. Dowlas boldly throws out a challenge to all specters ("let 'em come where there's company and candles"), even he for a moment is unnerved by the sudden apparition of the pale Silas, whose "strange unearthly eyes" cannot adjust to the tavern's light.

The chapter is important not only because it introduces the society which Silas now confronts (in the yard of the same Rainbow Tavern where at the end of the novel the bridal procession will gather), but also because the debate develops two clearly defined attitudes which are carried over into the explanations soon advanced to account for the theft of the miser's gold. In the light of what the reader already knows, neither explanation is correct. The crime has not been committed by a swarthy pedlar seen with a tinderbox, nor by the "preternatural felon" that Mr. Macey so doggedly believes in. And yet the battle rages between the advocates of common sense and the believers in supernatural occurrences:

The advocates of the tinder-box-and-pedlar view considered the other side a muddle-headed and credulous set, who, because they themselves were wall-eyed, supposed everybody else to have the same blank outlook; and the adherents of the inexplicable more than hinted that their antagonists were animals inclined to crow before they had found any corn— mere skimming-dishes in point of depth—whose clear-sightedness consisted in supposing that there was nothing behind a barn-door because they couldn't see through it; so that, though their controversy did not serve to elicit the fact concerning the robbery, it elicited some true opinions of collateral importance. (chap. 10, p. 116.)

As inferences of fact, the opinions are equally invalid. As in *Adam Bede*, where even the keen-eyed Mrs. Poyser and the visionary Dinah discover that some truths can elude either one, here too neither party can establish the total truth. But the controversy is as important to George Eliot's own objectives as those useless metaphysical disputations which engage Milton's angels are to the purpose of *Paradise Lost*. Playfully, she suggests that although they are deeply divided in their speculations, both parties actually have one point of agreement, for both are equally convinced of the veracity of Silas' story. It is his normal, human suffering which overcomes their resistance. And, as the stimulus for all our better feelings, this suffering contains all the truth that man needs to know. In "Amos Barton" or even in *Adam Bede*, this insight would have been conveyed by a hortatory narrator or one of the characters. In *Silas Marner*, however, it is unobtrusively introduced by an artist who has fully learned how to exploit her own self-division.

Around the time George Eliot began *Silas Marner*, George Henry Lewes published an amusing essay entitled "Seeing Is Believing," in which he attacked those who confused inference and fact: "when a man avers that he has 'seen a ghost,' he is passing far beyond the limits of visible fact, into that of inference. He saw *something* which he *supposed* to be a ghost."[26] Like Lewes, George Eliot has her fun with the spiritualists in Raveloe. But as a novelist whose art relies on the reader's inferences from simulated facts, she is also careful to suggest

[26] "Seeing is Believing" appeared in *Blackwood's Edinburgh Magazine*, LXXXVIII (October 1860), 382. It was ostensibly a review of a book by Robert Dale Owen (son of the celebrated British socialist Robert Owen), *Footfalls on the Boundary of Another World*.

that Mr. Dowlas' empirical view of reality cannot disallow certain necessary illusions. Empirically speaking, ghosts do not exist. But in the figurative mode of this tale, Dunstan's ghost hovers over the entire story. Shortly before Godfrey reports that his brother's skeleton has been found, Nancy has had a premonition. She looks at "the placid churchyard with the long shadows of the gravestones across the bright green hillocks," but the external beauty of this scene only impresses upon her "the presence of a vague fear . . . like a raven flapping its slow wing across the sunny air" (chap. 17, p. 240). Her foreboding proves correct. The ghost of the past now crosses the threshold of the Red House. Nancy's prescience resembles Dinah's. Yet while in Hayslope the visionary and the naturalistic seemed at odds, in Raveloe they remain in harmony. As in *Middlemarch*, where George Eliot was to rely on far more intricate balances, the craftsmanship of *Silas Marner* can persuade us that some power has meted out appropriate punishments and rewards.

Like the equanimous Mr. Snell, "accustomed to stand aloof from human differences as those of beings who were all alike in need of liquor," the author avoids the controversy of opposed systems of belief. If Chaucer uses his Host to control his opinionated pilgrims, George Eliot speaks through the landlord, who vows: "The truth lies atween you: you're both right and both wrong, as I allays say." Mr. Snell tries to prevent further dispute by inducing Mr. Macey to tell the oft-told and much cherished anecdote of the Lammeters' wedding. After going through "that complimentary process necessary to bring him up to the point of narration," the old parish clerk complies. His story is meant to restore harmony to the divided group at the inn; like children, his listeners delight in hearing the story over and over again. Appropriately enough, his story is about the conjunction of opposites, the union of disparate elements. Mr. Macey begins by contrasting the Lammeters from the Osgoods. The former have come "from a bit north'ard"; the latter have been rooted in Raveloe for generations. But the long-winded clerk admits that, after due consideration, this difference is not really appreciable: although "there's nobody rightly knows" the region from which old Mr. Lammeter came, it could not be "much different from this country, for he brought a fine breed o' sheep with him, so there must be pastures there." Having thus reassured his audience, Mr. Macey jumps right into the terrifying core of his story: the clergyman officiating at the Lammeter-Osgood wedding, Mr. Drumlow—"poor old gentleman, I was fond of him"—had put the questions to bride and bridegroom "by the rule o' contrary, like." Mr. Macey makes sure to stress his own presence of mind amidst this scene of disturbing confusion:

"Wilt thou have this man to thy wedded wife?" says he, and then he says, "Wilt thou have this woman to thy wedded husband?" says he. But the partic'larest thing of all is, as nobody took any notice on it but me, and they answered straight off "yes," like as if it had been me saying "Amen" i' the right place, without listening to what went before.

Skillful storyteller that he is, Mr. Macey aids the imagination of his hearers by dramatizing the division of his mind. He tells them that he felt as "if I'd been a coat pulled by the two tails, like," and then tops his own metaphor: "I was worreted as if I'd got three bells to pull at once." Having lingered on the climax, Mr. Macey now mercifully produces the long-awaited denouement: on confronting Mr. Drumlow with his mistake, the excited clerk was assured that the marriage was still valid. Mr. Macey transmits the parson's exact words: "he says, 'Pooh, pooh, Macey, make yourself easy' he says; 'it's neither the meaning nor the words—it's the re*g*ester does it—that's the glue' " (chap. 6, pp. 70–77).

In *Silas Marner* it is the "glue" of George Eliot's artistry which resolves the conflicts that had divided her previously. Through her choice of a perfect "re*g*ester," she was able to

yoke humor and high seriousness, to connect the probable with
the improbable by fusing the laws of observed experience with
the poetic justice of a fairy tale. In the marriage at the end
of the novel, the daughter of Godfrey is given away by her
"father" Silas. But this irregularity is no more disturbing than
Mr. Drumlow's carelessness. Coincidence and causality, redemption and punishment, Lantern Yard and Rainbow Yard have
been meticulously bonded. Though retaining the duality of the
earlier novels, *Silas Marner* blends these opposites in a union
as indissoluble as that of the couple wedded "by the rule o'
contrairy."

In his essay on superstition, Lewes had maintained: "What an
honest man tells me he saw, I will believe he saw, if it comes
within the possibilities of vision; my scepticism begins when he
ceases to narrate what he actually saw, and substitutes his *interpretation* of it."[27] Though not meant to be, his criterion can be
applied to George Eliot's novel. We believe in Silas' or Dolly's
confidence in "Them as know better nor we do," because the
conclusions these simple people form are within the range of
their own vision. When Dolly offers Silas the cakes with the
inscription "I.H.S." pricked on them, he is "as unable to interpret the letters as Dolly," although, in her words, "the letters
have held better nor common" (chap. 10, p. 126). George
Eliot makes it clear that Dolly's "simple Raveloe theology" is as
much predicated on the visible world as on the invisible "Them"
she alludes to in an unconscious relapse into polytheism. Silas
can believe in a just deity only through the gift of Eppie; Dolly
likewise suggests that Aaron is indispensable for her own faith:
"either me or the father must allays hev him in our sight—that
we must" (chap. 10, p. 129). But the novelist no longer senti-
mentalizes her religion of humanity; she does not try to
separate the "worldly" from the "otherworldly," as she did in

[27] *Ibid.*, 382.

"Amos Barton." Instead, she quietly suggests that all belief, natural and supernatural, stems from man's elemental need to confide in somebody other than the self. The truth of this insight is at once as simple and as complex as life itself.

Only ten years after George Eliot's death, *Silas Marner* had the misfortune to be chosen as a text for the "Student's Series of English Classics." Even today, the work has yet to recover from the resulting obloquy. In a play like *The Winter's Tale*, the sudden echoes of *Hamlet* or *King Lear* tend to remind us that Shakespeare merely carried into his stylized romances the same complicated questions about existence that were raised by his tragedies. *Silas Marner* is equally oblique. Although George Eliot's Victorian thoroughness had led her to interpret human experience in novels of increasing complexity and bulk, the compactness of *Silas Marner* contains the same riches which were spread out over *The Mill on the Floss*. Neither Silas nor Dolly, Godfrey nor Nancy, is profound. Yet their groping among half-shadows, their imperfect grasp of the bare letters of the alphabet, carries a greater authority than the flat rejections forced upon Dinah Morris, Latimer, or Maggie. By avoiding the explicitness of her earlier explanations, George Eliot made her insights seem deeper than those which she had expressed more openly. Dolly's creed is as self-limiting as that previously advanced by her creator. But it is far more credible in her broken words than if it had been spoken by an erudite narrator or affixed as the motto for "The Lifted Veil": "Give me no light great heaven but such as turns / To energy of human fellowship." For Dolly exhausts all the light she possesses in order to reconcile Silas to his fate. Her words seem less melancholic than Adam Bede's similar statement, because they actually do ease Silas' questionings: "And all as we've got to do is to trusten, Master Marner—to do the right thing as fur as we know, and to trusten. For if us as knows so little can see a bit o' good and rights, we may be sure as there's a good and a rights bigger nor what we can know." (chap. 16, p. 217.) Through Dolly, George Eliot expressed her own hope for "a good and a rights bigger nor what we can know." She had already demonstrated her ability to adopt the point of view of "us as knows so little" in the childhood portions of *The Mill*. It is the full exercise of that ability which makes *Silas Marner* so delightful a reading experience. As in *Middlemarch*, the author was able to divide herself among her characters without at all relinquishing the breadth of her own vast culture. Dolly's hopefulness, Nancy's elementary righteousness, even Priscilla Lammeter's satiric ability to laugh at human foibles stem from a distribution similar to the dispersion of qualities in *Middlemarch* among Dorothea Brooke, Mrs. Bulstrode, and Mary Garth. Even Silas Marner, that simple weaver of cloth, is a self-projection of the subtle intellect who was to devise the "web" of *Middlemarch*: "In this strange world, made a hopeless riddle to him, he might, if he had had a less intense nature, have sat weaving, weaving—looking towards the end of his pattern, or towards the end of his web, till he forgot the riddle." (chap. 2, p. 27.) If nobody among the Raveloers suspects that this alienated stranger is "the same Silas Marner who had once loved his fellow with tender love, and trusted an unseen goodness," very few of George Eliot's readers could suspect that this grotesque misanthrope who wants so badly to solve the riddle of existence is as much a projection of his creator as the puzzled Maggie had been.

Silas Marner refracts a view of reality which is more complicated than the artist had previously allowed herself to admit. In Wordsworth's "Michael," "a story unenriched with strange events" (1. 14), the city destroys the faith of the old peasant; in *Silas Marner*, events almost as strange as those in "The Ancient Mariner" allow "old Master Marner" to be integrated into a world of poetic belief. The unusual Latimer had shriveled into a misanthrope; Silas the misanthrope grows into a venerable Raveloe sage. His growth reverses Latimer's degeneration. If

Latimer's story is a study in disease, Silas' is therapeutic. Coming from the writer who, in the name of a harsh actuality, had thwarted the innocent Mr. Gilfil and so severely punished Hetty and Maggie, *Silas Marner* is an unusually joyous work. But the novel is not great simply because its comic powers generate the quality of joy which Arnold had despaired of in Victorian art, or because in it George Eliot overcame the philosophical nihilism which she had merely resisted in her earlier fiction. Its greatness stems rather from her surprising ability to merge the ordinary with the extraordinary, from the unexpected ease with which she accommodated the conflicting impulses which she had tried to methodize from "Amos Barton" to *The Mill on the Floss*. Without surrendering an iota of her and Lewes' belief in empirical fact, she managed to balance "rational explanation" and "impenetrable mystery" (chap. 10, pp. 115–116). She had devised an artistic construct whose truth could remain independent from that of the actual world. Only *Middlemarch* would repeat that accomplishment.

Silas Marner marks the end of George Eliot's first stage of development. Occasionally, as in the country setting for Romola's redemption or in the idyll of Fred Vincy's regeneration by the Garths, she would recur to the pastoralism exploited in this novel. But after the composition of *Silas*, the novelist ventured into a new territory. From *Romola* to *Daniel Deronda*, she went to history itself and examined its larger cyclical motions. The story of Silas rallied her trust in the temporal world. Just as the weaver becomes "arrested" as he is about to shut his door to the "goodness" beyond it, so did she become momentarily arrested by her urgent need to counter her mounting pessimism. From "Amos Barton" on, she had looked with increasing discomfort at the uprooting of the past. But change, so capricious and destructive in *The Mill on the Floss*, proved to be beneficent in *Silas Marner*, redirecting the weaver to his earlier trustfulness. George Eliot was herself now ready to visit the past.

New difficulties were in store for her. A new gap would arise when she tried to link the individual fates of her characters to the "grand political and social conditions" she now wanted to portray. George Eliot's experimentations with form were far from over. *Silas Marner* had arisen out of the first of her "mental phases"; *Middlemarch* was to result from the experiments to come. In her greatest novel, the artist in her would triumph once more over the philosopher who refused to compromise the truth that was so difficult.

Index

Index